Spicilegi

Containing Remains Of Bardesan, Meliton, Ambrose and Mara Bar Serapion

William Cureton

Alpha Editions

This edition published in 2020

ISBN: 9789354210518

Design and Setting By
Alpha Editions
www.alphaedis.com
email - alphaedis@gmail.com

I feel highly gratified, therefore, that the permission to dedicate it to your Lordship has afforded me such an occasion of recording my admiration and respect for your Lordship's talents and virtues; and my gratitude, in common with that of very many others, for your long continued efforts, through evil report and good report, to promote the civil and religious liberty of all classes of society—the best human means of securing both their temporal and eternal happiness;—as well as of expressing my deep sense and acknowledgment of favours and kindnesses, for which I had no claim of personal connection or private influence with your Lordship to afford me the slightest pretension.

I have the honour to be,

MY LORD,

Your Lordship's very faithful Servant,

WILLIAM CURETON.

CLOISTERS, WESTMINSTER ABBEY,
July 20, 1855.

NOTICE.

THE prudent advice which Horace has given to authors, "Nonumque prematur in annum,"[1] has been literally followed by me with respect to this book, although I cannot take the credit of having adopted it intentionally. It is now nine years since the Text of this volume was printed. Other more pressing occupations have hindered me from publishing it before the present time. In the Preface to " The Antient Syriac Version of the Epistles of St. Ignatius," which appeared in 1845, I made known my intention of editing the celebrated Dialogue of Bardesan on Fate which I had found; and as early as the year 1846 I communicated an English translation of the "Oration of Meliton" to the late venerable Dr. Routh, President of Magdalene College, Oxford. At that time he had just completed the first volume of " Reliquiæ Sacræ," in which he had collected all that was then known to remain of the genuine writings of the antient Bishop of Sardis. In the same year, when my " Vindiciæ Ignatianæ" appeared, I announced that the present volume was in the press, and early in 1847 the whole of the Syriac part was printed.

In 1852 M. Ernest Renan, a young orientalist, from whose zeal and diligence we may hope for much hereafter, in a Letter addressed to M. Reinaud, inserted in the "Journal Asiatique" an account of some Syriac Manuscripts which he had seen in the British Museum the year before, and amongst the rest, a notice of that in which are found the treatises comprised in this volume. Not having seen the announcement of my intended publication, he believed that he had been the first to discover the existence of these precious remains of antiquity. In writing to thank M. Renan for the copy of this Letter, which he had been good enough to send to me, I pointed out to him the fact that they had been already printed four years before. His reply, which is now in my hands, reflects far greater honour upon M. Renan, than the reputation of any such discovery could have done. He is most anxious to

---

[1] De Arte Poetica, v. 388.

repair an injury, which, although in ignorance and unintentionally, he thought that he had done to me by assuming to himself a discovery which I had already made, and to restore to me the full credit—if indeed there be any in so small a matter—by taking the earliest opportunity of stating in the "Journal Asiatique" how the case really stood. Nor did this satisfy him. In a brief notice prefixed to a Latin Translation of this tract of Meliton, which came into my hands in time for me to refer to it in the notes of this volume, he again alludes to the same matter.[1]

Besides the Syriac text which I had communicated to M. Renan, for the purpose of being inserted in the "Spicilegium Solesmense," edited by my very learned friend, M. Pitra, I also placed in the hands of the Chevalier Bunsen the English translation in manuscript, as well as the printed text, with full permission to make any use of it that he might deem proper, for the second edition of his work, "Hippolytus and his Age."

In the course of the present year, a writer who seems to have been altogether unaware of these facts has inserted, in the "Journal of Sacred Literature,"[2] a translation of the pieces attributed to Meliton, published in this volume. It appears to be the attempt of some young man who at present has but a very imperfect acquaintance with the language, as well as with what has been done in Syriac literature of late, or he could hardly have been ignorant that my volume was in

---

[1] Hæc ego, mense Septembri 1851, dum Musei Britannici codices assidue verso, non sine gaudio reperi, deque his, in *Journal asiatique*, april. 1852, breviter egi, simul et operis Melitoniani initium publici juris feci. **Mox** vero per litteras certior factus sum quæ primum nec reperisse credideram, eadem v. cl. GULIELMO CURETONIO bene jam cognita fuisse, imo virum doctissimum et honoratissimum apud se habere eadem fragmenta jam typis excusa, atque in *Spicilegio* illo *syriaco* quod omnes Europæ viri eruditi tanta expectatione præstolantur, proditura. Curetonii ergo laus sit Melitonem syrum primum detexisse. Vide autem quæ sit viri illius humanitas : nostris precibus motus, plagulas quibus textus Melitonianus continebatur nobiscum communicavit, easque per nos latinas fieri permisit.

[2] In the numbers for January and April 1855.

the press. It has been my duty, in the course of the Notes, to point out some of the errors into which he has fallen, although I could not undertake to notice them all.[1] Whoever he be, let him not take this amiss. He deserves encouragement for having applied himself at all to such studies; but he will certainly render a greater benefit to literature, and better consult his own reputation, if henceforth he will advisedly follow the caution of the Roman poet whose words I have quoted above.

---

[1] The reader will find these mentioned in the notes. I give one or two here as a specimen of this author's version. He signs himself B.H.C.

B.H.C.'s TRANSLATION.

I say that rejection is denounced against those.

Now the understanding is free and a knower of the truth: whether it is in these things consider with thyself. And if they dress up for thee the figure of a woman.

Against this generation.

But perhaps thou wilt say, How is my work not the God whom thou worshippest, and not an image?

And art thou not ashamed that blood should be required of the maker of it?

Wherein thou wallowest on the earth, and yet art favoured. For things which are destitute of consciousness are afraid of him who maketh the earth tremble.

Was seized by the shearer.

Thou didst lie down against rectitude of mind.

MY TRANSLATION.

I affirm that also the Sibyl has said respecting them.

But thou, a free intelligence and cognizant of the truth, enter into thyself, and if they clothe thee in the fashion of a woman.

Touching this matter.

But perchance thou mayest say, Why did not God create me, so that I should then have served Him, and not idols?

And art thou not ashamed, perchance it should be deficient to demand of him who made it?

Why rollest thou thyself upon the earth, and offerest supplication to things which are without perception? Fear him who shaketh the earth.

Was taken from the flock.

Thou wast reclining on a soft bed.

PREFACE.

The Manuscript from which the materials for the present volume have been chiefly derived, is one of those which were obtained by Archdeacon Tattam from the Syrian convent in the desert of Nitria in the year 1843. It is now numbered 14,658 amongst the Additional Manuscripts in the British Museum. Several leaves were added in 1847 from fragments subsequently acquired by M. Pacho ;[1] and four more were again supplied from other fragments procured also by him from the same source in the year 1850. At present the volume consists of one hundred and eighty-eight leaves. Originally it must have had more than two hundred and twenty ; for the last gathering as it now stands is numbered the twenty-second, and each gathering consisted of ten leaves. It is imperfect both at the beginning and the end, has suffered mutilations in several parts of the volume, and some of the leaves have been much stained by oil. It is written in a large bold hand in two columns : the headings of chapters and the titles of separate works are distinguished by red letters. It appears to have been transcribed about the sixth or seventh century of our era.

BARDESAN.

The first work printed from this Manuscript is the celebrated Treatise of Bardesan on Fate, said to have been addressed to the Emperor Marcus Antoninus, commonly known as

---

[1] See the account of the acquisition of the collection in the Preface to my edition of the *Festal Letters of Athanasius*.

Marcus Aurelius ; although, with the document now complete before us, we find no intimation of its having been so addressed. Eusebius calls it, Ὁ πρὸς Ἀντωνῖνον ἱκανώτατος αὐτοῦ περὶ εἱμαρμένης διάλογος :[1] Jerome, copying him, writes, " Clarissimus et fortissimus liber quem, Marco Antonino de fato tradidit.[2] Theodoretus speaks of the author in the following terms : Βαρδησάνης δὲ ὁ Σύρος, ἐξ Ἐδέσης ὁρμώμενος, ἐν τοῖς Οὐήρου Μάρκου Καίσαρος ἤκμασε χρόνοις. τοῦτον φασὶ πολλὰ τῆς Βαλεντίνου περικόψαι μυθολογίας. πολλὰ δὲ καὶ τῇ Σύρων συνέγραψε γλώττῃ, καὶ ταῦτα τινες μετέφρασαν εἰς τὴν Ἑλλάδα φωνήν. ἐντετύχηκα δὲ κἀγὼ λόγοις αὐτοῦ κατὰ εἱμαρμένης γραφεῖσι.[3] Epiphanius gives the same account in a rather extended form, supplying also the name of the person to whom Bardesan chiefly addressed himself in this Dialogue : Ὃς πολλὰ πρὸς Ἀβειδὰν τὸν Ἀστρονόμον κατὰ εἱμαρμένης λέγων συνελογήσατο.[4] Eusebius, in his *Ecclesiastical History*, speaks of the author thus : Βαρδησάνης, ἱκανώτατός τις ἀνὴρ, ἔν τε τῇ Σύρων φωνῇ διαλεκτικώτατος, πρὸς τοὺς κατὰ Μαρκίωνα καί τινας ἑτέρους διαφόρων προϊσταμένους δογμάτων διαλόγους συστησάμενος, τῇ οἰκείᾳ παρέδωκε γλώττῃ τε καὶ γραφῇ, μετὰ καὶ πλειστων ἑτέρων αὐτοῦ συγγραμμάτων ;[5] and again, in his *Preparatio Evangelica*, he prefaces an extract from the work now before us with these words : Παραθήσομαι δέ σοι καὶ τῶνδε τὰς ἀποδείξας ἐξ ἀνδρὸς, Σύρου μὲν τὸ γένος, ἐπ᾽ ἄκρον δὲ τῆς Χαλδαϊκῆς ἐπιστήμης ἐλαληκότος. Βαρδησάνης ὄνομα τῷ ἀνδρὶ, ὃς ἐν τοῖς πρὸς τοὺς ἑταίρους διαλογοις τὰ δὲ πῇ μνημονεύεται φάναι.[6] He then quotes the long extracts which I have printed, pp. 8—10 and 16—32. Photius, writing of Diodorus, Bishop of Tarsus, has the following words : ἅμα τε τὴν τῆς εἱμαρμένης κατασείων δόξαν, καὶ τὴν

---

[1] *Hist. Eccles.* b. iv. c. 30.
[2] *Catal. Script. Eccl.* Edit. Erasmus, vol. i. p. 180.
[3] *Hæret. Fabul. Comp.* b. i. c. 22.   [4] *Panarium,* edit. Petau, p. 477.
[5] *Hist. Eccles.* loc. cit.   [6] *Præp. Evang.* b. vi. c. 9.

Βαρδισάνου συνεπιρραπιζει.¹ And again, Ἐν ᾧ τοὺς ἀπὸ Βαρδισάνου αἱρετικοὺς διελέγχει, δέχεσθαι μὲν προσποιουμένους τοὺς προφήτας,
καὶ τὰς μὲν ψυχὰς γενέσεως ἐλευθέρας καὶ αὐτεξουσίους ὁμολογοῦντας,
τὸ σῶμα δὲ τῇ ταύτης ὑποτάττοντας διοικήσει· πλοῦτον γὰρ καὶ πενίαν
καὶ νόσον καὶ ὑγίειαν καὶ ζωὴν καὶ θάνατον καὶ ὅσα οὐκ ἐφ᾽ ἡμῖν ἔργον
εἶναι λέγουσι τῆς εἱμαρμένης.²

The title, indeed, of the work in this volume is *Book
of the Laws of Countries*, and the name of the person who
is introduced as having written down the dialogue is
Philip (see pages 5 and 7); but it is evident that it is the
same treatise as that alluded to by all these writers whose
words have been now quoted. It is a dialogue. Bardesan takes
the leading part in it : his discourse is addressed to his companions, one of whom is named Avida, or Abida. The subject-
matter is on Fate. It affirms the precise doctrine which is
attributed to Bardesan's treatise. The author declares himself
to be fully acquainted with the science of Chaldæan astrology,
and gives abundant proof of the same; and, further, all those
passages which have been quoted as extracts from Bardesan's
treatise, are found in this. Moreover, it is written in Syriac,
in which most of his works were composed, although he was
also well skilled in the Greek tongue, as Epiphanius³ informs
us. There can be no doubt, therefore, that we have now in
our hands, in the original language of the author, and in a
complete form, that celebrated Dialogue of Bardesan on Fate,
written about the middle of the second century,⁴ which has been

---

¹ See *Bibliotheca*, Cod. 223 : edit. Bekker, p. 208.

² *Ibid.* p. 221.

³ Λόγιός τις ὢν ἐν ταῖς δυσὶ γλώσσαις, Ἑλληνικῇ τε διαλέκτῳ, καὶ τῇ τῶν
Σύρων φωνῇ. *Panarium*, p. 476.

⁴ At page 30 he speaks of the recent conquest of Arabia by the Romans.
This took place under Marcus Aurelius : see Tillemont, *Hist. des Empe-*

so often referred to by subsequent writers, but of which only a comparatively small portion has hitherto been known to us.

Eusebius has inserted two long extracts from this treatise in his *Præparatio Evangelica*, probably from a Greek translation made by some of those friends of Bardesan, who, as the same author, in his *Ecclesiastical History*, as well as Theodoretus, informs us, translated his dialogues into Greek.[1] I have given both of these passages in this volume, on the same page with the English translation. Besides the Greek version preserved by Eusebius, there is also a Latin translation of the second extract, contained in the *Recognitions*, falsely attributed to Clement of Rome, which were modified and done into Latin by Ruffinus about the year 400.[2] I have printed this, as well as the Greek,[3] in juxtaposition with my own English translation, in order that the reader may at one view be enabled to compare the three, and to note their variations as well as their agreement. I have likewise appended an extract from the second Dialogue of Cæsarius, brother of Gregory of Nazianzum, in which, although the name of the author be not mentioned, much has been borrowed from that same part of Bardesan's dialogue which relates especially to the laws and habits of different nations. It may be interesting and useful to compare this also with the other versions, and with the original text.[4]

---

reurs, vol. ii. p. 402: thus confirming by internal evidence the account of the date of this work given by Eusebius, Theodoretus, Epiphanius, and others.

[1] Οὓς οἱ γνώριμοι (πλεῖστοι δὲ ἦσαν αἰτῷ δυνατῶς τῷ λόγῳ παρισταμένῳ) ἐπὶ τὴν Ἑλλήνων ἀπὸ τῆς Σύρων μεταβεβλήκασι φωνῆς. *Hist. Eccl.* b. 4. c. 30.

[2] See his Preface to Gaudentius.

[3] Pp. 16—33.

[4] In giving these extracts I have followed, for Eusebius, the edition of the *Preparatio Evangelica,* printed at the Clarendon Press in 4 vols.

With respect to the Author, Bardesan himself, so much has been already said by different writers,[1] that the subject seems to have been exhausted; and I am not aware that I am able to bring any additional facts to light, beyond what is supplied by the treatise itself, now, after the lapse of many centuries, for the first time exhibited in its original integrity. I will therefore only quote a few passages relating to Bardesan and his opinions, which I have extracted from the famous reply of Philoxenus, Bishop of Mabug, to an anonymous writer who had impugned the opinions which he had put forth in an Epistle addressed to the monks.[2] They are taken from one of the Nitrian Manuscripts obtained by Dr. Tattam in 1841, now in the British Museum, No. 12,164: ܠܐ ܕܝܢ ܐܬܕܟܪܬ ܠܗܘ ܡܦܩܢܟ ܒܪܕܝܨܢ ܕܢܓܝܪܘܬ ܪܘܚܐ ܘܒܒܣܝܡܘܬ ܦܬܓܡ̈ܐ ܗܘܦܟܐ ܕܠܘܬ ܟܠܢܫ ܡܫܬܒܚ ܠܗ ܬܠܡܝܕܘܗܝ ܒܟܬܒܝܗܘܢ "But thou hast not been mindful of thy instructor, Bardesan, whom his disciples celebrate in their books for his patience and polite answers to every man." fol. 125, b. ܡܢ ܕܡܬܘܪܐ ܠܗܘ ܠܘܩܒܠ ܕܐܬܐܡܪ ܡܢ

---

by the late Dr. Gaisford, Dean of Christ Church; for the *Recognitions*, that of Gersdorf, Lips. 1838; and for Cæsarius, that of Gallandi in the *Bibliotheca Veterum Patrum*. Venet. 1765. Vol. vi. The text of this last is in a very corrupt state. Several errors might, however, easily have been amended, but I deemed it better to copy the text as I found it.

[1] Two authors have written works expressly on this subject—FRID. STRUNZIUS, *Historia Bardesanis et Bardesanistarum*. 4to. Viteb. 1710; and AUGUSTUS HAHN, *Bardesanes Gnosticus Syrorum Primus Hymnologus. Commentatio Historico-Theologica*. 8vo. Lips. 1819. BEAUSOBRE has devoted an entire chapter: *De Bardesanes et de ses Erreurs*, c. 9, b. iv. vol. ii. in *Histoire de Manichée et du Manicheisme*. See also, Cave, Lardner, Tillemont, and others. Perhaps the most complete compendious notice is that by Gallandi, *Bibl. Veterum Patrum*, vol. i. Proleg. p. cxxii.

[2] See respecting this, Assemani. *Biblioth. Orient.* vol. ii. p. 27.

ܒܬܘܠܬܐ ܕܝܠܕܗ ܗܘ ܥܠܝܐ ܠܒܪܕܝܨܢ ܫܠܡ "Who so confesseth that boy which was born of the Virgin, that her child is the Highest, he assents to Bardesan." f. 127, b. ܡܛܠܗܕܐ ܐܦ ܗܕܐ ܕܥܬܝܩ ܥܠܡܐ ܛܠܝܐ ܗܘܐ ܠܘ ܗܘ ܢܣܒܢ ܡܢ ܒܪܕܝܨܢ ܐܠܐ ܗܘ ܐܬܚܫܚ ܒܗ ܐܝܟ ܕܠܐܟܣܝܘܬܐ ܕܛܥܝܘܬܗ ܘܫܩܠܗ ܡܢ ܠܘܬܢ ܡܢ ܡܠܦܢܘܬܐ ܕܥܕܬܐ "Therefore this also, that 'the Antient of Eternity was a boy,' we have not taken this from Bardesan, but he has made use of it as a means of concealing his own error, and took it from the doctrine of the Church." f.164. ܐܝܬ ܡܢܗܘܢ ܕܐܡܪܝܢ ܕܡܢ ܫܡܝܐ ܐܚܬ ܡܠܬܐ ܦܓܪܐ ܐܝܟ ܕܐܡܪܬ ܐܢܬ ܗܫܐ ܘܫܠܡܬ ܐܢܬ ܠܒܪܕܝܨܢ ܡܠܦܢܟ . . . . . ܕܠܐ ܐܕܪܟܬ ܡܕܡ ܗܘ ܪܥܝܢܗ ܕܒܪܕܝܨܢ ܕܡܢ ܫܡܝܐ ܣܐܡ ܠܗ ܠܦܓܪܗ ܕܡܫܝܚܐ "There are some of them who say, that he sent down the Word a body from heaven, as thou saidest just now, and didest assent to thy teacher Bardesan . . . . . Because thou hast not comprehended the mind of Bardesan, who assumeth the body of Christ to be from heaven." f. 171. b.

MELITON.[1]

The second tract in this volume bears the title of "An Oration of Meliton the Philosopher," addressed to Antoninus Cæsar. Nor is there any thing contained in it, so far as I am competent to form an opinion, which in any way should lead

[1] Respecting Meliton, and the writings attributed to him, see Eusebius' account printed in this volume, p. 56, and the notes thereon; Cave's "Life of Saint Melito, Bishop of Sardis," in his *Lives of the most eminent Fathers of the Church that flourished in the first Four Centuries*, and the Notice in his *Historia Litteraria*. Fabricius, *Bibl. Græc.* vol v. p. 184; and Piper, *De vita et Scriptis Melitonis*, in "*Theolog. Stud. u. Kritik*," by Ullmann and Umbreit, A.D. 1838, p. 54. Dr. Routh has published all that was then known to remain of the genuine writings of Meliton in his *Reliq. Sacr.* vol. i. p. 113.

us to doubt of the correctness of this inscription, or to question the genuineness of the work.

It is true, as M. Bunsen states, that it appears to be entire, and yet does not contain that passage quoted by Eusebius [1] from the most famous of all Meliton's writings, his *Apology* to the Emperor Marcus Antoninus in defence of the persecuted Christians. Had indeed that learned ecclesiastical historian been fully acquainted with all the works of Meliton, and also distinctly stated that no other address had been made by him to any one bearing the name of Antoninus Cæsar than that in which was contained the passage that he has quoted, it would then have been sufficiently evident that the work before us could not be by Meliton, if indeed it be, as it appears to me to be, complete, and not an abridgment or extract from a larger *Apology* : this, however, may seem to some to be uncertain. [2] Eusebius himself, however, has given us to understand plainly that he did not profess to exhibit a full and exact account of all the writings, either of Meliton or of Apollinaris, [3] but only of such as had come to his own knowledge. His silence, therefore, as the late venerable Dr. Routh [4] has justly observed, is not of itself to be construed as an argument against the genuineness or authority of any work bearing a name not mentioned by him, if there be no positive external testimony against it, nor any internal evidence in the work itself which

[1] See p. 57.

[2] M. Renan thinks it a fragment. " Melitonis Episcopi Sardium Apologiæ ad Marcum Aurelium imperatorem fragmentum."

[3] See p. 57, l. 15.

[4] " Neque auctori *Præfationis* magis deneganda est fides, quam aliis temporum eorundem scriptoribus, ex quorum testimonio multi recepti sunt libri veterum, neque ab Eusebio, neque ab alio quoquam æqualium ejus memorati; præsertim quam infra asserat Eusebius, pervenisse opera certa quædam ex multis Apollinarii libris." *Reliq. Sacr.* vol. i. p. 167.

may render it doubtful or suspected. Maximus,[1] in his Preface
to the writings attributed to Dionysius the Areopagite, says
that there were very many works which Eusebius omitted to
notice, because they had never fallen into his hands. And as
a case in point we may observe that Eusebius has not said one
word respecting the *Apology* of Athenagoras, presented also to
Marcus Antoninus about the same time, and containing many
things in common with this address, and with the other
Apologies offered to the Roman Emperors at that period.

There is no reason why we must suppose that Meliton
should not have written two Addresses to the Roman Emperor
as well as Justin Martyr, or that one of them might not have
escaped the knowledge of Eusebius, or at least have had no
mention of it made by him, as well as that of Athenagoras.
The *Apology* cited by Eusebius was probably amongst the latest,
or indeed the last of all the works [2] which Meliton wrote ; and
internal evidence has led critics to conclude that it was presented to the Emperor Marcus Antoninus in the tenth year of
his reign, after the death of his associate in the Empire, Lucius
Aurelius Verus, about A.D. 169-70. External testimony by
the author of the *Chronicon Paschale* attributes it to the same
date, A.D. 169.[3] But the same writer, five years before, A.D.

---

[1] Πάμπολλα παρῆκεν Εὐσέβιος οὐκ ἐλθόντα παρὰ χεῖρας οἰκείας· καὶ γὰρ οὔτε
φησὶν ἅπαντα καθάπαξ συναγηοχέναι· μᾶλλον γε μὴν ὁμολογεῖ καὶ ἀριθμοῦ κρείτ-
τονα βιβλία καθεστάναι μηδαμῶς εἰς αὐτὸν ἐληλυθότα. καὶ πολλῶν ἐδυνάμην
μνημονεῦσαι μὴ κτηθέντων αὐτῷ, καὶ ταῦτα τῆς αὐτοῦ χώρας : cited by Dr.
Routh, *Reliq. Sacr.* vol. i. p. 167.

[2] Eusebius writes—Ἐπὶ πᾶσι καὶ τὸ πρὸς Ἀντωνῖνον βιβλίδιον, which
Ruffinus translates, " Et post omnia Liber ad Antoninum Verum." b. 4. c. 26.

[3] In the cxxxvii. Ol. A. C. 169 : Μελίτων, Ἀσιανὸς τῆς Σάρδεων πόλεως
ἐπίσκοπος, καὶ Ἀπολλινάριος Ἱεραπόλεως ἐπίσκοπος, καὶ ἄλλοι πολλοὶ τοῦ
καθ' ἡμᾶς λόγου βιβλίον ἀπολογίας Αὐρηλίῳ Ἀντωνίνῳ ἐπέδωκαν, Ἰουστίνου
καὶ ἄλλων πολλῶν, κ.τ.λ., p. 484 *ibid.*

164-65,[1] speaks also of an *Apology* presented by Meliton to the Emperor. Unless, therefore, we assume that he was not sufficiently well and clearly informed, and has therefore given a confused account—an assumption for which the silence of Eusebius cannot afford sufficient grounds—we can hardly draw any other conclusion from his words than that Meliton presented two Apologetical addresses to the Roman Emperors—the one before us, which contains rather a defence of the true religion against the Polytheism, idolatry, and incorrect ideas of the Deity entertained by Pagans ; and the other, as the extract preserved by Eusebius would lead us to infer, against the persecution of the Christians on account of their faith, Indeed the passage which the author of the *Chronicon Paschale* cites as from Meliton's *Apology*, and which, from its having been given before he mentions the later date, would lead us, if there were two, to refer it to the former, seems to be sufficiently near to be almost identified with expressions found in the work before us, if we bear in mind, that it must necessarily have undergone some change in phraseology, by the translation out of Greek into Syriac, and also suppose it not to have been intended for an exact and verbatim quotation,[2] but only as an allusion.

Judging merely from what we read in the Address itself, I should have been disposed to fix the date about four years earlier than that in which mention is first made of Meliton by the

---

[1] Ἀλλὰ καὶ Μελίτων Ἀσιανὸς, Σαρδιανῶν ἐπίσκοπος, βιβλίον ἀπολογίας ἔδωκεν τοῖς λελεγμένοις βασιλεῦσιν (Μάρκῳ Αὐρηλίῳ καὶ Ἀντωνίνῳ Βήρῳ), καὶ ἕτεροι δὲ πολλοὶ, ὧν ὁ δηλωθεὶς Ἰουστῖνος, κ.τ.λ.: p. 482. in the ccxxxvi. Olympiad. A. Mund. 5672 : A.D. 164-65. edit. Dindorf. p. 482.

[2] Compare Οὐκ ἐσμὲν λίθων οὐδεμίαν αἴσθησιν ἐχόντων θεραπευταὶ, ἀλλὰ μόνου Θεοῦ, τοῦ πρὸ πάντων καὶ ἐπὶ πάντων, p. 483, *ibid.*, with "*There is one God the Lord of all* ———— embracing *stones* ————, and are willing while they themselves are endowed with senses to *serve that which is insensible,* p. 47, and within whom he is, and *above* whom," &c., p. 49.

Chronicon Paschale, either to the end of 160, or the beginning of 161, a short time before the death of Antoninus Pius, and probably when his health had sensibly begun to decline. Unless, indeed, the expression be intended as generally applicable to every one whose father is still alive, the words " Be solicitous respecting thy father—so long as thy solicitude may be of avail to help him," would imply that Antoninus Pius was still surviving, although perhaps in a state to cause anxiety. In the inscription, Marcus Antoninus is designated Cæsar, and not Autocrat, or Emperor. His being associated with Antoninus Pius, and taking a part in the administration of the empire, would be sufficient grounds for Meliton to address him ; and in the words of the *Apology* cited by Eusebius, he alludes to the part which he took in the government: " During the time that thou also with him wast governing every thing." The prospect of his early succession to be the head of the state, might also have prompted Meliton to offer his opinion as to the surest means of governing a realm in peace—by knowing the truth, and living conformably thereto. At the end of the Address he refers to the children of Antoninus. Of these he had several, both sons and daughters.[1]

In forming an opinion from the internal evidence of the work, I cannot think with the Chevalier Bunsen, that " it bears the stamp of a late and confused composition." It seems certain, indeed, that the writer alludes most clearly to the Second Epistle of St. Peter ;[2] but inasmuch as I do not hold the same views as my very learned and dear friend respecting the authenticity

---

[1] His two sons, Commodus and Annius Verus, were made Cæsars upon the occasion of the triumph of Lucius Verus, A.D. 166. See Tillemont, *Hist. Emp.* vol. ii. p. 391.

[2] See p. 50, and the note on the passage, p. 95 below.

of that Epistle,[1] I do not recognise, in the fact of its having
been clearly alluded to in the work which we have now
before us, any evidence of the "lateness" of the composition.
As to the Address being "confused," it does not seem to me
in this respect to differ in its method from the rest of the
Apologies of the second century; with which, indeed, it has
very many things in common, even to some evident mistakes, such as that of confounding the Egyptian god Serapis
with the Patriarch Joseph.[2] Some of the views of this writer
as to the origin of Polytheism and idolatry in certain places
are uncommon. They have probably been gathered from tra-
ditions at that time current in the East, but of which in these
days very little is known.

I will not, however, pursue this subject further at present,
but, committing the document into the hands of the reader,
leave him to judge and draw his own conclusions for himself.

For an account of the other extracts attributed to Meliton,
and the sources from which they have been gathered, I must
refer to the notes in this volume.

AMBROSE.

The short work bearing the inscription of *Hypomnemata*,
and attributed to Ambrose, a "chief man of Greece," is the
same, with some modifications, as that known by the title of
Λόγος πρὸς Ἕλληνας—"Oratio ad Gentiles," which, in several
copies, is attributed to Justin Martyr, and indeed has been

---

[1] M. Bunsen puts the following in the mouth of Hippolytus in his
Apology: "You will, on your side, kindly abstain from quoting what you
call the Second Epistle of St. Peter. I might have been induced to do so,
in order to prove my theory about the coming of Antichrist, and the end
of the world after 6000 years. But I could not in good conscience. The
antient Churches did not know such a letter." Vol. iv. p. 33.

[2] See p. 43, and notes, p. 89.

very generally received as his.   Many, however, have doubted the authorship, and others have not hesitated to state their conviction that it bears internal evidence of being by a different hand from the undoubted work of Justin, *The Dialogue, with Trypho the Jew.*[1]   Assuming the authorship as it is given here to be correct, there seems to be an easy explanation why it might have come to be attributed to Justin, in the fact of its having been often classed in the same volume with his *Apologies,* which have in a great measure the same object in view ; and thence having been supposed to be by Justin himself, a transition which the small bulk of the work may readily account for.

The Ambrose here mentioned as *a chief man of Greece,* and a *senator,* can hardly be understood to be any other than the friend and disciple of Origen, whom Epiphanius designates as one of those illustrious in the palaces of kings,[2] and whose wealth enabled him to supply his master with all the necessary expenses for completing his Hexaplar edition of the Scriptures,[3] and who also himself suffered martyrdom for the Christian faith.   Certainly the inscription of this tract and its contents would well concur with what we know of Ambrose.[4]

---

[1] See Oudin, *Com. de Scriptoribus Ecclesiæ Antiquæ,* vol. i. p. 190. Otto classes it in his edition with Justin's *Opera addubitata.*

[2] Ἀμβροσίῳ τινὶ τῶν διαφανῶν ἐν αὐλαῖς βασιλικαῖς : see *Panar.* p. 526.

[3] See Eusebius, *Hist. Eccl.* vi. 23.

[4] See Cave, *Historia Literaria,* and *Life of Origen,* § x ; Halloix, *Origenes Defensus,* b. i. c. 8.   The name Ambrose, among later Syriac writers, seems to have been still further contracted from ܐܡܒܪܘܣܝܘܣ, Ambrose, to ܐܒܪܝܣ.   Thus, in the work called ܕܟܘܪܢܝܬܐ, or the *Bee,* c. 51, we read ܐܒܪܝܣ ܐܬܟܠܝ ܡܢܐ ܐܬܟܪܙܝܐ ܐܟܣܘܡܘܣ ܕܝܠ ܡܦܝ ܡܐ ܕܩܒܪܗ ܠܐ ܝܕܝܥ, " Abres.   He is called in Greek, Ambrosius.   The place of his sepulture is not known." See also Jo. Saluca, cited by Assemani, *Bibl. Orient.* vol. i. p. 533.   Respecting the *Bee,* see my *Corpus Ignatianum,* p. 360.

MARA, SON OF SERAPION.

We have no information respecting this author beyond what is supplied in the letter itself addressed to his son. Mara, or as Assemani[1] writes it in Latin, Maras, is not an uncommon appellation amongst the Syrians, and there have been many who have borne the name of Serapion[2].

The author speaks of himself as one whose city had been ruined, and himself also taken and detained as prisoner in bonds by the Romans, together with others whom the victors treated in a tyrannical manner, as distrustful of their fidelity to the Roman government. He describes the misery of his friends and companions belonging to the city of Samosata, and the distresses which he and they suffered when they joined themselves together on the road to Seleucia. He alludes to the destruction of Jerusalem and the dispersion of the Jews as an act of divine vengeance for their having murdered Jesus ; but he makes no direct mention of the name of Christ, and only designates him as the " wise king," who, although put to death, still lived in the " wise laws which he promulgated."

From these facts it is evident that the author wrote at a time when the Romans not long before had been making fresh conquests, or repressing rebellion in the parts of Syria about Samosata and Seleucia, and probably at a period when, on account of the persecution of the Christians, it would not have been prudent or safe to have spoken in more direct terms of Christ. Comagena and its capital Samosata were taken by the Romans in the reign of Vespasian, A.D. 72, or two years after the capture

---

[1] See *Bibl. Orient.* vol. i. p. 643.
[2] Fabricius, *Bibl. Græc.* vol. viii. p. 192.

of Jerusalem by Titus.[1] About twenty-three years later the
persecution under Domitian began, A.D. 95.[2] There would be
nothing therefore incongruous in assigning, from its internal
evidence, the date of this Epistle to the close of the first century. Nor would the allusion to the catastrophe of Samos at
all militate against this, if it be referred to the earthquake in
the reign of Augustus, from which several of the neighbouring
islands also suffered.[3]

The mention, however, of that island having been covered
with sand, as a punishment for the burning of Pythagoras,
seems to me to have a direct reference to the Sibylline verses;"[4]

$$"Οττι βροτοὶ φαῦλον ζωῆς ἀδίκουτ' ἐνέχοντο,$$
$$'Εσται καὶ Σάμος ἄμμος, ἐσεῖται δὲ Δῆλος ἄδηλος$$
$$Καὶ 'Ρώμη ῥύμη.[5] τὰ δὲ θέσφατα πάντα τελεῖται.$$

I cannot therefore, in my own mind, come to any other conclusion than that this Epistle ought to be assigned to a period
when the Sibylline verses were frequently cited, the age of Justin
Martyr, Meliton, and Tertullian. This date, too, will perhaps
otherwise coincide quite as well with what is read in the
letter as the former. The troubles to which the writer alludes
as having befallen himself and his city will apply to those
inflicted by the Romans upon the countries about the Tigris
and Euphrates which had been excited to rebel against them

---

[1] See Tillemont, *Hist. des Empereurs*, vol. ii. p. 30.

[2] *Ibid.* p. 121.

[3] See Gale, *Sibyll. Orac.* p. 406.

[4] *Ibid.* p. 405.

[5] Lactantius alludes to this line: " Et vero cum caput illud orbis occi-
deret, et ῥύμη esse cœperit, quod Sibyllæ fore aiunt," &c. *Inst. Div.* b. vii.
p. 25.

by Vologeses, in the Parthian war under the command of
Lucius Verus, A.D. 162—165.[1] I have not found the name
of Samosata especially mentioned as having suffered more
than other cities in this war; but it is stated that Seleucia
was sacked and burned by the Romans, and five or six thousand slain.[2] The persecution under Marcus Antoninus followed very close upon this war, and as these facts equally
agree with the allusions made in this Epistle of Mara, it
may perhaps be nearer the truth to assign its date to the
latter half of the second century rather than to the close of
the first.

If indeed such be the period at which this Letter was written,
there is no improbability in supposing, that the Serapion, to
whom it is addressed, may be the same as he who succeeded
Maximinus[3] as eighth Bishop of Antioch, about the year 190,
and who himself also wrote short epistles, similar to this in
purpose and tendency, for which indeed his father's might have
set him a pattern.[4]

---

[1] See Tillemont, *Hist. des Emp.* vol. ii. p. 385.

[2] *Ibid.* p. 389.

[3] See Eusebius, *Hist. Eccl.* b. v. c. 19; and Cave's *Histor. Litter.*

[4] See Jerome, *De Viris Illus.* c. xii. " Leguntur et sparsim ejus breves
Epistolæ auctoris sui ἀσκήσει et vitæ congruentes." Dr. Routh has given
all the remains of Serapion in his *Reliq. Sacr.* vol. i. p. 449.

BARDESAN.

THE BOOK

OF THE

LAWS OF COUNTRIES.

A few days ago we went up to visit Shemashgram, our brother. And Bardesan came and found us there; and when he had felt him, and seen that he was well, he asked us, "What were you talking about, for I heard your voice from without as I was coming in?" For he was accustomed, whenever he found us talking about any 5 thing before him, to ask us, "What were you saying?" that he might converse with us about it. We therefore said to him, "This Avida was saying to us: 'That if God be one, as you say, and He created mankind, and willeth that you should do that which you are commanded, why did He not create men so that they 10 should not be able to go wrong, but always should do what is good; for by this His will would be accomplished.'"

Bardesan saith to him, "Tell me, my son Avida, why dost thou think that the God of all is not one, or that He is one, and doth not will that men should conduct themselves holily and uprightly?" 15

Avida saith, "I, my Lord, asked these of my own age in order that they might give me a reply."

Bardesan saith to him, "If thou desirest to learn, it would be advantageous for thee, that thou shouldest learn from one who is older

than they: but if to teach, it is not requisite that thou shouldest
question them, but that thou shouldest persuade them to ask
thee what they desire. For teachers are usually asked, and do not
themselves ask. And whenever they do put a question, it should be
5 to direct the mind of the questioner so that he may ask properly,
and they may know what his desire is. For it is a good thing
that a man should know how to put questions."

Avida saith, " I am desirous of learning, but I began first to
question these my brethren, because I was ashamed of asking
10 thee."

Bardesan saith, " Thou speakest cleverly. Nevertheless know
that he who putteth [2] his inquiries properly, and is willing to be
convinced, and draweth near to the way of truth without obsti-
nacy, needeth not be ashamed, because he will certainly give
15 pleasure to him to whom the inquiry is directed, by those things
which I have mentioned. If therefore, my son, thou hast any
thing in thy mind respecting this about which thou wast in-
quiring, tell it to us all; and if it please us also, we shall partici-
pate with thee; and if it please us not, necessity will compel us
20 to shew thee why it does not please us. And if thou wert only
desiring to know this word, without having any thing in thy
mind respecting it, as a man who has lately attached himself to
the Disciples and is a recent inquirer, I will inform thee, in order
that thou mayest not depart from us without profit; and if those
25 things which I tell thee please thee, we have also for thee other
things respecting this matter, but if they please thee not, we for
our part shall have spoken without any ill feeling."

Avida saith, " I even greatly desire to hear and to be convinced,
because it is not from any other I have heard this word; but I
30 have spoken it of my own mind to these my brethren, and they
were not willing to convince me, but say, ' Believe really, and thou
wilt be able to know every thing;' but I am not able to believe
unless I be convinced."

Bardesan saith, " Not Avida alone is unwilling to believe, but
35 also many, because they have in them no faith, are not even able to
be convinced, but always are pulling down and building up, and are

found destitute of all knowledge of the truth. Nevertheless, because Avida is not willing to believe, lo! I will speak to you who
do believe concerning this which he inquireth, and he will hear
something more."

And he began to say to us, " There are many men who have ⁵
not faith, and have not received knowledge from the wisdom
of the truth. And on this account they are not competent to
speak and to instruct, and do not easily incline themselves to hear.
For they have not the foundation of faith to build upon, and they
have no confidence upon which they may hope And because they ¹⁰
also doubt respecting God, they likewise have not within them
that fear of Him which would liberate them from all fears: for
whoso hath not the fear of God within him, he is subject to every
fear. For even with respect to that,⁽³⁾ whatever it may be, which
they do not believe, they are not sure that they properly disbe- ¹⁵
lieve; but they are unstable in their minds, and are not able
to stand, and the taste of their thoughts is insipid in their mouth,
and they are always timid and hasty and rash. But as to
what Avida was saying, 'Why did not God create us so that
we should not sin and be guilty?'—if man had been created ²⁰
so, he would not have been for himself, but would have been the
instrument of him who moved him; and it is known that whoso
moveth as he chuseth he moveth him either to good or to evil.
And how then would a man differ from a harp, upon which another
playeth, or from a ship, which another steereth: but the praise and ²⁵
the blame stand in the hand of the artist, and the harp itself knoweth
not what is played upon it, nor the ship whether it be well steered
and guided; but they are instruments which are made for the
use of him who possesseth in himself the science. But God in his
kindness did not will that he should create man so. But he ³⁰
exalted him by Free-will above many things, and made him equal
with the angels. For observe the sun and the moon and the sphere,
and the rest of those creatures which are greater than we in
some things, that there is not given to them Free-will of themselves, but they are all fixed by ordinance that they should do that ³⁵
only which is ordained for them, and nothing else. For the sun

never saith, that I will not rise at my time; nor the moon, that I
will not change, and not wane, and not increase; nor does any
one of the stars say, that I will not rise, and I will not set; nor the
sea, that I will not bear the ships, and I will not stand within my
5 bounds; nor the hills, that we will not continue in the places in
which we are set; nor do the winds say that we will not blow;
nor the earth, that I will not bear and sustain whatsoever is upon
me: but all these things serve and are subject to one ordinance,
for they are the instruments of the wisdom of God which erreth
10 not. For if every thing ministered, who would be he that is
ministered unto; and if every thing were ministered unto, who
would be he that ministered? And there would not be one
thing differing from another. For that which is single and hath
no difference in it, is a Being which up to this hour has not been
15 established. But those things, which are requisite for ministration,
have been fixed in the power of man, because in the image[4] of Elohim
he was created. On this account there has been given to him these
things in kindness, that they might minister to him for a season;
and it has been given to him to govern himself by his own will, and
20 that whatever he is able to do, if he will he should do it, and if he
will not, he should not do it; and he should justify or condemn himself. For if he had been made so that he would not be able to do
evil by which he may be condemned, in the same manner also the
good which he should do would not be his, and he would not be
25 able to be justified by it. For whoso should not of his own will do
that which is good or evil, his justification and his condemnation
would stand in that Fortune for which he is created. On this
account, let it be manifest to you, that the goodness of God has
been great towards man, and that there has been given to him
30 Free-will more than to all those Elements of which we have been
speaking; that by this same Free-will he may justify himself, and
govern himself in a godlike manner, and associate with the
angels, who also are possessed of Free-will for themselves; for we
know, that even the angels, if they had not been possessed of
35 Free-will for themselves, would not have had intercourse with
the daughters of men, and would not have sinned nor fallen from

their places. And in the same manner therefore those others which did the will of their Lord, by their power over themselves were exalted and sanctified, and received mighty gifts. For every one that exists stands in need of the Lord of all; and there is no end to his gifts. But nevertheless know ye, that even those things 5 of which I have said that they stand by ordinance, are not entirely devoid of all freedom, and on this account at the last day they all shall be subject to judgment."

I say to him, "And how can those things which are fixed be judged?"

10

He saith to me, "Not in so far as they are fixed, oh, Philip, will the Elements be judged, but in so far as they have power; for Beings when they are set in order are not deprived of their natural property, but of their force of energy, being diminished by the mingling of one with another, and they are subdued by the 15 power of their Creator; and in so far as they are subject, they will not be judged, but in that which is their own."

Avida saith to him, "Those things which thou hast said are very good. But lo! the commandments which have been given to men are severe, and they are not able to perform them."[5] 20

Bardesan saith, "This is the answer of such an one as doth not desire to do that which is good; and more especially of him who has obeyed and submitted to his enemy. For men are not commanded to do any thing but what they are able to do. For there are two commandments set before us such as are 25 suitable and just for Free-will: one that we separate ourselves from every thing which is evil and which we should dislike to be done to ourselves; and the other that we should do that which is good and which we love, and desire that it should also be done to us likewise. What man, therefore, is there who is unable to 30 avoid stealing, or to avoid lying or committing adultery and fornication, or that he should be guilty of hatred and falsehood? For lo! all these things are subject to the mind of man, and it is not in the power of the body they are, but in the will of the soul. For even if a man be poor and sick and old, or impotent in his 35 limbs, he is able to avoid doing all these things; and as he is able to

avoid doing these things, so is he able to love, and to bless, and to
speak the truth, and to pray for that which is good for every one
whom he knoweth: and if he be in health and have the use of
his hands, he is able too to give something of that which he hath;
5 also to support by the strength of body him who is sick and
broken down, this too he is able to do. Who, therefore, it
is that is not able to do what those devoid of faith murmur
about, I know not. For I think, that it is in these commandments more than in any thing man has power. For they are
10 easy, and there is nothing that is able to hinder them. For we
are not commanded to carry heavy burthens of stones, or of
timber, or of any thing else, which those only who are powerful in body are able to do; nor that we should build fortresses and found cities, which kings only are able to do; nor
15 that we should steer ships, which mariners only are skilled in
steering; nor that we should measure and divide the earth, which
geometricians only know how to do; nor any one of those arts
which some men possess, and the rest are devoid of them; but there
has been given to us according to the goodness of God command-
20 ments without grudging, such as every man who possesses a soul
within him can do rejoicing; for there is no man who rejoiceth not
when he doeth that which is good; nor is there any one who doth
not delight within himself when he refraineth from wicked things,
with the exception of those who were not made for this grace, and
25 are called Tares: for would not[6] that judge be unjust who
should blame a man for such a thing as he is not able to do?"

Avida saith to him, "Respecting these deeds, oh Bardesan,
sayest thou that they are easy to perform?"

Bardesan saith, "To him who desireth, I have said, and do
30 say, that they are easy; for this is the good conduct of a free
mind, and of that soul which hath not rebelled against its Governors.
For there are many things which impede the action of the body,
and more especially old age, and sickness, and poverty."

Avida saith, "Perchance a man may be able to avoid wicked
35 things, but to do good things who among men is able?"

Bardesan saith, "It is more easy to do good than to abstain from evil. For the good is the man's own, **and** on this account he rejoiceth whenever he doeth good; but the evil is the operation of the enemy, and on this account, when a man is troubled and not sound in his nature, he doeth wicked things. For know, my son, that it is an easy thing for a man to praise and bless his friend; but that a man should not blame and revile him that he hates is not easy. But nevertheless, this is possible to be; and whenever a man doeth that which is good, his mind is cheerful and his conscience tranquil, and he is pleased that every one should see what he does; but whenever a man acts wrongly, and committeth an injury, he is agitated and troubled, and full of rage and anger, and is tormented in his soul and in his body: and when he standeth in this mind, he is not pleased to be seen by every one; and those things in which he rejoiceth, which even praise and blessing follow, are rejected by him; but upon those things by which he is agitated and troubled followeth the curse of blame. But perhaps a man may say, that even fools are pleased when they do vile things:—but not in the doing of them, and not in being commended, and not for good hope; and this pleasure doth not continue with them. For the enjoyment which is in a sound state for good hope is one; and the enjoyment in an unhealthy state for bad hope is another. For lust is one thing and love is another; and friendship is one thing and sodality another; and we ought plainly to understand that the unrestrained ardour of love is called lust, which [7] although there may be in it enjoyment for a moment, nevertheless is far removed from that true love, whose enjoyment is for ever uncorruptible and indissoluble."

I say to him, " After this manner again was this Avida saying, ' That it is from his Nature man acteth wrongly; for if he had not been formed naturally to do wrong, he would not do wrong.'"

Bardesan saith, " If all men did one deed and acted with the one mind, it would then be known that it was their Nature governed them, and they would not have the Free-will of which I spake to you. Nevertheless, in order that ye may understand what is Nature and what is Free-will, I will proceed to inform you.

The Nature of man is this : that he should be born, and grow
up, and rise in stature, and beget children, and grow old, by
eating and by drinking, and sleeping, and waking, and that he
should die.   These because they are of Nature, belong to all
5 men, and not to all men only, but also to all animals which have
a soul in them ; and some of them also to trees.   For this is a
physical operation which performeth and produceth and esta-
blisheth every thing as it has been ordained.   But Nature also
is found to be maintained by animals too in their actions.   For the
10 lion eateth flesh, by his Nature ; and on this account all lions are
eaters of flesh.   And the sheep eateth grass ; and for this reason all
sheep are eaters of grass.   And the bee maketh honey by which it
sustains itself ; for this reason all bees are honey-makers.   And the
ant layeth up for itself a store in summer, that it may sustain itself
15 from it in the winter ; and for this reason all ants do likewise.
And the scorpion striketh with its sting him who hath not hurt
it ; and so likewise all scorpions strike.   And all animals maintain their Nature ; and those which feed upon grass do not eat
flesh ; nor do those that feed upon flesh eat grass.   But men are
20 not governed in this manner ; but in the things belonging to their
bodies they maintain their Nature like animals, and in the things

---

"Κατὰ φύσιν ὁ ἄνθρωπος γεννᾶται, τρέφεται, ἀκμάζει, γεννᾷ,
ἐσθίει, πίνει, κοιμᾶται, γηρᾷ, ἀποθνήσκει· καὶ τοῦτο παντὸς
ἀνθρώπου καὶ παντὸς ἀλόγου ζῴου.   Καὶ τὰ μὲν ἄλλα ζῷα ψυχικὰ
ὄντα, καὶ διόλου κατὰ συμπλοκὴν γεγενημένα, διόλου σχεδὸν κατὰ
φύσιν φέρεται.   Λέων σαρκοφαγεῖ, καὶ ἀμύνεται εἴ τι ἀδικηθῇ· καὶ
διὰ τοῦτο πάντες οἱ λέοντες σαρκοφαγοῦσι καὶ ἀμύνονται.   Καὶ
ἀμνάδες χορτοφαγοῦσι, καὶ κρεῶν οὐχ ἅπτονται, καὶ ἀδικούμεναι
οὐκ ἀμύνονται· καὶ ὁ αὐτὸς τρόπος πάσης ἀμνάδος.   Σκορπίος γῆν
ἐσθίει, καὶ τοὺς μὴ ἀδικήσαντας ἀδικεῖ, κέντρῳ ἰοβόλῳ πλήσσων·
καὶ ἡ αὐτὴ κακία πάντων σκορπίων.   Μύρμηξ κατὰ φύσιν οἶδε
χειμῶνος παρουσίαν, καὶ δι' ὅλης θερείας κάμνων, ἀποτίθεται
ἑαυτῷ τροφάς· καὶ ὁμοίως πάντες μύρμηκες ἐργάζονται.   Μέλισσα
μέλι γεωργεῖ, ἐξ οὗ καὶ τρέφεται· καὶ ἡ αὐτὴ γεωργία πάσαις με-
λίσσαις.   Καὶ ἦν πολλὰ εἴδη ἐκθέσθαι ἡμῖν τῶν ζῴων, ἅτινα τῆς
φύσεως μὴ δυνάμενα ἐκστῆναι, πολὺν θαυμασμὸν παρασχεῖν ὑμῖν
ἐδύνατο· ἀλλ' αὐτάρκη ἡγησάμην ἐκ τῶν παρακειμένων τὴν ἀπό-

which belong to their minds they do that which they wish, as
being free and with power, and as the likeness of God : for there
are some of them that eat flesh, and do not touch bread ; and
there are some of them that make a distinction in the eating of
flesh ; and there are some of them that do not eat the flesh of any 5
animal in which there is a soul ; and there are some of them that
have connexion with their mothers, and with their sisters,[6] and
with their daughters ; and there are some that never approach
women at all ; and there are some that avenge themselves like
lions and like leopards ; and there are some that injure him who 10
has not done them any harm, like scorpions ; and there are some
that are led like sheep, and do not hurt those who govern them ;
and there are some who conduct themselves with virtue, and some

---

δειξιν ποιήσασθαι, ὅτι τὰ μὲν ἄλλα ζῷα κατὰ τὴν κοινότητα καὶ
τὴν διαφορὰν κατὰ φύσιν δοθεῖσαν ἑκάστῳ ἐξ ἀνάγκης ἡδέως φε-
ρεται, ἄνθρωποι δὲ μόνοι τὸ ἐξαίρετον ἔχοντες, τόν τε νοῦν καὶ τὸν
ἐκ τούτου προφερόμενον λόγον, κατὰ μὲν τὴν κοινότητα ἕπονται τῇ
φύσει, ὡς προεῖπον, κατὰ δὲ τὸ ἐξαίρετον οὐ κατὰ φύσιν πολιτεύον-
ται. Οὐδὲ γὰρ μία βρῶσις ἢ τῶν ἁπάντων· ἄλλοι μὲν γὰρ κατὰ τοὺς
λέοντας τρέφονται, ἄλλοι δὲ κατὰ τὰς ἀμνάδας· οὐχ ἓν ἔχοντες
σχῆμα φορημάτων, οὐκ ἔθος ἕν, οὐχ εἷς νόμος πολιτείας ἐν
αὐτοῖς, οὐ μία κίνησις ἐπιθυμίας τῶν πραγμάτων· ἀλλ' ἕκαστος
τῶν ἀνθρώπων κατὰ τὴν ἰδίαν θέλησιν αἱρεῖται ἑαυτῷ βίον, τὸν
πλησίον μὴ μιμούμενος, πλὴν ἐν οἷς βούλεται. Τὸ γὰρ ἐλεύθερον
αὐτοῦ οὐχ ὑπόκειται δουλείᾳ, καὶ εἴ ποτε ἑκὼν δουλεύσει, καὶ τοῦτο
τῆς ἐλευθερίας αὐτοῦ ἐστι, τὸ δύνασθαι δουλεύειν ἑκόντα. Πόσοι
τῶν ἀνθρώπων, καὶ μάλιστα τῶν Ἀλαναίων, ὡς τὰ ἄγρια ζῷα,
κρεοβοροῦσιν ἄρτου μὴ γευόμενοι, καὶ οὐ διὰ τὸ μὴ ἔχειν, ἀλλὰ διὰ
τὸ μὴ θέλειν ; Ἄλλοι κρεῶν οὐ γεύονται, ὡς τὰ ἥμερα ζῷα· ἄλλοι
ἰχθυοφαγοῦσι μόνον· ἕτεροι δὲ ἰχθύων οὐ γεύονται, οὐδ' ἂν λιμώσ-
σωσιν. Οἱ μὲν ὑδροποτοῦσιν, οἱ δὲ οἰνοποτοῦσιν, οἱ δὲ σίκερα
πίνουσι. Καὶ ἁπλῶς πολλὴ διαφορὰ βρωμάτων καὶ πομάτων ἐν
τῇ ἀνθρωπότητι, μέχρι καὶ ἐν τῇ τῶν λαχάνων καὶ ὀπωρῶν βρώσει
διαφερόμενοι. Ἀλλὰ καὶ οἱ μὲν, ὡς σκορπίοι καὶ ὡς ἀσπίδες, μὴ
ἀδικηθέντες ἀδικοῦσιν· οἱ δὲ, ὡς τὰ ἄλογα ζῷα, ἀδικούμενοι ἀμύνονται. Ἕτεροι δὲ, ὡς λύκοι ἁρπάζουσι, καὶ ὡς γαλαῖ κλέπτουσιν·
ἄλλοι δὲ ὡς ἀμνάδες καὶ μηκάδες ὑπὸ τῶν ὁμοιοπαθῶν ἐλαύνονται,
καὶ τοὺς ἀδικοῦντας οὐκ ἀδικοῦσι· καὶ οἱ μὲν λέγονται ἀγαθοὶ, οἱ

c

with righteousness, and some with vice.   And if any one should
say, they have each individually a Nature to do so, let him see
that it is not so.   For there are some who were fornicators and
drunkards, and when the admonition of good counsels reached
5 them, they became chaste and temperate, and abandoned the lust
of their bodies.   And there are some who conducted themselves
with chastity and temperance ; and when they became negligent
of right admonition, and despised the commands of the Deity, and
of their instructors, fell from the way of truth, and became forni-
10 cators and prodigals ; and there are some who repented again
after their fall ; and fear came upon them, and they returned
to the truth in which they stood.   What, then, is man's Nature ?
for lo ! all men differ one from another in their conduct, and in
their desires ; and those who stood in one will and in one counsel
resemble one another : but those men whose lust is enticing
15 them up to the present moment, and whose passion governs
them, desire to attribute whatsoever they do wrong to their
Creator ; so that they themselves may be found without fault,
and He who created them may be condemned by a vain plea ;
and they do not see that Nature has no law, for a man is not blamed
20 because he is tall in his stature or little, or white or black ;
or because his eyes be large or small ; or for any one of the defects
of the body : but he is blamed if he steal, or lie, or practise
deceit, or poisoneth, or curseth, or doeth such things as are like
these ; for lo ! from hence it is evident, that as to those things
25 which are not done by our hands, but which we have from
Nature, we are not indeed condemned by these ; neither by these
are we justified ; but those things which we do by our own Free-
will, if they be good, by them we are justified and praised, and if
they be wicked, by them we are condemned and blamed."

δὲ κακοὶ, οἱ δὲ δίκαιοι. Ὅθεν ἐστὶ νοεῖν, μὴ πάντως κατὰ φύσιν
ἄγεσθαι τὸν ἄνθρωπον· (ποίαν γὰρ αὐτοῦ ἐροῦμεν φύσιν ;) ἀλλὰ πῇ
μὲν φέρεται κατὰ φύσιν, πῇ δὲ κατὰ προαίρεσιν. Διὸ τὸν ἔπαινον,
καὶ τὸν ψόγον, καὶ τὴν καταδίκην ἔχει ἐν τοῖς κατὰ προαίρεσιν· ἐν
δὲ τοῖς κατὰ φύσιν ἔχει τὴν ἀνεγκλησίαν οὐ κατὰ ἔλεος, ἀλλὰ κατὰ
λόγον.

Again we asked him, and said to him, " There are others who
say, that by the decree of Fortune men are governed, at one time
wickedly, and at another time well."

He said to us, " I likewise, O Phillip and Baryama, know
that there are men [9] who are called Chaldeans, and others who love 5
this knowledge of the art, as I also once loved it; for it has been
said by me, in another place, that the soul of man is capable of knowing that which many do not know, and the same men meditate to
do; and all that they do wrong, and all that they do good, and
all the things which happen to them in riches and in poverty, and 10
in sickness and in health, and in defects of the body, it is from the
influence of those Stars, which are called the Seven, they befal them,
and they are governed by them. But there are others which say
the opposite of these things,—how that this art is a lie of the Chaldeans, or that Fortune does not exist at all, but it is an empty name; 15
and all things are placed in the hands of man, great and small : and
bodily defects and faults happen and befal him by chance. But
others say that whatsoever a man doeth, he doeth of his own
will, by the Free-will that has been given to him, and the faults
and defects and evil things which happen to him, he receiveth as 20
a punishment from God. But as for myself, in my humble opinion,
it appeareth to me that these three sects are partly true, and partly
false. They are true, because men speak after the fashion which
they see, and because, also, men see how things happen to them, and
mistake ;—because the wisdom of God is richer than they, which 25
has established the worlds and created man, and has ordained the
Governors, and has given to all things the power which is suitable
for each one of them. But I say that God and the Angels, and
the Powers, and the Governors, and the Elements, and men and
animals have this power : but all these orders of which I have 30
spoken have not power given to them in every thing. For he that
is powerful in every thing is One ; but they have power in some
things, and in some things they have no power, as I have said :
that the goodness of God may be seen in, that in which they have
power, and in that in which they have no power they may know 35
that they have a Lord. There is, therefore, Fortune, as the Chal-

deans say : but that every thing is not in our will is apparent from hence—that the majority of men have wished to be rich and to have power[10] over their fellows, and to be healthy in their bodies, and that things should be subject to them as they desire : yet wealth is
5 not found but with few; nor power, except with one here and there; nor health of body with all men; neither do those who are rich have entire possession of their riches ; nor those who are in power have all things obedient to them as they wish : and sometimes they are disobedient in a manner which they do
10 not wish : and at one time the rich are wealthy as they desire, and at another time they become poor in a manner which they do not desire ; and those who are perfectly poor dwell in a manner that they do not wish, and live in the world in a manner that they do not desire ; and they covet things, and they flee from
15 them. And many beget children, and do not bring them up ; and others bring them up, and they do not inherit ; and others inherit, and become a disgrace and an affliction : and others are rich as they wish, and have ill health as they do not wish; and others are healthy as they desire, and are poor as they do not desire. There are
20 some who have many of the things which they wish, and few of those which they do not wish ; and there are some who have many of the things which they do not wish, and few of those which they do wish : and thus it is found, that riches, and honours, and health, and sickness, and children, and various objects of desire, are
25 placed under Fortune, and are not in our own power. But with such as are according as we wish, we are pleased and delighted ; and towards such as we do not wish we are drawn by force. And from those things which befal us when we do not wish, it is evident, also, with respect to those things which we do wish, that it is not
30 because we wish them that they befal us, but that they happen as they do happen ; and with some of them we are pleased and with some not. And we men are found to be governed by Nature equally, and by Fortune differently, and by our Free-will each as he wishes.
35   "But let us speak now, and shew with respect to Fortune, that it has not power over every thing; for this very thing itself

which is called Fortune is an order of procession which is given to the Powers and the Elements by God; and according to this procession and order, intelligences are changed by their coming down to be with the soul, and souls are changed by their coming down to be with the body: and this alternation itself is called the 5 Fortune, and the Nativity of this assemblage, which is being sifted and purified, for the assistance of that which by the favour of God and by grace (1) has been assisted, and is being assisted, till the consummation of all. The body, therefore, is governed by Nature, the soul also suffering with it and perceiving; and the body is not con- 10 strained nor assisted by Fortune in all the things which it does individually; for a man does not become a father before fifteen years, nor does a woman become a mother before thirteen years. And in the same manner, also, there is a law for old age; because women become effete from bearing, and men are deprived of the 15 natural power of begetting; while other animals which are also governed by their own Nature, before those ages which I have specified, not only procreate, but also become too old to procreate, in the same manner as also the bodies of men when they are grown old do not procreate; nor is Fortune able to give them children at that time at which the body has not the Nature to give them. Neither, again, is Fortune able to preserve the body of man in life, without eating and without drinking; nor even when it has meat and drink, to prevent it from dying, for these and many other things pertain to Nature itself; but when the times and 20 manners of Nature are fulfilled, then comes Fortune apparent among these, and effecteth things that are distinct one from another; and at one time assists Nature and increases, and at another hinders it and hurts; and from Nature cometh the growth and perfection of the body; but apart from Nature and by Fortune 30 come sicknesses and defects in the body. From Nature is the connexion of males and females, and the pleasure of the both heads; but from Fortune comes abomination and a different manner of connexion, and all the filthiness and indecency which men do for the cause of connexion through their lust. From Nature is birth and 35 children; and from Fortune sometimes the children are deformed;

and sometimes they are cast away, and sometimes they die untimely. From Nature there is a sufficiency in moderation for all bodies; and from Fortune comes the want of food, and affliction of the bodies; and thus, again, from the same Fortune is gluttony and extravagance which is not requisite. Nature ordains that old men should be judges for the young, and wise for the foolish; and that the valiant should be chiefs over the weak, and the brave over the timid. But Fortune causeth that boys should be chiefs over the aged, and fools over the wise; and that in time of war the weak should govern the valiant, and the timid the brave.[12] And know ye distinctly that, whenever Nature is disturbed from its right course, its disturbance is from the cause of Fortune, because those Heads and Governors, upon whom that alternation is which is called Nativity, are in opposition one to the other. And those of them which are called Right, they assist Nature, and add to its excellency, whenever the procession helps them, and they stand in the high places, which are in the sphere, in their own portions; and those which are called Left are evil: and whenever they, too, occupy the places of height, they are opposed to Nature, and not only injure men, but, at different times, also animals, and trees and fruits, and the produce of the year, and the fountains of water, and every thing that is in the Nature which is under their control. And on account of these divisions and sects which exist among the Powers, some men have supposed that the world is governed without any superintendence, because they do not know that these sects and divisions and justification and condemnation proceed from that influence which is given in Free-will by God, that those actors also by the power of themselves may either be justified or condemned: as we see that Fortune crushes Nature, so we can also see the Free-will of man repelling and crushing Fortune itself: but not in every thing, as also Fortune itself doth not repel Nature in every thing; for it is proper that the three things, Nature and Fortune and Free-will, should be maintained in their lives until the procession be accomplished, and the measure and number be fulfilled, as it seemed good before Him who ordained how should be the life and perfection of all creatures, and the state of all Beings and Natures."

Avida saith, " That it is not from his Nature a man doeth wrong 5 I am persuaded by those things which thou hast shewed, and that all men are not governed equally. But if thou art also able to shew this, that it is not from Fortune and Fate those act wrongly who do act wrongly, then it will be right to believe, that man holds his own Free-will, and by his Nature is brought near to 10 those things which be good, and warned from the things which are wicked, and on this account he will also justly be judged in the last day."

Bardesan saith, " From this, that men are not equally governed, (13) art thou persuaded that it is not from their Nature they act 15 wrongly ? Therefore the matter constrains thee to believe that neither also from their Fortune do they altogether act wrongly, if we be able to shew thee that the decree of the Fortunes and the Powers does not move all men equally, but we have Free-will in ourselves to avoid serving Physical nature and being moved by 20 the control of the Powers."

Avida saith, " Prove me this, and I will be convinced by thee, and whatever thou shalt charge me I will do."

Bardesan saith, " Have you read the books of the Chaldeans which are in Babylon, in which are written what the stars effect by 25 their associations at the Nativities of men ? And the books of the Egyptians, in which are written all the modes which happen to men?"

Avida saith, " I have read the books of Chaldeism, but I do not know which belong to the Babylonians and which to the Egyptians."

Bardesan saith, " The doctrine of both countries is the same." 30

Avida saith, " It is known that it is so."

Bardesan saith, " Hear now and understand, that it is not what the stars decree in their Fortune and in their portions, that all men equally do who are in all the earth ;

for men have established laws in different places, by that Free-will which has been given to them by God. Because the gift itself is opposed to that Fortune of the Powers, which assume for themselves that which has not been given to them. I will begin
5 to speak so far as I remember from the east, the head of the whole world.

"*The Laws of the Seres.* The Seres have laws that they should not kill, and not commit fornication, and not worship idols; and in the whole country of the Seres there are no idols, nor
10 harlots, who killeth a man, nor who is killed; while they too are born at all hours, and upon all days. And Mars the fierce, when he is placed in the midst of the heavens, doth not force the Free-will of the Seres that a man should shed the blood of his neighbour with a weapon of iron. Nor does Venus, when she is
15 placed with Mars, force any one of the men of the Seres that he should have connexion with his neighbour's wife, or with another

---

"Νόμους ἔθεντο διαφόρους οἱ ἄνθρωποι ἐν ἑκάστῃ χώρᾳ, τινὰς γεγραμμένους, τινὰς δὲ ἀγράφους· ἐξ ὧν διηγήσομαι, ὡς οἶδα, καὶ ὧν μέμνημαι, ἀρξάμενος ἐκ τῆς τοῦ κόσμου ἀρχῆς.

Νόμος ἐστὶ παρὰ Σήραις μηδένα φονεύειν, μήτε πορνεύειν, μήτε κλέπτειν, μήτε ξόανα προσκυνεῖν· καὶ ἐν ἐκείνῃ τῇ μεγίστῃ χώρᾳ οὐ ναόν ἐστιν ἰδεῖν, οὐ γυναῖκα πορνικὴν, οὐ μοιχαλίδα ὀνομαζομένην, οὐ κλέπτην ἑλκόμενον ἐπὶ δίκην, οὐκ ἀνδροφόνον, οὐ πεφονευμένον. Οὐδενὸς γὰρ τὸ αὐτεξούσιον ἠνάγκασεν ὁ τοῦ πυριλαμπέος Ἄρεος ἀστὴρ μεσουρανῶν ἄνδρα σιδήρῳ ἀνελεῖν, οὐ Κύπρις σὺν Ἄρει τυχοῦσα ἀλλοτρίᾳ γυναικὶ μιγῆναί τινα παρ' ἐκείνοις, πάντως πάσῃ ἡμέρᾳ μεσουρανοῦντος τοῦ Ἄρεος, καὶ πάσῃ ὥρᾳ καὶ ἡμέρᾳ γεννωμένων τῶν Σηρῶν.

Παρὰ Ἰνδοῖς καὶ Βάκτροις εἰσὶ χιλιάδες πολλαὶ τῶν λεγομένων Βραχμάνων, οἵτινες κατὰ παράδοσιν τῶν προγόνων καὶ νόμων οὔτε φονεύουσιν, οὔτε ξόανα σέβονται, οὐκ ἐμψύχου γεύονται, οὐ μεθύσκονταί ποτε, οἴνου καὶ σίκερος μὴ γευόμενοι, οὐ κακίᾳ τινὶ κοινωνοῦσι προσέχοντες τῷ Θεῷ, τῶν ἄλλων Ἰνδῶν φονευόντων, καὶ ἑταιρευόντων, καὶ μεθυσκομένων, καὶ σεβομένων ξόανα, καὶ πάντα σχεδὸν καθ' εἱμαρμένην φερομένων. Ἔστι

woman; but rich and poor, and sick and healthy, and rulers [14] and subjects, are there: because these things are given to the power of the Governors.

" *Laws of the Brahmins which are in India.* Again, among the Indians, the Brahmins, among whom there are many thousands [5] and tens of thousands, have a law that they should not kill at all, and not revere idols, and not commit fornication, and not eat flesh, and not drink wine; and among them not one of these things takes place. And there are thousands of years to these men, lo! [10] since they govern themselves by this law which they have made for themselves. *Another Law which is in India.* And there is another law in India, and in the same Clime, belonging to those, which are not of the family of the Brahmins, nor of their doctrine; that they should serve idols, and commit fornication, and kill, and [15] do other abominable things, which do not please the Brahmins.

Leges sunt in unaquaque regione vel regno ab hominibus positæ, sive scriptura sive etiam usu durantes, quas nemo facile transgreditur.

Denique primi Seres, qui initio orbis terræ habitant, legem habent neque homicidium neque adulterium neque scortum nosse, neque furtum committere, neque idola venerari, et in illa omni regione quæ est maxima, neque templum invenitur neque simulacrum neque meretrix neque adultera, neque fur ad judicium deducitur, sed neque occisus ibi homo fertur aliquando, et tamen nullius libertas arbitrii compulsa est secundum vos a stella Martis ignita, ut ferro uteretur ad hominis necem, nec Venus cum Marte posita alienum matrimonium compulit vitiari, cum utique apud eos per singulos dies Mars medium cœli circulum teneat. Sed est apud Seres legum metus vehementior quam Genesis constellatio.

Sunt similiter et apud Bactros in regionibus Indorum immensæ multitudines Bragmanorum, qui et ipsi ex traditione majorum, moribus legibusque concordibus, neque homicidium neque adulterium committunt, neque simulacra colunt neque animantia edere in usu habent, nunquam inebriantur, nunquam malitiose aliquid gerunt, sed deum semper timent; et quidem hæc illi, cum cæteri Indorum et homicidia et adulteria committant, et simulacra colant, et inebrientur, atque alia

D

And in the same Clime of India there are men that by custom
eat the flesh of men in the same manner as the rest of the nations
eat the flesh of animals. But the evil stars have not forced the
Brahmins to do evil and abominable things; nor have the good
5 stars persuaded the rest of the Hindoos to abstain from evil things;
nor have these stars which are well arranged in the places which
it is proper for them, and in the signs of Zodiac which relate to
humanity, persuaded those who eat the flesh of men to abstain
from using this abominable and odious food.

10 "*Laws of the Persians.* And, again, the Persians have made
laws for themselves that they may take for wives their sisters,
and their daughters, and their daughters' daughters; and there
are some that go further, and take even their mothers. Of
these same Persians some have been scattered, and are in
15 Media and the country of Parthia, and in Egypt, and in

δὲ ἐν τῷ αὐτῷ κλίματι τῆς Ἰνδίας φυλή τις Ἰνδῶν, οἵτινες τοὺς
ἐμπίπτοντας ξένους ἀγρεύοντες καὶ τούτους θύοντες ἐσθίουσι· καὶ
οὔτε οἱ ἀγαθοποιοὶ τῶν ἀστρων κεκωλύκασι τούτους μὴ μιαιφονεῖν
καὶ μὴ ἀθεμιτοφαγεῖν, οὔτε οἱ κακοποιοὶ ἠνάγκασαν τοὺς Βραχμᾶνας κακουργεῖν.

Παρὰ Πέρσαις νόμος ἦν, γαμεῖν τὰς θυγατέρας καὶ τὰς ἀδελφὰς καὶ
τὰς μητέρας· καὶ οὐ μόνον ἐν τῇ χώρᾳ ἐκείνῃ καὶ ἐν ἐκείνῳ τῷ κλίματι
τούτους τοὺς ἀνοσίους γάμους οἱ Πέρσαι ἐποίησαν, ἀλλὰ καὶ ὅσοι
αὐτῶν τῆς Περσίδος ἐξελήμησαν, οἵτινες καλοῦνται Μαγουσαῖοι, τὴν
αὐτὴν ἀθεμιτίαν διαπράττονται, παραδιδόντες τοῖς αὐτοῖς νόμους
καὶ τὰ ἔθη τοῖς τέκνοις κατὰ διαδοχήν. Ἐξ ὧν εἰσὶ μέχρι νῦν πολλοὶ
ἐν Μηδίᾳ, καὶ ἐν Αἰγύπτῳ, καὶ ἐν Φρυγίᾳ, καὶ ἐν Γαλατίᾳ. Καὶ οὐ
δήπου Κύπρος ἐν ὁρίοις καὶ οἴκοις Κρόνου, σὺν Κρόνῳ ἐφομαρτοῦντος
τοῦ Ἄρεως ἐν ταῖς τῶν πάντων γενέσεσιν εὑρίσκετο.

Παρὰ Γήλους νόμος ἐστί, τὰς γυναῖκας γεωργεῖν, καὶ οἰκοδομεῖν καὶ πάντα τὰ ἐργατικὰ πράσσειν, καὶ κοινωνεῖν οἷς ἂν βού-
λωνται, καὶ μὴ ἐγκαλεῖσθαι ὑπὸ τῶν ἀνδρῶν, μήτε καλεῖσθαί
τινα μοιχαλίδα, τῷ πάσας ἐργατικὰς εἶναι, καὶ πᾶσι κοινωνεῖν,
μάλιστα δὲ τοῖς ξένοις. Καὶ οὔτε μυρίζονται Γήλισσαι γυναῖκες,
οὐχ ἱμάτια βαπτὰ φοροῦσιν, ἀνυπόδητοι δέ εἰσι πᾶσαι, καίτοι τῶν

Phrygia, and they are called Magi: and in all countries and Climes in which they are, they govern themselves by this law which was established for their fathers: but we cannot say that for all the Magi and the rest of the Persians. Venus was placed with the Moon, and with Saturn in the mansion of Saturn in his portions, while Mars witnessed them. And there are many places in the kingdom of the Parthians where men kill their wives, and their brethren, and their children, and incur no vengeance: while among the Romans and the Greeks, whoso killeth one of these incurreth capital punishment, the greatest of vengeance.

" *Laws of the Geli.* Among the Geli the women sow and reap, and build, and perform all the things of labourers, and do not wear dresses of colours: nor do they put on shoes, nor use sweet ointments: neither does any one blame them when they commit adultery with strangers, or when they have connexion

---

hujusmodi flagitia exerceant. Sed et in ipsius Indiæ nihilominus occiduis partibus regio quædam est, ubi hospites cum inciderint, capti immolantur et comeduntur: et neque bonæ stellæ vetuerunt eos ab hujusmodi flagitiis et ab exsecrandis cibis, neque malignæ stellæ compulerunt Bragmanas, ut aliquid agerent mali.

Est rursus mos apud Persas, matres accipere in conjugium et sorores et filias, et sub illo omni axe incesta Persæ ineunt matrimonia. Ac ne forte liceat his qui mathesim sequuntur uti illo perfugio quo dicunt, certas quasdam esse plagas cœli, quibus propria quædam habere conceditur, ex ipsa Persarum gente aliquanti ad peregrina profecti sunt, qui Magusæi appellantur, ex quibus usque in hodiernum sunt alii in Media, alii in Parthia, sed et in Ægypto nonnulli, plures autem in Galatia et Phrygia, qui omnes incestæ hujus traditionis formam indeclinabilem servant, ac posteris custodiendam transmittunt etiam cum plagam cœli mutaverint: nec tamen eos Venus cum Luna in finibus et domibus Saturni, cum Saturno adtestante etiam Marte, compulit habere inter cæteros Genesim.

Apud Gelos quoque mos est, ut mulieres agricolentur, ædificent, et omne opus virile perficiant, sed et misceri quibus volunt licet, nec incusantur a viris aut adulteræ appellantur, passim enim concubitus

with the slaves of their houses ; but their husbands, the Geli,
put on garments of colours, and ornament themselves with gold
and jewels, and anoint themselves with sweet unguents ; nor is it on
account of effeminacy they conduct themselves so, but on account
5 of a law which is established among them ; and all the men are
lovers of hunting, and makers of war : but we cannot say that,
for all the women of the Geli, Venus was placed in Capricorn, or
in Aquarius, in a place of ill-luck ; nor for all the Geli is it
possible for us to say that Mars and Venus were placed in Aries,
10 where it is written that vigorous and lascivious men are born.

Γήλων ἀνδρῶν κοσμουμένων ἐν φορήμασι μαλακοῖς καὶ ἐν διαφόροις χρώμασι, καὶ χρυσοφορούντων, καὶ μυριζομένων· καὶ οὐ κατά
τινα ἄλλην μαλακίαν, εἰσὶ γὰρ ἀνδρεῖοι, καὶ πολεμικώτατοι, καὶ
κυνηγετικώτατοι.   Καὶ οὐ πᾶσαι αἱ τῶν Γήλων γυναῖκες ἔλαχον ἐν
Αἰγοκέρωτι ἢ ἐν Ὑδρηχόῳ κακοδαιμονοῦσαν τὴν Κύπριν· οὔθ' οἱ
ἄνδρες αὐτῶν πάντες ἔχουσιν ἐν Κριῷ σὺν Ἄρει τὴν Παφίην, ἔνθα
τοὺς ἀνδρείους καὶ σπατάλους οἱ Χαλδαΐζοντες λέγουσι.

Παρὰ Βάκτροις αἱ γυναῖκες παντὶ κόσμῳ διαφέροντι καὶ παντὶ μύρῳ
χρῶνται, ὑπηρετούμεναι ὑπὸ παιδίσκων καὶ νεανίσκων μᾶλλον ἢ οἱ
ἄνδρες· προερχόμεναι μετὰ πολλῆς φαντασίας ἔφιπποι, κοσμοῦσαι
πολλῷ χρυσῷ καὶ λίθοις βαρυτίμοις τοὺς ἵππους. Καὶ οὐ σω-
φρονοῦσιν, ἀλλ' ἀδιαφόρως κοινωνοῦσι τοῖς δούλοις καὶ τοῖς ξένοις,
ἄδειαν ἔχουσαι τοιαύτην, καὶ ὑπὸ τῶν ἀνδρῶν μὴ ἐγκαλούμεναι,
σχεδὸν κυριεύουσιν αὐτῶν. Καὶ οὐ πάντως ἐν πάσῃ γενέσει τῶν ἐν
Βακτρίᾳ γυναικῶν μεσουρανεῖ μετὰ Διὸς καὶ Ἄρεος ἐν ἰδίοις ὅροις
ἡ φιλόγελως Ἀφροδίτη.

Ἐν δὲ τῇ Ἀραβίᾳ, καὶ τῇ Ὀσροηνῇ, οὐ μόνον αἱ μοιχαλίδες φονεύονται, ἀλλὰ καὶ αἱ ὑποπτευόμεναι οὐκ ἀφίενται ἀτιμώρητοι.

Παρὰ Πάρθοις καὶ Ἀρμενίοις οἱ φονεῖς ἀναιροῦνται, ποτὲ μὲν ὑπὸ
τῶν δικαστῶν, ποτὲ δὲ ὑπὸ τῶν καθ' αἷμα τῶν φονευθέντων. Καὶ ἐάν
τις φονεύσῃ γυναῖκα αὑτοῦ, ἢ ἀδελφὸν ἄτεκνον, ἢ ἀδελφὴν ἄγαμον,
ἢ υἱὸν, ἢ θυγατέρα, οὐκ ἐγκαλεῖται ὑπό τινος, νόμου τοιούτου ὑπ-
άρχοντος ἐν ταῖς χωραις ἐκείναις· παρ' Ἕλλησι δὲ καὶ Ῥωμαίοις
μείζονι τιμωρίᾳ ὑποβάλλονται οἱ τῶν οἰκείων καὶ συγγενῶν φονευταί.

" *The Laws of the Bactrians.* Amongst the Bactrians, which are called Cashani, the women adorn themselves with the goodly raiment of the men, and with much gold and goodly jewels ; and their male and female slaves minister to them more than to their husbands; and they ride horses ; and some adorn themselves with 5 vestments of gold and with precious stones. And these women do not observe chastity, but have connexion with their slaves, and with strangers which come to that country, and their husbands do not blame them ; and they have no fear, because the Cashani esteem their wives as mistresses ; but we cannot say that, for 10 all the Bactrian women, Venus is placed, and Mars, and Jupiter, in the mansion of Mars in the midst of the heavens, where women that are rich, and adulterers, and keep under their husbands in every thing, are born.

" *The Laws of the Racami, and of the Edesseans, and the* 15 *Arabians.* Amongst the Racami, and the Edesseans, and the Arabians, not only is she that committeth adultery put to death, but she also, that has the name of adultery against her, has capital punishment.

---

miscent et præcipue cum hospitibus, unguenta nesciunt, non induuntur veste fucata, non calceis ; e contra viri Gelonum ornantur, pectuntur, indumentis mollibus et variis induuntur, auro compositi unguentisque delibuti, et hæc non pro dissolutione virium, sunt enim bellicosissimi et venatores acerrimi : nec tamen universæ Gelonum mulieres, in Capræcornu aut Aquario cacodæmonem Venerem nascentes habuere, neque viri eorum in Ariete cum Marte Venerem positam, per quod schema effeminatos et dissolutos nasci adserit viros Chaldaica disciplina.

Porro vero in Susis mulieres unguentis et quidem optimis utuntur, ornamentis comtæ ex lapidibus preciosis, ministeriis quoque ancillarum fultæ procedunt multo majore ambitione quam viri, nec tamen pudicitiam colunt, sed indifferens eis cum quibuscunque voluerint usus est et servis et hospitibus, tali licentia a viris permissa ; et non solum non culpantur pro hoc, sed et dominantur in viros. Nec tamen omnium Genesis mulierum Susidarum in medictate cœli cum Jove et Marte Venerem in Jovis domibus habent.

"*The Laws in Hatra.* There is a law established in Hatra that whosoever committeth the small crime of a theft even of little value should be stoned. Amongst the Cashani, whoso committed such a theft as this, they spit in his face. Amongst the Romans, whoso

5 committeth a little theft is scourged and dismissed. On the other side the Euphrates, and towards the East, he who is reviled either as a thief or as a murderer, does not feel very angry ; but if a man be reviled as an arsenocœte, he then avenges himself even to the putting to death.

10 " *Laws of* [16]   *   * boys   * and are not   *   * Again, in all the country of the East, those who have been insulted, and are known, their fathers and their brothers kill them, and oftentimes they do not even make known their graves.

15 " *Laws of the Orientals.* But in the north, and in the country of the Germans, and those that are near to them, such boys among them as are handsome become as wives to the men, and they

---

Ἐν Ἄτροις ὁ κλέπτων τι ὀβολοῦ ἄξιον λιθάζεται· παρὰ Βάκτροις ὁ ὀλίγα κλέπτων ἐμπτύεται, παρὰ Ῥωμαίοις πληγαῖς αἰκίζεται· τοιοῦτοι γὰρ οἱ νόμοι. Ἀπὸ Εὐφράτου ποταμοῦ, καὶ μέχρι τοῦ Ὠκεανοῦ, ὡς ἐπὶ ἀνατολὰς, ὁ λοιδορούμενος ὡς φονεὺς, ἢ ὡς κλέπτης, οὐ πάνυ ἀγανακτεῖ· ὁ δὲ ὡς ἀρσενοκοίτης λοιδορούμενος, ἑαυτὸν ἐκδικεῖ μέχρι καὶ φόνου.

Παρ' Ἕλλησι δὲ καὶ οἱ σοφοὶ ἐρωμένους ἔχοντες οὐ ψέγονται. Ἐν τῇ αὐτῇ ἀνατολῇ ὑβριζόμενοι, ἐὰν γνωσθῶσιν, ὑπὸ ἀδελφῶν, ἢ πατέρων καὶ συγγενῶν φονεύονται, καὶ ταφῆς προδήλου οὐκ ἀξιοῦνται.

Παρὰ δὲ Γάλλοις οἱ νέοι γαμοῦνται μετὰ παρρησίας, οὐ ψόγον τοῦτο ἡγούμενοι διὰ τὸν παρ' αὐτοῖς νόμον. Καὶ οὐ δυνατόν ἐστι πάντας τοὺς ἐν Γαλλίᾳ οὕτως ἀθέως ὑβριζομένους λαχεῖν ἐν ταῖς γενέσεσι Φωσφόρον μεθ' Ἑρμοῦ, ἐν οἴκοις Κρόνου καὶ ὁρίοις Ἄρεος δύνοντα.

Ἐν Βρεττανίᾳ πολλοὶ ἄνδρες μίαν γυναῖκα ἔχουσιν· ἐν δὲ τῇ Παρθίᾳ, πολλαὶ γυναῖκες ἕνα ἄνδρα, καὶ πᾶσαι σωφρονοῦσι πειθόμεναι αὐτῷ κατὰ τὸν νόμον.

Αἱ δὲ Ἀμαζόνες πᾶσαι ἄνδρας οὐκ ἔχουσιν, ἀλλ' ὡς τὰ ἄλογα ζῷα, ἅπαξ τοῦ ἔτους περὶ τὴν ἐαρινὴν ἰσημερίαν ὑπερβαίνουσαι τοὺς ἰδίους ὅρους κοινωνοῦσι τοῖς πλησιοχώροις, ἑορτήν τινα ταύτην

have also marriage-feasts; and this is not considered by them as a disgrace, nor as a reproach, on account of a law which they have: but it is not possible that all those that are in Gallia, who are disgraced by this disgrace, should have at their nativity Mercury placed for them with Venus, in the mansion of Saturn, and in the 5 limits of Mars, and in the signs of the Zodiac at the west. For respecting those men who have their nativity thus, it is written that they are disgraced as women.

" *Laws of the Britons.* Amongst the Britons many men take one wife.
10

" *Laws of the Parthians.* And amongst the Parthians one man takes many wives, and all of these are obedient to his command in chastity, on account of a law which is established there in the country.

" *Laws of the Amazons.* As to the Amazons, all of them, the en- 15 tire nation, have no husbands, but, like beasts, once in the year, at the season of spring, they go out from their coasts, and pass the river, and when they are over they make a great festival on the mountain, and the men from those quarters come, and abide with them fourteen days, and have intercourse with them, and they become 20 pregnant by them, and then pass again to their own country; and at the time of birth such as are males, they expose, and bring up the

---

In ulterioribus Orientis partibus, si puer muliebri se substernat injuriæ, cum agnitum fuerit, a fratribus aut parentibus vel quibuslibet proximis interficitur, nec sepultura donatur.

Et rursus apud Gallos lex prisca constituit nuptum tradi publice pueros, nec opprobrium ex hoc aliquod duci; et numquid possibile est, ut omnes qui tam turpiter succumbunt apud Gallos, Luciferum cum Mercurio in domibus Saturni et finibus Martis habuerint?

In Britanniæ partibus plures viri unam habent uxorem, in Parthia multæ mulieres unum habent virum, et utraque orbis pars moribus suis atque institutis obsequitur.

Amazones omnes non habent viros, sed sicut animalia semel in anno circa vernale æquinoctium proprios egressæ terminos, finitimæ gentis viris miscentur, solennitatem quandam per hoc observantes, ex quibus cum conceperint redeunt, et si marem pepererint abjiciunt, feminas

females: and it is a known thing, that according as Nature ordains, because they all become pregnant in one month, they also are delivered in one month, a little more and a little less; and as we have heard, all of them are vigorous and warlike: but not
5 one of the stars is able to help all those males, which are born, from being exposed."

" *Book of the Chaldeans.* It is written in the Book of the Chaldeans, that whenever Mercury is placed with Venus in the mansion of Mercury, it produceth painters and sculptors, and
10 money-changers; but when they are in the mansion of Venus, they produce perfumers, and dancers, and singers, and poets. And in all the country of the Tayites and of the Saracens,[17] and in Upper Lybia, and amongst the Mauritanians, and in the country of the Nomades, which is at the mouth of the ocean, and in outer
15 Germania, and in Upper Sarmatia, and in Hispania, and in all

ἡγουμένοις· ἐξ ὧν συλλαμβάνουσαι ὑποστρέφουσι, καὶ ἀναγκαίως ἐν ἑνὶ καιρῷ ἀποκυΐσκουσι κατὰ τὸν τῆς φύσεως νόμον, καὶ τοὺς μὲν γεννωμένους ἄρρενας ῥίπτουσι, τὰς δὲ θηλείας ἀνατρέφουσι· πολεμικαί τέ εἰσι, καὶ γυμνασίων προνοούμεναι.

Ἑρμῆς μετὰ Ἀφροδίτης ἐν οἴκοις Ἑρμοῦ ποιεῖ πλάστας, καὶ ζωγράφους, καὶ τραπεζίτας· ἐν οἴκοις δὲ Ἀφροδίτης μυρεψοὺς, ἢ φωνάσκους καὶ ὑποκριτὰς ποιημάτων. Καὶ παρὰ Ταϊνοῖς καὶ Σαρακηνοῖς, καὶ ἐν τῇ ἀνωτέρᾳ Λιβύῃ, καὶ παρὰ Μαύροις, καὶ παρὰ τοῖς παρὰ τὸ στόμα τοῦ Ὠκεανοῦ Νομάσι, καὶ ἐν τῇ ἐξωτέρᾳ Γερμανίᾳ, καὶ ἐν τῇ ἀνωτέρᾳ Σαρματίᾳ, καὶ ἐν τῇ Σκυθίᾳ, καὶ ἐν πᾶσι τοῖς ἐξ Ἀρκτικῶν μερῶν τοῦ Πόντου ἔθνεσι, καὶ ὅλῃ τῇ Ἀλανίᾳ, καὶ Ἀλβανίᾳ, καὶ Ὠτηνῇ καὶ Σαυνίᾳ, καὶ ἐν Χρυσῇ, οὐκ ἔστιν ἰδεῖν οὐ τραπεζίτην, οὐ πλάστην, οὐ ζωγράφον, οὐκ ἀρχιτέκτονα, οὐ γεωμέτρην, οὐ φώνασκον, οὐχ ὑποκριτὴν ποιημάτων, ἀλλ' ἐστέρηται ὁ τῆς τοῦ Ἑρμοῦ καὶ τῆς Ἀφροδίτης ἐνεργείας τρόπος ἐν ὅλῳ τῷ κύκλῳ τούτῳ τῆς οἰκουμένης. Οἱ Μῆδοι πάντες τοῖς μετὰ σπουδῆς τρεφομένοις κυσὶ τοὺς νεκροὺς ἔτι ἐμπνέοντας παραβάλλουσι· καὶ οὐ πάντες σὺν τῇ Μήνῃ τὸν Ἄρεα ἐφ' ἡμερινῆς γενέσεως ἐν Καρκίνῳ ὑπὸ γῆν ἔχουσιν. Ἰνδοὶ τοὺς νεκροὺς καίουσι, μεθ' ὧν συγκαίουσιν ἑκούσας τὰς γυναῖκας· καὶ οὐ δήπου πᾶσαι αἱ καιόμεναι ζῶσαι Ἰνδῶν γυναῖκες ἔχουσιν ὑπὸ γῆν ἐπὶ νυκτερινῆς γενέσεως

the countries which are to the north of Pontus, and in all the
country of the Alanians, and amongst the Albanians, and amongst
the Zazi, and in Brusa which is beyond the Duro, one seeth not
either sculptors, nor painters, nor perfumers, nor money-
changers, nor poets. But this decree of Mercury and Venus is
inhibited from the circumference of the whole world. In the whole
of Media, all men when they die, even while life is still re-
maining in them, are cast to the dogs, and the dogs eat the
dead of the whole of Media; but we cannot say that all the
Medians are born while the Moon is placed for them with Mars in
Cancer during the day below the Earth: for thus it is written
that those whom the dogs eat are born. The Hindoos, all of
them when they die are burnt with fire, and many of their wives
are burnt with them alive; but we cannot say, that all those
women of the Hindoos which are burnt had at their nativity
Mars and the Sun placed in Leo in the night below the Earth,
as those men are born which are burnt with fire. All the Germans

nutriunt. Cumque unius temporis sit omnium partus, absurdum est, ut
in maribus quidem putetur Mars cum Saturno in tempore æquis esse
portionibus, in feminarum vero Genesi nunquam.

Sed neque Mercurium cum Venere habuisse in domibus propriis positum, ut vel pictores ibi vel sculptores vel trapezitas
efficiat, aut in domibus Veneris, ut unguentarios vel vocales vel
poetas producat. Apud Sarracenos et superiores Libes et Mauros et
circa ora maris Oceani habitantes, sed et in extremis Germaniæ
partibus et apud Sarmatas et Scythas atque omnes quæ sub axe
septentrionis jacent Pontici littoris gentes, et in Chrysea insula,
nunquam invenitur trapezita, nec sculptor, aut pictor, aut archi-
tectus, aut geometres, aut tragœdus, aut poeta; ergo deficit apud
eos Mercurii Venerisque constellatio. Ex omni orbe terrarum
Medi tantummodo summa observantia adhuc spirantes homines
canibus devorandos abjiciunt, et non ob hoc Martem cum Luna
per diurnam Genesim in Cancro positos habent. Indi mortuos
suos incendunt, cum quibus et uxores defunctorum sponte se offe-
rentes exuruntur. Sed non ideo omnes quæ vivæ incenduntur Indorum mulieres, in nocturna Genesi sub terra habent Solem cum Marte

E

die by suffocation, except those which are killed in battle; and it
is not possible that at the nativity of all the Germans the Moon and
Hora should have been placed between Mars and Saturn. But, in
all places, every day and at all hours, men are born in nativities
5 which are distinct one from the other, and the laws of men overcome the Decree, and they govern themselves according to their
customs; and Fortune does not compel the Seres to kill at all when
they do not wish; nor the Brahmins to eat flesh; nor restrain
the Persians from marrying their daughters and their sisters;
10 nor the Hindoos from being burnt; nor the Medians from being
devoured by dogs; nor the Parthians from taking many wives;
nor the Britons from many men taking one wife; nor the

σὺν Ἄρει τὸν Ἥλιον ἐν Λέοντι ὁρίοις Ἄρεος. Γερμανῶν οἱ πλεῖστοι
ἀγχονιμαίῳ μόρῳ ἀποθνήσκουσι, καὶ οὐ πάντως τὸ πλῆθος τῶν
Γερμανῶν τὴν σελήνην καὶ τὴν ὥραν μεσολαβουμένας ὑπὸ Κρόνου
καὶ Ἄρεος ἔχει. Παντὶ ἔθνει, καὶ πάσῃ ἡμέρᾳ καὶ παντὶ τόπῳ τῆς
γενέσεως γεννῶνται ἄνθρωποι· κρατεῖ δὲ ἐν ἑκάστῃ μοίρᾳ τῶν ἀνθρώπων νόμος καὶ ἔθος διὰ τὸ αὐτεξούσιον τοῦ ἀνθρώπου· καὶ οὐκ
ἀναγκάζει ἡ γένεσις τοὺς Σῆρας μὴ θέλοντας φονεύειν, ἢ τοὺς
Βραχμᾶνας κρεοφαγεῖν, ἢ τοὺς Πέρσας ἀθεμίτως μὴ γαμεῖν, ἢ τοὺς
Ἰνδοὺς μὴ καίεσθαι, ἢ τοὺς Μήδους μὴ ἐσθίεσθαι ὑπὸ κυνῶν, ἢ
τοὺς Πάρθους μὴ πολυγαμεῖν, ἢ τὰς ἐν τῇ Μεσοποταμίᾳ γυναῖκας
μὴ σωφρονεῖν, ἢ τοὺς Ἕλληνας μὴ γυμνάζεσθαι γυμνοῖς τοῖς σώ-
μασιν, ἢ τοὺς Ῥωμαίους μὴ κρατεῖν, ἢ τοὺς Γάλλους μὴ γαμεῖσθαι,
ἢ τὰ ἄλλα βάρβαρα ἔθνη ταῖς ὑπὸ τῶν Ἑλλήνων λεγομέναις Μού-
σαις κοινωνεῖν· ἀλλ᾽, ὡς προεῖπον, ἕκαστον ἔθνος καὶ ἕκαστος τῶν
ἀνθρώπων χρῆται τῇ ἑαυτοῦ ἐλευθερίᾳ, ὡς βούλεται καὶ ὅτε βούλεται, καὶ δουλεύει τῇ γενέσει καὶ τῇ φύσει δι᾽ ἣν περίκειται σάρκα,
πῇ μὲν ὡς βούλεται, πῇ δὲ ὡς μὴ βούλεται. Πανταχῇ γὰρ καὶ
ἐν παντὶ ἔθνει εἰσὶ πλούσιοι καὶ πένητες, καὶ ἄρχοντες καὶ ἀρχό-
μενοι, καὶ ἐρρωμένοι καὶ νοσοῦντες, ἕκαστος κατὰ τοὺς τῆς γενέσεως
αὐτοῦ κλήρους.

Ταῦτα, ὦ Βαρδησάνη, ἄκρως ἡμᾶς πέπεικε, φημὶ αὐτῷ. Οἱ
δὲ ἀστρονόμοι φασὶ τὴν γῆν ταύτην μεμερίσθαι εἰς ἑπτὰ κλίματα, καὶ ἄρχειν ἑκάστου κλίματος ἕνα τῶν ἑπτὰ ἀστέρων· καὶ

Edesseans from being chaste; nor the Greeks from practising gymnastics * * *; nor the Romans from always seizing upon countries; nor the Gauls from marrying one for another; nor *constrain* the Amazons to bring up the males; neither does the Nativity compel any at the circumference of the world to use [18] the art of the 5 Muses; but as I have said, in every country, and in every nation, all men use the Free-will of their Nature as they wish, and do service to Fortune and to Nature, on account of the body with which they are clad, at one time as they wish, at another as they do not wish; for in every country and in every nation there are rich 10 and poor, and rulers and subjects, and healthy and sick, each of them, according as Fortune and Nativity has reached him.

I say to him, "Thou has convinced us of these things, Father Bardesan, and we know that they are true. But thou art aware that the Chaldeans say, that the Earth is divided into seven por- 15 tions, which are called Climes; and over these same portions those Seven *Stars* have authority, each one over one of them; and in

---

in partibus Martis. Germanorum plurimi laqueo vitam finiunt, nec idcirco omnes Lunam cum Hora, Saturno et Marte circumcinctas habent. Sed non in omni gente, et in omni die per omnem diversitatem Genesis nascuntur homines? Ex quibus omnibus apparet, quia metus legum in unaquaque regione dominatur, et arbitrii libertas quæ est hominibus insita per spiritum, obtemperat legibus, nec cogere potest Genesis aut Seres homicidium committere, aut Bragmanos carnibus vesci, aut Persas incesta vitare, vel Indos non exuri, aut Medos non a canibus devorari, Parthos non habere plures uxores, aut mulieres Mesopotamiæ non servare pudicitiam, Græcos non exerceri palæstris, Gallorum pueros non pati muliebria, vel gentes barbaras Græcorum studiis institui, sed ut diximus, unaquæque gens suis legibus utitur pro libertatis arbitrio, et decreta Genesis legum severitate depellit.

Sed dicet aliquis eorum qui in disciplina mathesis eruditi sunt, Genesim in septem partes dirimi, quæ illi climata appellant, dominari vero unicuique climati unam ex septem stellis, et istas quas exposuimus diversas leges non ab hominibus positas, sed ab istis principibus

each one of those same places the will of its Power prevails; and this is called Law."

He said to me, "Know first, my son Phillip, that for the purpose of deceit the Chaldeans have invented this saying: For although the earth be divided into seven portions, nevertheless, in each one of the same portions there are found many laws which differ one from the other. For there are not found in the world seven laws according to the number of the Seven Stars; nor twelve according to the number of the Signs of the Zodiac; nor also thirty-six according to the number of the Decani: but there are many laws in each kingdom, and in each country, and in each circuit, and in every habitation, which are different from their neighbours. For ye remember what I said to you, that in one Clime of the Hindoos there are men that do not eat the flesh of animals, and there are others that eat the

---

τοὺς διαφόρους νόμους μὴ τοὺς ἀνθρώπους τεθεικέναι ἑαυτοῖς, ἀλλ' ἑκάστου ἄρχοντος πλεονάζειν τὸ θέλημα ἐν τῇ ἰδίᾳ χώρᾳ, ὃν νόμον νενομίκασιν οἱ κρατούμενοι.

Ἀπεκρίνατο. Οὐκ ἀληθὴς ἡ ἀπόκρισις αὕτη, ὦ Φίλιππε. Εἰ γὰρ καὶ διῄρηται ἡ οἰκουμένη εἰς μέρη ἑπτά, ἀλλ' οὖν γε ἐν μιᾷ μερίδι εὑρίσκομεν πολλὰς διαφορὰς νόμων. Οὐδὲ γὰρ ἑπτὰ νόμοι εἰσὶ κατὰ τοὺς ἑπτὰ ἀστέρας, οὐδὲ δώδεκα κατὰ τὰ ζώδια, οὐδὲ τριακονταὲξ κατὰ τοὺς δεκανούς, ἀλλὰ μυρίοι. Μνημονεύειν τε ὀφείλετε ὧν προεῖπον, ὅτι καὶ ἐν ἑνὶ κλίματι καὶ ἐν μιᾷ χώρᾳ τῶν Ἰνδῶν εἰσιν ἀνθρωποφάγοι Ἰνδοί, καί εἰσιν οἱ ἐμψύχων ἀπεχόμενοι, καὶ ὅτι οἱ Μαγουσαῖοι οὐκ ἐν Περσίδι μόνῃ τὰς θυγατέρας γαμοῦσιν, ἀλλὰ καὶ ἐν παντὶ ἔθνει, ὅπου ἂν οἰκήσωσι, τοὺς τῶν προγόνων φυλάσσοντες νόμους καὶ τῶν μυστηρίων αὐτῶν τὰς τελετάς. Ἀλλὰ καὶ πολλὰ βάρβαρα ἔθνη κατελέξαμεν, τά τε ὄντα ἐν μεσημβρίᾳ, καὶ δύσει, καὶ ἀνατολῇ, καὶ ἄρκτῳ, τουτέστιν ἐν διαφόροις κλίμασι, μὴ μετέχοντα Ἑρμαϊκῆς ἐπιστήμης. Πόσοι, νομίζετε, σοφοὶ ἄνδρες παρήγαγον τοὺς κακῶς κειμένους νόμους; Πόσοι δὲ νόμοι ὑπὸ τῆς ἀπορίας κατελύθησαν; Πόσοι βασιλεῖς κρατήσαντες ἐθνῶν, παρήγαγον τοὺς πρὸ αὐτῶν νόμους, καὶ ἔθεντο τοὺς ἰδίους; Καὶ οὐδεὶς τῶν ἀστέρων ἀπώλεσε τὸ ἴδιον κλίμα.

flesh of men. And again, I told you respecting the Persians and the Magi, that it was not in the Clime of Persia only they have taken for wives their daughters and their sisters, but in every country to which they have gone, they have used the law of their fathers, and observed the mysteries of what they delivered to them. And again, remember that there are many people I told you, which surround all the world, that are not in one Clime, but in all the winds, and in all the Climes; and they have not the art which Mercury and Venus give when they are in configuration one with the other. And if the laws pertained to the Climes this could not be; but it is known, because those men are distant from the intercourse of men they are many in the manners of their living.[16] How many wise men, think ye, have abrogated from their own countries those laws which seemed to them not to be well made? And how many laws are there which have been broken on account of necessity? And how many kings are there, who, having taken those countries which did not belong to them, have abrogated the laws of their establishing, and instituted such laws as they desired?

---

secundum uniuscujusque voluntatem; et hoc quod stellæ visum est, legem ab hominibus observatam.

Ad hæc ergo respondebimus, quod primo quidem non est in septem partes orbis terræ divisus, tum deinde et si ita esset, in una parte et in una regione invenimus multas differentias legum, et ideo neque septem sunt secundum numerum Stellarum, neque duodecim secundum numerum Signorum, neque triginta et sex secundum numerum Decanorum, sed sunt innumeræ. Meminisse autem debemus eorum quæ supra enumerata sunt, quod in una Indiæ regione sunt et qui hominum carnibus vescantur, et sunt qui etiam a pecudibus vel avibus omnibusque animantibus abstineant, et quia Magusæi non solum in Perside matres ac filias accipiunt in matrimonium, sed et in omni gente ubicunque habitaverint, malorum suorum incesta instituta custodiunt. Tum præterea et innumeras gentes memoravimus, quæ penitus studia nesciunt literarum. Sed et aliquanti sapientes viri ipsas leges in nonnullis commutaverunt locis, aliæ vero etiam sponte pro sui vel impossibilitate vel inhonestate derelictæ sunt. Certe quod in promptu est noscere, quanti imperatores

And whenever these things took place, no one of the Stars was able to preserve the law. But this is at hand for you to see; because but as yesterday the Romans took Arabia, and abrogated all their ancient laws ; and more especially that circumcision with
5 which they circumcised. For he that has the power in himself obeyeth such law as is ordained for him by another, who also is possessed of the power of himself. But I will tell you what may avail more than any thing to persuade the foolish, and those lacking of faith. All the Jews, who have received the law at the
10 hand of Moses, circumcise their male children on the eighth day, and do not wait for the coming of the Stars; neither do they respect the law of the country ; nor does the Star, which has authority in the Clime, govern them by force ; but whether they be in Edom, or in Arabia, or in Greece, or in Persia, or in the North,
15 or in the South, they fulfil this law which was established for them by their fathers ; and it is known that this which they do is not from Nativity, for it is not possible that Mars should rise for all the Jews on the eighth day when they are circumcised, so that steel should pass over them, and their blood be shed. And

---

Χθὲς οἱ Ῥωμαῖοι τῆς Ἀραβίας κρατήσαντες τοὺς τῶν βαρβάρων νόμους ἤλλαξαν· ἔπεται γὰρ τὸ αὐτεξούσιον τῷ αὐτεξουσίῳ. Τὸ δὲ δυνάμενον πεῖσαι καὶ τοὺς ἀπίστους ἐκθήσομαι ὑμῖν. Ἰουδαῖοι πάντες οἱ διὰ Μωσέως δεξάμενοι νόμον τοὺς γεννωμένους ἄρρενας παῖδας ἐν τῷ ὀγδόῃ ἡμέρᾳ αἱμάσσουσι περιτέμνοντες, οὐκ ἀστέρος παρουσίαν ἀναμένοντες, οὐ κλίματος ἐξουσίαν ἐκτρεπόμενοι, οὐχ ὑπὸ νόμου ἀλλοτρίας χώρας ἀγόμενοι· ἀλλ᾽ εἴτε ἐν Συρίᾳ τυγχάνουσιν, εἴτε ἐν Γαλλίᾳ, εἴτε ἐν Ἰταλίᾳ, εἴτε ἐν Ἑλλάδι, ἢ ἐν Παρθίᾳ ἢ ὅπου ἂν ὦσι, τοῦτο ποιοῦσιν. Ὅπερ οὐκ ἔστι κατὰ γένεσιν, οὐ γὰρ δύνανται πάντες, Ἰουδαῖοι μίαν γένεσιν ἔχειν. Ἀλλὰ καὶ δι᾽ ἡμερῶν ἑπτὰ πάντες ὅπου ἂν ὦσιν, ἀργοῦσιν ἐκ παντὸς ἔργου, καὶ οὔτε ὁδεύουσιν, οὔτε πυρὶ χρῶνται· οὔτε ἀναγκάζει ἡ γένεσις Ἰουδαῖον, οὐ κτίσαι οἶκον, οὐ καταλῦσαι, οὐκ ἐργάσασθαι, οὐ πωλῆσαι, οὐκ ἀγοράσαι ταῖς ἡμέραις τοῦ σαββάτου, καὶ τοι ἐν τῇ αὐτῇ ἡμέρᾳ γεννώντων Ἰουδαίων καὶ γεννωμένων, καὶ νοσούντων καὶ ἀποθνησκόντων. Ταῦτα γὰρ οὐκ ἔτι ἐστὶ τοῦ αὐτεξουσίου. Ἐν τῇ Συρίᾳ

all of them, wherever they are, abstain from worshipping idols ; and
one day in seven they and their children abstain from all work,
and from all building and from all travelling, and from buying
and selling; neither do they kill an animal on the sabbath-day,
nor kindle fire, nor judge a cause ; and there is not found amongst 5
them a man whom Fortune commands that on the Sabbath day he
should either go to law and gain his cause, or go to law and lose it,
or should pull down or build up, or do any one of those things
which all such men as have not received this law do.   They have
also other things, in which they are not governed like the 10
rest of mankind, while on this same day they both beget, and
are born, and fall sick, and die, for these things are not [20] in the
power of man.   In Syria and in Edessa men used to cut off their
foreskins to Tharatha : but when Abgar the king was converted

---

gentium quas vicerant leges et instituta mutarunt, et suis eas legibus sub-
jecerunt. Quod evidenter a Romanis factum docetur, qui omnem pæne
orbem omnesque nationes propriis primo et variis legibus institutisque
viventes, in Romanorum ius et civilia scita verterunt. Superest ergo ut
et stellæ gentium, quæ a Romanis victæ sunt, climata sua partesque per-
diderint. Addam adhuc rem, quæ possit etiam valde incredulis satisfacere.
Judæi omnes qui sub lege Moysi vivunt, filios suos octava die absque
ulla dilatione circumcidunt, et infantis teneri sanguinem fundunt; a
sæculo autem nullus ex gentibus hoc die octava perpessus est, et
e contra Judæorum nullus omisit.   Quomodo ergo in hoc ratio Genesis
stabit ? cum per cunctas orbis terræ partes omnes Judæi admixti gentibus vivant, et octava ferrum perferant die unius in membri loco, et
nemo gentilium, sed ipsi soli ut dixi, hoc faciunt, non stella cogente
nec perfusione sanguinis perurgente, sed lege religionis adducti, et in
quocunque orbis loco fuerint, hoc est eis insigne vernaculum.   Sed et
quod unum nomen omnibus inest ubicunque fuerint, numquid et hoc
per Genesim venit ? et quod nunquam apud eos infans natus exponitur,
et quod septimo quoque die omnes, ubicunque fuerint, otium gerunt, nec
iter incedunt nec igni utuntur ?   Quid est ergo, quod nullum Judæorum in illa die cogit Genesis aut iter agere, aut ædificare, aut vendere
aliquid, aut emere ?

to Christianity, he commanded that every one that cut off his foreskin should have his hand cut off. And from that day, and up to this hour, no man cutteth off his foreskin in the country of Edessa. What, then, shall we say respecting the new race of
5 ourselves who are Christians, whom in every country and in every region the Messiah established at His coming; for, lo! wherever we be, all of us are called by the one name of the Messiah—Christians; and upon one day, which is the first of the week, we assemble ourselves together, and on the appointed days we abstain
10 from food. Neither do the Brethren which are in Gallia take

---

καὶ ἐν τῇ Ὀσροηνῇ, ἀπεκόπτοντο πολλοὶ τῇ Ῥέᾳ, καὶ ἐν τούτῳ μιᾷ ῥοπῇ ὁ βασιλεὺς Ἄβγαρος ἐκέλευσε τῶν ἀποκοπτομένων τὰ αἰδοῖα ἀποκόπτεσθαι καὶ τὰς χεῖρας, καὶ ἐκ τότε οὐδεὶς ἀπεκόψατο ἐν τῇ Ὀσροηνῇ. Τί δὲ ἐροῦμεν περὶ τῆς τῶν Χριστιανῶν αἱρέσεως, ἧς ἡμεῖς οἱ δοξασταὶ πολλοὶ ὄντες καὶ ἐν διαφόροις ἀνέστημεν κλίμασιν, ἐν παντὶ ἔθνει καὶ κλίματι, οἵτινες πολλοὶ ὄντες, ἑνὶ ὀνόματι κεκλήμεθα; Καὶ οὔτε οἱ ἐν Παρθίᾳ Χριστιανοὶ πολυγαμοῦσι, Πάρθοι ὑπάρχοντες, οὔθ' οἱ ἐν Μηδίᾳ κυσὶ παραβάλλουσι τοὺς νεκρούς· οὐχ οἱ ἐν Περσίδι γαμοῦσι τὰς θυγατέρας αὐτῶν, Πέρσαι ὄντες, οὐ παρὰ Βάκτροις καὶ Γάλλοις φθείρουσι τοὺς γάμους· οὐχ' οἱ ἐν Αἰγύπτῳ θρησκεύουσι τὸν Ἄπιν ἢ τὸν κύνα ἢ τὸν τράγον ἢ αἴλουρον· ἀλλ' ὅπου εἰσὶν, οὔτε ὑπὸ τῶν κακῶς κειμένων νόμων καὶ ἐθῶν νικῶνται, οὔθ' ἡ ὑπὸ τῶν ἀρχῶν πρυτανευομένη γένεσις αὐτοὺς ἀναγκάζει τοῖς ἀπειρημένοις κακοῖς ὑπὸ τοῦ διδασκάλου αὐτῶν χρῆσθαι, νόσῳ δὲ, καὶ πενίᾳ καὶ πάθεσι καὶ ταῖς νομιζομέναις ἀτιμίαις ὑπόκεινται. Ὥσπερ γὰρ ὁ ἐλεύθερος ἡμῶν ἄνθρωπος δουλεύειν οὐκ ἀναγκάζεται, κἂν ἀναγκασθῇ, ἀνθίσταται τοῖς ἀναγκάζουσιν, οὕτως οὐδὲ ὁ φαινόμενος ἡμῶν δοῦλος ἄνθρωπος τῆς ὑποταγῆς ἐκφεύγειν ῥᾳδίως δύναται. Εἰ γὰρ πάντα ἐδυνάμεθα, ἡμεῖς ἂν ἦμεν τὸ πᾶν, ὥστε εἰ μηδὲν ἐδυνάμεθα, ἄλλων ἦμεν, ὡς προεῖπον, ὄργανα καὶ οὐχ ἑαυτῶν. Θεοῦ δ' ἐπινεύσαντος πάντα δυνατὰ καὶ ἀνεμπόδιστα· τῇ γὰρ ἐκείνου βουλήσει οὐδὲν ἀντιστῆναι δύναται. Καὶ γὰρ τὰ δοκοῦντα ἀνθίστασθαι, αὐτοῦ χρηστοῦ ὄντος, καὶ συγχωροῦντος ἑκάστῃ φύσει ἔχειν τὴν ἰδιότητα καὶ τὸ αὐτεξούσιον τοῦ θελήματος, ἀνθίσταται."

males for wives; nor those which are in Parthia take two wives; nor those which are in Judea circumcise themselves; nor do our sisters which are amongst the Geli and amongst the Cashani have connexion with strangers; nor do those which are in Persia take their daughters for wives; nor those who are in Media fly from their dead, or bury them alive, or give them for food to the dogs; nor do those who are in Edessa kill their wives that commit fornication, or their sisters, but withdraw themselves from them, and commit them to the judgment of God. Nor do those who are in Hatra stone the thieves. But whereever they be, and in whatever place that they are, the laws of the countries do not separate them from the laws of their Messiah; neither does the Fortune of the Governers compel them to make use of things which are impure to them; but sickness and health, and riches and poverty—this which does not appertain to their Freewill, befals them wherever they are. For as the Free-will of men is not governed by the necessity of the Seven, and whenever it is governed it is able to stand against its influences, so also is this visible man not able readily to deliver himself from the commands of his Governers, for he is a slave and a subject. For if we were able to do every thing we should be every thing; and if nothing came within the reach of our hands to do, we should be the instruments of others. But whenever God pleaseth, all things are possible to be, without hindrance. For there is nothing which can hinder that great and

---

Quin imo et majorem fidem rerum præsentium dabo. Ecce enim ex adventu justi et veri prophetæ vixdum septem anni sunt, in quibus ex omnibus gentibus convienientes homines ad Judæam, et signis ac virtutibus quæ viderant, sed et doctrinæ maiestate, permoti, ubi receperunt fidem ejus, abeuntes ad regiones suas, illicitos quosque gentilium ritus et incesta sprevere conjugia. Denique apud Parthos, sicut nobis Thomas qui apud illos evangelium prædicat, scripsit, non multi jam erga plurima matrimonia diffunduntur, nec multi apud Medos canibus objiciunt mortuos suos, neque Persæ matrum conjugiis aut filiarum incestis matrimoniis delectantur, nec mulieres Susides licita ducunt adulteria; nec potuit ad crimina Genesis compellere, quos religionis doctrina prohibebat.

F

holy will. For even such as think that they stand against Him, it is
not in strength they stand, but in evil and in error; and this may
subsist a short time, because He is kind, and permitteth all Natures [21] that they should stand in what they are, and be governed by
their own will, but being bound nevertheless by the deeds which are
5 done, and by the plans which have been devised for their help.
For this order and government which have been given, and
association of one with another, softens down the force of the Natures, that they should not be altogether injurious, nor be altogether injured, as they were injuring and injured before the creation
10 of the world. And there will be a time, when also this injury
which remaineth in them shall be brought to an end by the instruction which will be in another association. And at the
establishment of that new world, all evil motions will cease, and
all rebellions will be brought to an end, and the foolish will be
15 persuaded, and deficiencies will be filled up, and there will be peace
and safety, by the gift of Him who is the Lord of all Natures.

HERE ENDETH THE BOOK OF THE LAWS OF COUNTRIES.

CÆSARII,

FRATRIS GREGORII THEOLOGI

DIALOGUS II.

Πεῦσις ρθ'.

Τῆς ὑμετέρας ἁγιωσυνῆς λέγειν μοι ἐπιτρεπούσης, ἐντεῦθεν τοῦ
λόγου ἄρχομαι, οὐ λυμήνασθαι τοὺς παρόντας, ἀλλ' ἀποθέσθαι
τὴν λύμην βουλόμενος. αὐτίκα γοῦν Ἄρης κέντρον λαβὼν, οἰκείῳ
20 οἴκῳ ἐκ τετραγώνου ἐπιθεωρῶν Κρόνον σὺν Ἑρμῇ ἐπὶ κέντρον,
Σελήνης ἐπ' αὐτὸν πλήρους ἀρχομένης, ἐπὶ ἡμερινῆς γεννήσεως,
ἐκτελεῖ ἀνδροφόνους καὶ κτεινομένους, ἐπωμότας, καὶ αἱμοπότας,
μεθύσους, λάγνους, δαιμονῶντας, μυστηρίων ἀποκρύφων ἴστορας,
μάγους θύτας, καὶ τὰ τούτοις ἀκόλουθα, ἐξαιρέτως μηδενὸς τῶν

ἀγαθοποιῶν ἀστέρων ἐπιθεωροῦντος. αὐτὸς δὲ πάλιν Ἄρης πρὸς
Ἀφροδίτην σχῆμα τετράγωνον, μοιρικῶς ἐπὶ κέντρον μὴ ἐπιθεω-
ροῦτός τινος ἀγαθοποιοῦ, μοιχοὺς ἀποτελεῖ, ἀδελφαῖς καὶ μητράσι
μιγνυμένους. Κύπρις σὺν Μήνῃ ἐν ὁρίοις καὶ οἴκοις Κρόνου, σὺν
Κρόνῳ, ἐπιμαρτυροῦντος τοῦ Ἄρεος, ἀποτελεῖ γυναῖκας γεωργοὺς 5
καὶ οἰκοδόμους, καὶ πάντων ἀνδρείων ἔργων ἐπιστήμονας, καὶ
κοινοῦσθαι καὶ συγκαθεύδειν οἷς δ᾽ ἂν βούλοιντο, καὶ μὴ κωλύεσθαι
ὑπὸ τῶν οἰκείων ἀνδρῶν. ἀνδρείους οὖν ἀποτελεῖ γυναῖκας ἐν Αἰγοκέρῳ, Ὑδροχόῳ, κακοδαίμονας ἐν Ἀφροδίτῃ, ἐπ᾽ ἀνδρῶν δὲ τοὐναντίον
σὺν Ἄρεϊ οὖσα, ἐν Κριῷ. ὅθεν οὐχ οἷόν τε φόβῳ ἢ τινος ἀπειλῇ ἢ 10
μηχανῇ ἐπισχεῖν τὰς ἐπιθυμίας διὰ τὴν τῶν ἄστρων ἀποκλήρωσιν.

Ἀπόκρισις.

Ἐπιστημόνως πάνυ τῆς Ἑλλήνων πλάνης τοὺς μύθους ἀπήγγει-
λας. αὖθις οὖν κἀγὼ θαρραλέως ἀποδύσομαι πρὸς τὰ ὑπὸ σοῦ
ῥηθέντα, καὶ σφενδόνῃ ἢ τοξίᾳ τῷ λόγῳ χρώμενος, καθεῖλαι πειρά-
σομαι Ἄρεα καὶ Ἀφροδίτην τοὺς ἡμετέρους ἀστέρας, ὅπως μοι
ἀστροκτονιάς γένεσιν ἐπιφημίσῃς. πρότερον δὲ ἀξιῶ παιδευθῆναί σε, 15
οἷόν τε ὑπάρχειν, τὸν βουλόμενον, τὰς ἐπιθυμιάς καὶ ἐνεργείας ἢ
κολάζειν, ἢ παντελῶς ἀποσείεσθαι. σείω δὲ ἐκ τοῦ συνειδότος
αἰκιζομένου, καὶ μνήμῃ τοῦ ἀκλινοῦς κριτηρίου, τῶν καλῶν εἰργό-
μενου. ἀλλὰ καὶ οἱ τῶν ἀρχόντων νόμοι οἷοί τε πρὸ τῆς πείρας τῶν
στρεβλωτηρίων, καὶ πηγάνων, καὶ καταπέλτων, τῇ ἀκοῇ καὶ μόνῃ 20
τῶν φοβερῶν τῆς κακίας ἀνταμείψεως, σωφρονῆσαι τὴν ἀκόλαστον,
καὶ ἀμβλῦναι τὴν σφριγῶσαν ἀκμὴν τῆς νεότητος, ἐν ἑκάστῃ χώρᾳ,
ἐγγράφως ἢ ἀγράφως ὑπάρχοντες παρ᾽ ἡμῖν τε καὶ ἔθνεσιν· ἐν τοῖς
μὲν τὸ γράμμα, ἐν τοῖς δὲ ἡ συνήθεια.

Νόμος γὰρ ἀνόμοις τὰ πάτρια δοκεῖ· ὧν πρῶτοι Σῆρες οἱ τὸ 25
ἄκρον τῆς χέρσου οἰκοῦντες, νόμον ἔχοντες τὸ πατρῷον ἔθος, μὴ
ἑταιρίζεσθαι, μηδὲ συλᾶν, μὴ μοιχᾶσθαι, μὴ ξοάνοις προσκυνεῖν,
ἢ ποτνιᾶσθαι δαίμοσι, μηδ᾽ ὅλως ἐν αὐτοῖς ὑπάρχειν εἴδωλον, ἢ
ἑταίραν, ἢ μοιχαλίδα, οὐ συλώτην, οὐ φονέα, οὐ λωποδύτην· καὶ
ὅμως οὐδενὸς τὸ αὐτεξούσιον ἠνάγκασεν ὁ τοῦ κατὰ σὲ πυριλαμ- 30
ποῦς Ἄρεος ἀστήρ. οὐδὲ ἐβιάσατό τινα αὐτῶν φασγάνῳ τὸν πέλας
ἀναιρεῖν, ἢ λίθῳ πατάξαι· οὐκ Ἀφροδίτης σὺν Ἄρει ἔπεισεν αὐτοὺς
ἐπιλυττῆσαι τῇ γυναικὶ τοῦ γείτονος· πανημέρινον μεσουρανοῦντος

τοῦ Ἄρεος, καὶ ὅμως ἰσχυρότερος τῆς ἀνάγκης τῶν ἄστρων παρὰ Σῆρσιν ὁ πάτριος νόμος.

Νόμος δὲ καὶ παρὰ Βακτριανοῖς ἤτοι Βραγμανοῖς, ἡ ἐκ προγονων παιδεία, μὴ μεθύειν, μηδὲ ἀψύχων ἀπογεύεσθαι, οὐκ οἴνου ἁπλοῦ ἡ
5 νόθου μετέχειν, Θεὸν τὸν ἐμὸν δεδοικότας· καίτοι τῶν παρακειμένων αὐτοῖς Ἰνδῶν μιαιφονούντων, καὶ οἰνοφλογούντων, καὶ μονιῶν ἀγρίων ἡ συῶν δίκην θηλυμονούντων, καὶ τῷ πάθει κραδαινομένων. ἐν δὲ τοῖς Ἑσπερίοις κλίμασιν ἐνδοτέρω τῶν ἐκεῖσε Ἰνδῶν, ξενόβοροι τινὲς ὑπάρχοντες τοὺς ἐπήλυδας ἀναιροῦντες ἐσθίουσι, καὶ οὐδεὶς τῶν
10 ἀγαθοποιῶν ἀστερων τῆς μιαιφονίας αὐτοὺς ἀπωσθῆναι ἴσχυσε μέχρι τήμερον.

Ἕτερος νόμος Χαλδαίοις τε καὶ Βαβυλωνίοις μητρογαμεῖν καὶ ἀδελφοφθορεῖν, καὶ ταῖς σφῶν παισὶν ἐπιμαίνεσθαι, καὶ μιαιφθορεῖν, εἰ καὶ πόρρω τῆς ἐνεγκαμένης γένωνται, καὶ τοῖς σφῶν κεχρῆσθαι
15 νόμοις, φανερῶς καὶ λεληθότως διακελεύομενοι· ἐξ ὧν τινες αὐτῶν μέχρι καὶ νῦν ὑπάρχουσιν, ἐν Μήδοις καὶ Πάρθοις καὶ Ἐλαμίταις καὶ Αἰγυπτίοις, ἐν Φρυξὶ καὶ Γαλάταις, ἔν τισι κώμαις μιαιβιοῦντες· καὶ οὐδέπω Κύπρις σὺν Μήνῃ ἐν ὁρίοις καὶ οἴκοις Κρόνου, ἐπιμαρτυροῦντος τοῦ Ἄρεος, ἐν ταῖς πάντων αὐτῶν γενέσεσιν εὑρίσκεσθαι
20 οἴατε.

Θάτερος δὲ παρὰ Γήλαις νόμος· γυναῖκας γεωργεῖν καὶ οἰκοδομεῖν, καὶ τὰ ἀνδρῶν πράττειν· ἀλλὰ καὶ κοινωνεῖν οἷς δ᾽ ἂν βούλονται τῶν ἐπηλύδων, οὐκ ἐπιτιμώμεναι ὑπὸ τῶν προεχόντων ἀνδρῶν, οὐδὲ ζηλούμεναι. οὐ μυρίζονται δὲ, οὐδὲ φυκίοις τὴν ὄψιν
25 νοθεύονται, σφῶν παρειὰς ἐπιχρωννῦσαι, καθὼς αἱ παρ᾽ ἡμῖν ἀλλότριαι ὑποδύνουσαι προσωπεῖον. οἱ δὲ ἄνδρες στιβάζονται ἐσθῆτι μαλακῇ καὶ ἀνθοβάφῳ περιβολῇ. ὑπάρχουσι δ᾽ ἐν αὐταῖς καὶ πολεμικώταται, καὶ θηροῦσαι τὰ μὴ λίαν ἰσχυρὰ τῶν θηρίων. πῶς οὖν πᾶσαι αἱ Γήλων γυναῖκες οὐκ ἔλαχον Αἰγοκέρῳ ἢ Ὑδροχόῳ,
30 κακαδαιμονοῦσι τῇ Κύπριδι; οὔτ᾽ αὖ πάλιν οἱ ἄνδρες αὐτῶν ἔλαχον ἐν Κριῷ σὺν Ἄρει τὴν Ἀφροδίτην, ἔνθα τοὺς ἀνδρείους καὶ σπατάλους φασὶν οἱ τῇ γνώμῃ Χαλδαῖοι;

Ἐν δὲ Σούσοις τῆς Βαβυλῶνος αἱ γυναῖκες παντὶ μύρῳ διαφέροντι, καὶ κόσμῳ χρῶνται, ὑπηρετούμεναι καὶ φαιδρῶς προϊοῦσαι
35 σὺν βλωσυρίᾳ, καὶ διαχύσει πολλῇ· πᾶσι δὲ Ἕλλησιν ἀδεῶς τε καὶ ἀναιδῶς συγκαθεύδουσιν, ἄρχουσαι μᾶλλον τῶν οἰκείων ἀνδρῶν.

καὶ οὐ πάντως ἐν πάσῃ γενέσει τῶν Σουσίδων γυναικῶν μεσουρανεῖ μετὰ Διὸς καὶ Ἄρεος ἐν Διὸς ὅροις ἡ Ἀφροδίτη.

Ἐν δὲ τῇ Ἐώᾳ οἱ ἀρρενοφθοροῦντες, οἱ παρὰ Χριστιανοῖς, ἐὰν
γνωσθῶσιν ὑπὸ τῶν ὁμαίμων ἀφειδῶς τιμωροῦνται.

Ἐν Βρεττανίᾳ πλεῖστοι ἄνδρες μιᾷ συγκαθεύδουσι γυναικί· 5
ὡσαύτως καὶ πολλαὶ γυναῖκες ἑνὶ ἑταιρίζονται ἀνδρί.

Καὶ πᾶσι τοῖς πατρίοις τὰ ἔθνη ὥσπερ νόμῳ στοιχοῦσιν ἀδάκνως
καὶ ἀπόνως.

Ἀμαζόνες δὲ ἄνδρας οὐκ ἔχουσιν· ἀλλ᾿ ὡς τὰ ἄλογα ζῶα, ἅπαξ
τοῦ ἔτους περὶ τὴν ἐαρινικὴν ἰσημερίαν ὑπερόριοι γίνονται, μισγόμε- 10
ναι τοῖς γειτνιῶσιν ἀνδράσιν, οἷον πανήγυρίν τινα, καὶ ἑορτὴν τὸν
καιρὸν τῆς ἑταιρείας ἡγούμεναι. ἐξ ὧν κατὰ γαστρὸς φέρουσαι,
παλινδρομοῦσιν οἴκαδε ἅμα πᾶσαι. τῷ δὲ καιρῷ τῆς ἀποκυήσεως,
τὸν μὲν ἄρρενα φθείρουσι, τὸ δὲ θῆλυ ζωογονοῦσι καὶ τιθηνοῦσιν
ἐπιμελῶς. ἄτοπον δὲ πιστεῦσαι ἐπὶ μὲν τῇ τῶν ἀρρένων σπορᾷ 15
Ἄρεα μετὰ Κρόνου ἐπὶ τῆς ὥρας ἰσομοίρως τυχεῖν· ἐπὶ δὲ τοῦ
θήλεως οὐδέποτε. καὶ πῶς ἐν τῷ αὐτῷ νυχθημέρῳ πάντων ἐν ταῖς
ὑποδεξαμέναις καταβληθέντων, καὶ ὁμοῦ πάλιν ὡς ἐκ μιᾶς νηδύος
προερχομένων, τὰ μὲν διαφθείρεται, τοῦ ἅμα τοῦ βίου γεύσασθαι,
καὶ ὑπὸ τῶν μιαιφόνων θανατούμενα πρὸ τοῦ σπᾶσαι γάλα, ἢ 20
ῥῆξαι φωνὴν, τὰ δὲ ζωογονεῖται, καὶ περιέπεται ἐν τοῖς ἀνόμοις
κόλποις τὰ κακὰ ἐνσκαίροντα; πῶς ἐν ταὐτῷ καιρῷ αἱ παρ᾿ ἡμῖν
γυναῖκες καὶ συλλαμβάνουσι καὶ ἀποκύουσαι πλεῖσται, καὶ διτο-
κοῦσαι ἄμφω τὰ βρέφη περιποιοῦνται, μηδὲν ὑπὸ τῶν ἄστρων
βιαζόμεναι διαφθείρειν, ἢ τῷ ἐδάφει προσαράττειν, καὶ τῇ γῇ προσ- 25
αναλύειν, ὡς Ἀμαζόνες τὰ δείλαια· ἀλλὰ τὸν σφῶν αὐχένα τῆς
ἐκείνων σφαγῆς προϋπεχούσας, ἑαυτὰς μᾶλλον ἢ τὰ ὑπότιτθα τοῦ
ζῆν ἱμειρόμενα ἀπορρήγνυσθαι.

Εἰ δὲ καὶ Ἑρμῆς, ὥς φατε, μετὰ Ἀφροδίτης ἐν οἴκοις ἰδίοις ἐπι-
τελεῖ πλάστας, ζωγράφους, κερματιστὰς, ἐν οἴκοις δὲ Ἀφροδίτης, 30
μυρεψοὺς, φωνάσκους, ὑποκριτὰς, ποιητάς· παρὰ δὲ Ἠλείοις καὶ
Σαρακηνοῖς καὶ τοῖς ἐν τῇ ἀνωτέρᾳ Λιβύῃ καὶ Μαύροις κατὰ τοὺς
ἠϊόνας καὶ ὄχθας τοῦ Ὠκεανοῦ ποταμοῦ οἰκοῦσι, καὶ ἐν τῇ ἐξωτέρᾳ
Γερμανίᾳ, καὶ ἐν τῇ ἀνωτέρᾳ Σαρματίᾳ, καὶ ἐν Σκυθίᾳ, καὶ ἐν πᾶσι
τοῖς ἐξωτικοῖς μέρεσι τοῦ Πόντου ἔθνεσιν, οὐχ οἷόν τε εὑρεῖν κολλυ- 35
βιστὴν, ἢ πλάστην, ἢ ζωγράφον, οὐκ ἀρχιτέκτονα, οὐ φωνάσκον,

οὐχ ὑποκριτὴν ποιημάτων, ὡς παρ᾽ ἡμῖν· διὰ τί Ἑρμῆς καὶ Ἀφροδίτη οὐ παρέσχον, κατ᾽ ἐνιαυτὸν ἐπιτυχεῖν γεννωμένῳ τοῖς ἐκλεί-
πουσι παρ᾽ αὐτοῖς ἐπιτηδεύμασι;

Μῆδοι δὲ πάντες μετὰ σπουδῆς ἔτι ἐμπνέοντας τοὺς κάμνοντας
5 κυσὶ βορὰν προτιθέασιν ἀναλγήτως; σὺν τῇ Μήνῃ, ὥς φατε, τὸν
Ἄρεα ἐπὶ ἡμερινῆς γενέσεως ἐν Καρκίνῳ Μῆδοι ἔλαχον;

Ἰνδοὶ τοὺς νεκροὺς ἑαυτῶν τεφροποιοῦσι πυρί· μεθ᾽ ὧν καταφ-
λέγουσί τινων τὰς συμβίους. καὶ οὐδήπου πᾶσαι αἱ πυριάλωτοι
Ἰνδῶν γυναῖκες, ἢ αἱ ζῶσαι, ἔλαχον ὑπὸ τῆς νυκτερινῆς συνελεύ-
10 σεως τῶν γονέων σὺν Ἄρει τὸν Ἥλιον, ἐν νυκτὶ μὴ φαίνοντα ἐν
μοίραις Ἄρεως.

Γερμανῶν οἱ πλείους ἀγχόνῃ τὸ ζῆν ἀμείβονται· καὶ οὐ πάντως
τὸ πλῆθος Γερμανῶν τὴν Σελήνην καὶ τὴν ὥραν μεσολαμβανομένας
ὑπὸ Κρόνου καὶ Ἄρεος ἔχουσιν. ἀλλ᾽ εἰ παντὶ ἔθνει ἡμέραι βρο-
15 τοῖς γένωνται, οὐ κρείττονες ἢ χείρονες κατὰ ἄστρων συμπλοκήν,
ὡς ὑμεῖς φατε, ἀλλ᾽ ἐν ἑκάστῃ χώρᾳ νόμοι τινὲς καὶ πάτρια ἔθη
κρατεῖ, ἐξ ὧν τὸ αὐτεξούσιον καὶ τὸ ἐφ᾽ ἡμῖν τὰ πρακτέα ὑπάρχειν
παιδευόμεθα πάντες. οὐ γὰρ οἷά τε ἡ καθ᾽ ὑμᾶς γένεσις ἀναγκάσαι
Σῆρας ἀνακεῖν, ἢ Βραχμᾶνας κρεωβορεῖν καὶ σικεροποτεῖν, ἢ
20 Πέρσας μὴ μητρογαμεῖν, καὶ ἀδελφοφθορεῖν, ἤ Ἰνδοὺς μὴ πυρὶ
διδόναι τοὺς νεκρούς, ἢ Μήδους μὴ κυσὶ τοὺς θνηξομένους προτι-
θέναι, ἢ Πάρθους μὴ πολυγαμεῖν, ἢ τοὺς Μεσοποταμίτας μὴ
ἄκρως σωφρονεῖν, ἢ Ἕλληνας μὴ σωμασκεῖσθαι, ἢ τὰ βάρβαρα
ἔθνη ταῖς ὑφ᾽ Ἑλλήνων προσαγαρευομέναις κοινωνεῖν· ἀλλ᾽ ὡς
25 προέφην, ἕκαστος βροτῶν χρῆται τῇ τοῦ νόμου ἐλευθερίᾳ, τὰ ἐκ
τῶν ἄστρων μυθουργούμενα καθ᾽ Ἕλληνας παραπεμπόμενος, τῷ
ἐκ τῶν νόμων δέει, ἢ τῷ ἐξ ἔθνους ἔθει πατρίῳ τῶν φαύλων εἰργό-
μενος· αἱ μὲν γὰρ τῶν ἀρετῶν ὑπάρχουσι προαιρετικαί, αἱ δὲ περι-
στατικαί, ἀνάγκῃ ἐπὶ τὸ κρεῖττον χωροῦντος τοῦ ζητουμένου ὑπὸ
30 τῶν νόμων.

Πεῦσις ρί´.

Ἀλλ᾽ ἑπτὰ ὄντων τῇ γενέσει ἡμῶν ἀνακειμένων ἀστέρων, εἰς
ἑπτὰ λέγομεν κλίματα τὴν γῆν διαιρεῖσθαι, καὶ ἄρχεσθαι ἕκαστον
κλῖμα ὑφ᾽ ἑνὸς τῶν ἀστέρων, καὶ πρὸς ἐκείνων συμπλοκὰς ἄγεσθαι,
καὶ ἀποτελεῖσθαι τοὺς ἀρχομένους· ὅπερ νόμον τινὲς τὴν τοῦ
35 ἄστρου ἐνέργειαν λέγουσιν.

Ἀπόκρισις.

Καὶ πῶς εἰ ἑπταχῶς διαιρεῖται ἡ οἰκουμενη, ἐν μιᾷ μερίδι πολ-
λοὺς καὶ διαφόρους νόμους εὑρίσκομεν ; καὶ οὔτε ἑπτὰ μόνον κατὰ
τοὺς ἀστέρας, οὔτε δὶς ἓξ κατὰ τοὺς ζωδικούς, οὐδ᾽ αὖ πάλιν τριά-
κοντα ἓξ κατὰ τοὺς δεκάνους, ἀλλὰ μύριοι μνημονεύονται νόμοι, πάλαι ἀμειφθέντες, καὶ νῦν ὑπάρχοντες. πῶς δὲ ἐν ταυτῷ τμήματι 5
τοὺς ἀνθρωποβόρους Ἰνδους, καὶ τοὺς ἐμψύχων καὶ θοίνης ἁπάσης
ἀπεχόμενους Βραχμαίους οἰκοῦντας ὁρῶμεν; πῶς δὲ οἱ ἐν Βαβυλῶνι,
ὅποι δ᾽ ἂν γίνωνται, τῇ μιαιγαμίᾳ τῶν ὁμαίμων παροινοῦσι ; πῶς
δ᾽ ἐν ἑτέρῳ τμήματι ὄντες οἱ Σκλαυηνοὶ καὶ Φυσωνῖται, οἱ καὶ
Δανούβιοι προσαγορεύομενοι, οἱ μὲν γυναικομαστοβοροῦσιν ἡδέως, 10
διὰ τὸ πεπληρῶσθαι τοῦ γάλακτος, μυῶν δίκην τοὺς ὑποτίτθους
ταῖς πέτραις ἐπαράττοντες· οἱ δὲ καὶ τῆς νομίμης καὶ ἀδιαβλήτου
κρεωβορίας ἀπέχονται ; καὶ οἱ μὲν ὑπάρχουσιν αὐθάδεις, αὐτόνομοι,
ἀνηγεμόνευτοι, συνεχῶς ἀναιροῦντες, συνεσθιόμενοι ἢ συνοδεύοντες,
τῶν σφῶν ἡγεμόνα καὶ ἄρχοντα, ἀλώπεκας καὶ τὰς ἐνδρύμους 15
κάττας καὶ μονιοὺς ἐσθίοντες, καὶ τῇ λύμων ὠρυγῇ σφᾶς προσκα-
λούμενοι· οἱ δὲ καὶ ἀδδηφαγίας ἀπέχονται, καὶ τῷ τυχόντι ὑπο-
ταττόμενοι καὶ ὑπείκοντες ;

Καὶ πολὺς ὁ λόγος περὶ Λογγοβάρδων καὶ Νόρων καὶ Γάλλων
τῶν Ἐσπερίων τῶν Ἑρμαϊκῆς καὶ Κρονικῆς ἀμοιρούντων ἐπιστημης 20
τῶν ἄστρων. πόσοι βασιλεῖς καὶ ἄρχοντες παρήγαγον τοὺς κακῶς
κειμένους νόμους, αὐτοὶ τὸ δοκοῦν νομοθετοῦντες ; ἢ αὖ πάλιν τοὺς
κρείττονας οἱ ἐνιαυτίοι ἀπώσαντο, ὑπ᾽ οὐδενὸς τῶν ἄστρων πρὸς τὰ
αἱρεθέντα εἰργόμενοι ; ἐν δὲ φάναι βούλομαι, ὃ καὶ τῶν ἀπίστων
πάντων ἀποῤῥάψει τὰ στόματα, Ἰουδαῖοι πάντες τὸν διὰ Μωσέως 25
δεξάμενοι νόμον, πᾶν ἄῤῥεν λογικὸν αὐτοῖς γινόμενον τῇ ὀγδόῃ
ἡμέρᾳ περιτέμνοντες αἱμάττουσιν. ἀπὸ δὲ τοῦ αἰῶνος, οὐδεὶς Ἑλλήνων ἢ Χριστιανῶν περιτομὴν ἐδέξατο. πλείστων Ἰουδαίων καὶ
Ἑλλήνων καὶ Χριστιανῶν κατὰ τοὺς αὐτοὺς μῆνας καὶ ἑβδομάδας
καὶ ἡμέρας καὶ ὥρας γενωμένων, Ἄρης, ἢ Ἑρμῆς, ἢ Κύπρις, ἢ ὁ 30
λοιπὸς Ἑλλήνων μῦθος, ἑνὸς κύκλου ἐμπεριέχοντος τὰ πάντα, καὶ
μηδενὸς ὑπὸ ἀστέρων βιαζομένου. οὐ γὰρ πάντες Ἕλληνες, ἢ Ἰουδαῖοι, ἢ Χριστιανοὶ ἐν τῇ αὐτῇ ἡμέρᾳ ἢ ὥρᾳ ἐν τῇ μητρῴᾳ κατε-
βλήθησαν νηδύϊ, οὐδ᾽ αὖ πάλιν πάντες ἅμα ἀπεκυήθησαν· πῶς οὖν

οἱ πλεῖστοι αὐτῶν Χριστῷ συνέθεντο, τὴν πατρῴαν ἀρνησάμενοι πλάνην, μὴ ἰσχύσαντος τοῦ ἄρχοντος ἀστέρος τῆς χερσαίου μερίδος ἐμποδῆσαι αὐτοὺς πρὸς θεοσέβειαν;

Bardesan, a man of antiquity, and renowned for the knowledge of events, has written in a treatise composed by him touching the synods of the heavenly luminaries with one another, saying thus: Two circuits of Saturn are 60 years; 5 circuits of Jupiter 60 years; 40 circuits of Mars 60 years; 60 circuits of the Sun 60 years; 72 circuits of Venus 60 years; 150 circuits of Mercury 60 years; 720 circuits of the moon 60 years; and this is one synod of them all, that is to say, the time of one synod of them; so that hence it appears, that for 100 of such synods there would be six thousand years, in this manner: 200 circuits of Saturn 6 thousand years; 500 circuits of Jupiter 6 thousand years; 4 thousand circuits of Mars 6 thousand years; six thousand circuits of the Sun six thousand years; 7 thousand and 200 circuits of Venus 6 thousand years; 12 thousand circuits of Mercury 6 thousand years; 72 thousand circuits of the Moon 6 thousand years: and Bardesan made these calculations when he was desirous of shewing that this world would stand only six thousand years.

(22)

AN ORATION OF MELITON THE PHILOSOPHER;

WHO WAS IN THE PRESENCE OF ANTONINUS CÆSAR, AND
BADE THE SAME CÆSAR KNOW GOD, AND SHEWED HIM THE
WAY OF TRUTH; AND HE BEGAN SPEAKING AFTER THIS
MANNER:

MELITO saith: It is not an easy matter readily to bring into the
right way that man who has been a long time pre-occupied by
error. But nevertheless it is possible to be done; for when a man
has been turned from error a little, the mention of the truth is
acceptable to him; for in the same manner as, when the cloud 5
has been broken a little, there is fine weather, so also a man, too,
when he is turned towards God, the thick cloud of error which
hindered him from the true vision, is quickly removed from his
face. For error, like passion and sleep, holdeth for a long time
those who alight under it; but truth, using the word as a stimulus, 10
and smiting such as are asleep, also awaketh them; and when
they are awake, seeing the truth, they also understand, and hearing,
they also distinguish that which exists from that which doth not
exist. For there are men that call wickedness righteousness, and 15
so then they suppose that this is righteousness when a man shall
be in error together with the many. But I say that this is not a
good excuse, that a man be in error with the many: for if one
only act foolishly his folly is great; how much greater, then,
must the folly be when the many are foolish together? 20

But the folly of which I speak is this, if a man should leave
that which really exists, and serve that which really does not exist:
but there is that which really exists, and is called God, and He
really exists, and by His power every thing subsists; and This
same was not made, nor yet brought into being, but exists 25
from eternity, and will exist for ever and ever. He undergoes no
change, while all things are changed. No sight is able to behold Him; nor understanding able to comprehend Him, nor

G

words to describe Him; and those who love Him [23] call him after
this manner—Father and God of Truth.

And if, therefore, a man abandon the light, and say that
there is another God, it is found from his own words that
5 he calleth some created thing God. For if a man call fire God,
it is not God, because it is fire; and if a man call the waters
Gods, they are not God, because they are waters; and if this
earth which we tread upon, and if those heavens which are seen
by us, and if the sun, or the moon, or one of those stars which
10 run their course by ordinance and rest not, nor proceed by their
own will,—and if a man call gold and silver Gods; are not these
things that we use as we please? And if that wood which we burn,
and if those stones which we break—how then are these Gods?
for, lo! they are for the use of men. How will not they be found
15 in great sin, who change the great God by their word into those
things which stand by ordinance so far as they do stand?

But I say nevertheless, that so long as a man not having heard,
neither discerneth nor understands that there is a Lord over
these creatures, perhaps he is not to be blamed, because no one
20 blameth the blind when he walketh badly. For in the same
manner also men, while they were seeking after God, stumbled
against stones and stocks; and such of them as were rich, stumbled against gold and silver, and by their stumbling were
kept back from that which they were seeking after. But now
25 that a voice has been heard in all the earth that there is a God
of truth, and an eye has been given to every man to see withal, they
are without excuse who are influenced by a feeling of shame towards
the many with whom they have been in error, but otherwise
desire to walk in the right way. For those who are ashamed to
30 be saved, necessity compels them to die. On this account I
counsel them that they open their eyes and see; for, lo! light
without envy is given to all of us, that we may see thereby;
and if, when light hath arisen upon us, any one closeth his eyes
that he may not see, his course is to the ditch. For why is a
35 man influenced by feelings of shame towards those who have been
in error together with himself? Rather it behoveth him to per-

suade them to follow in his steps, and if they be not persuaded
by him, he should save himself from amongst them. For there are
some men who are not able to raise themselves up from their mother
earth: for this cause, also, they make for themselves Gods from the
earth their mother.[24] And they are condemned by the judgments 5
of truth, because they affix that name which is unchangeable to
those things which subject to change, and fear not to designate
as Gods that which has been made by the hands of man ; and
dare to make an image for God whom they have not seen.

But I affirm that also the Sybil has said respecting them, that it 10
is the images of kings, who are dead, they worship. And this is
easy to understand ; for, lo! even now they worship and honour
the images of those belonging to the Cæsars, more than those
former *Gods :* for from those their former Gods, both tribute and
produce are *paid* to Cæsar as to one, who is greater than they. 15
And on this account those are slain who despise them, and diminish the revenue of Cæsar. For also to the treasury of other kings
in various places it is appointed how much the worshippers supply,
and how many sacks full of water from the sea. And this is the
wickedness of the world, of such as worship and fear that which 20
hath no perception ; and many of those who are cunning, either
for the sake of profit, or on account of vain-glory, or for the sake
of swaying the many, both worship themselves, and instigate the
deficient in understanding to worship that which hath no perception.   25

But I, according as I know, will write and shew how and for
what causes images were made for kings and tyrants, and they
became as gods. The people of Argos made images for Hercules,
because he was one of their own citizens and was brave, and
slew by his valour noisome beasts, and more especially because 30
they were afraid of him, for he was violent, and carried away
the wives of many, for his lust was great, like that of Zuradi the
Persian, his friend.

Again, the people of Acte worshipped Dionysius, a king, because
he originally introduced the vine into their country.   35

The Egyptians worshipped Joseph, a Hebrew, who was called

Serapis, because he supplied them with sustenance in the years
of famine.

The Athenians worshipped Athene, the daughter of Zeus, king of
the island of Crete, because she built the citadel Athens, and made
5 Ericthippus (Ericthonius) her son king there, whom she had
by adultery with Hephæstus, a smith, the son of a wife of her
father; and she always was making companionship with Hercules, because he was her brother on her father's side. For Zeus
'the king fell in love with Alcmene, the wife of Electryon, who
10 was from Argos, and committed adultery with her, and she gave
birth to Hercules.[25]

The people of Phœnicia worshipped Balthi, queen of Cyprus,
because she fell in love with Tamuz, son of Cuthar, king of
the Phœnicians, and left her own kingdom, and came and dwelt
15 in Gebal, a fortress of the Phœnicians, and at the same time she
made all the Cyprians subject to the king Cuthar: for before
Tamuz she had been in love with Ares, and committed adultery with him, and Hephæstus her husband caught her, and was
jealous over her, and came and slew Tamuz in Mount Leba-
20 non, while he was hunting wild boars; and from that time Balthi
remained in Gebal, and she died in the city Aphaca, where
Tamuz was buried.

The Elamites worshipped Nuh, daughter of the King of Elam.
When the enemy had taken her captive, her father made for her
25 an image and a temple in Shushan, a palace which is in Elam.

The Syrians worshipped Athi a Hadibite, who sent the
daughter of Belat, who was skilled in medicine, and she cured
Simi, daughter of Hadad, king of Syria; and after a time, when
the leprosy attacked Hadad himself, Athi entreated Elishah, the
30 Hebrew, and he came and cured him of his leprosy.

The people of Mesopotamia also worshipped Cuthbi, a Hebrew
woman, because she delivered Bacru, the patrician of Edessa,
from his enemies.

But touching Nebo, which is in Mabug, why should I write to
35 you; for, lo! all the priests which are in Mabug know that it is
the image of Orpheus, a Thracian Magus. And Hadran is the

image of Zaradusht, a Persian Magus, because both of these
Magi practised Magism to a well which is in a wood in Mabug,
in which was an unclean spirit, and it committed violence and
attacked the passage of every one who was passing by in all that
place in which now the fortress of Mabug is located; and these 5
same Magi charged Simi, the daughter of Hadad, that she should
draw water from the sea, and cast it into the well, in order that
the spirit should not come up *and* commit injury, according to
that which was a mystery in their Magism. And in like manner,
also, the rest of mankind made images of their kings, and wor- 10
shipped them, of which I will not write further.

But thou, a free intelligence and cognizant of the truth, if thou
wilt consider these things, enter into thyself; and if they clothe
thee in the fashion of a woman, remember that thou art a man, and
be a believer in Him who really is God, and to Him open thy 15
mind, and to Him commit thyself, and He is able to give thee ever-
lasting life, which dieth not;[26] for every thing cometh through
His hands: and all other things so let them be esteemed by thee as
they are, images as images, sculptures as sculptures; and let not
any thing which has been made be put by thee in the place of 20
Him who is not made. But let Him, the ever-living God,
be always running in thy mind; for thy mind itself is his likeness,
for it, too, is invisible and impalpable, and without form; and by
its will the whole body is moved. Know thou, therefore, that if
thou wilt always be serving Him that is immoveable, as He exists 25
for ever, so thou also, when thou shalt have put off this which
is visible and corruptible, shalt stand before Him for ever,
living and endowed with knowledge; and thy works shall be for
thee riches which fail not, and possessions that do not lack. But
know thou that the chief of all thy good works is this: that thou 30
shouldest know God and serve Him. And know that He asketh
not for any thing of thee: he needeth nothing.

Who is that God? He who is himself truth, and his word
truth. But what is truth? That which is not fashioned, and not
made, and not formed; that is, that which, without having been 35
brought into existence, does exist, and is called truth. But if, then,

a man worship that which has been made by hands, it is not the
truth he worshipeth, neither also the word of truth. But for
myself I have much to say touching this matter; but I am
influenced by a feeling of shame for those who do not under-
5 stand that they are better than the work of their own hands;
nor do they understand how they give gold to the artists, that
they may make for them a god, and give them silver for their ornament and their honour, and they transfer their riches from one
place to another, and then worship them. And what disgrace can
10 be greater than this, that a man should worship his riches, and
abandon Him who bestowed upon him the riches? and that he
should revile man, but worship the image of man, and slay a beast,
but worship the likeness of a beast. And it must be acknowledged that is the workmanship of their fellow-men that they
15 worship; for they do not worship the materials while they are
laid by in bundles, but when the artists have fashioned images from
them they worship them; neither do they worship the sub-
stance of gold or of silver, until the sculptors have engraven them,
then they worship them. Deficient of understanding! What
20 additional thing has been imparted to the gold that now thou
worshippest it? If it be because it resembles a winged animal,
why dost thou not worship the winged animal itself? And if
because it resembles a voracious beast, lo! the voracious beast
itself[27] is before thee. And if it be the artist's skill itself that
25 please thee, then let the artistic skill of God please thee, who made
every thing, and in His own likeness made the artists, and they
endeavour to do like Him, but resemble Him not.

But perchance thou mayest say, Why did not God create me so
that I should then have served Him, and not idols? By this that
30 thou speakest in such a manner, thou wouldest seek to become an
idle instrument, and not a living man. For God made thee so well
as it seemed good to Him, and gave thee a mind endowed with
Free-will. He set before thee abundant things that thou mightest
distinguish each thing, and choose for thyself that which is good.
35 He has set before thee the heavens, and he has placed in them
the stars. He hath set before thee the sun and the moon, and

they every day fulfil their course therein. He hath set before thee many waters, and restrained them by his word. He hath set before thee the vast earth, which is still, and continueth before thee in one fashion. And in order that thou mayest not suppose that of its own nature it continueth, He also maketh it 5 quake whensoever He desireth. He hath set before thee the clouds which by ordinance bring water from above and satisfy the earth: that from these things thou mightest understand, that He who moveth these is greater than they all, and that thou mightest accept the goodness of Him, who hath given to thee a 10 mind by which thou mayest distinguish these things. Therefore I counsel thee that thou shouldest know thyself, and shouldest know God. For understand how there is within thee that which is called the soul: by it the eye seeth, by it the ear heareth, by it the mouth speaketh: and how it employeth the whole body. 15 And whensoever He pleaseth to remove the soul from the body, it falleth and goeth to decay. From this, therefore, which exists within thyself and is invisible, understand how God also moveth the whole world by his power, like the body, *and* that whensoever it pleaseth Him to withdraw his power, the whole world also, 20 like the body, will fall and go to decay.

For what end, therefore, this world was created, and why it passeth away, and why the body exists, and why it falleth, and why it standeth, thou art not able to know until thou shalt have lifted up thy head from this sleep in which thou art sunken, and 25 have opened thine eyes, and seen that there is one God, the Lord of all, and have served Him with all thy heart. Then will He grant thee to know His will; for every one who is far removed from the knowledge of the living God is dead and buried in his body. On this account thou rollest thyself upon the ground be- 30 fore demons and shadows, and askest vain petitions from such as hath not what to give. But thou, stand thou up [28] from amongst those who are lying on the earth and embracing stones, and giving their sustenance as food for the fire, and offering their clothes to idols, and are willing, while they themselves are endowed with 35 senses, to serve that which is insensible. And do thou ask peti-

tions which will not fail from God who faileth not, for thy soul which is not liable to decay, and immediately thy Free-will will be evident, and of it be careful ; and give thanks to God who made thee, and gave thee a free mind, that thou mightest con-
5 duct thyself as thou wishest. He hath set before thee all these things, and sheweth thee, that if thou followest after evil thou shalt be condemned for thy evil deeds ; but if after goodness thou shalt receive from Him many good things, together with eternal life which never dieth.

10 There is nothing, therefore, which hindereth thee from changing thy evil manner of life, because thou art endowed with Free-will ; and from seeking and finding who is the Lord of all, and from serving Him with all thy heart, because with Him there is no jealousy of giving the knowledge of himself to those that seek it,
15 so that they are able to know Him.

Let it be thy care first, not to deceive thyself. For if thou sayest with regard to that which is not God, This is God, thou deceivest thyself, and sinnest before the God of truth. Fool ! is that God which is bought and sold ? Is that God which
20 standeth in need ? Is that God which must be watched ? How buyest thou him as a slave, and servest him as master ? How askest thou of him as of one who is rich to give to thee, and thyself givest to him as to one who is poor ? How canst thou expect of him that he will make thee victorious in battle ; for, lo !
25 when thine enemies have vanquished thee, they also strip him too ?

Perchance one who is a sovereign may say that I am not able to conduct myself well, because I am a sovereign. It behoveth me to do the will of the many. He who should plead thus, truly deserves to be laughed at. For why should not the sovereign be himself the
30 leader in all good things, and persuade the people which is sub-ject to him, that they should conduct themselves with purity, and know God in truth, and set them in himself examples of all good deeds ? Because so it becometh him. For it is an absurd thing that a sovereign, while he conducts himself badly, should be the
35 judge, and condemn those who go wrong.

But my opinion is this: that in this way a realm may be governed in peace, whenever the sovereign shall be acquainted with the God of truth,[29] and through fear of Him shall be withheld from injuring those who are his subjects, but shall judge every thing with equity, as one who knoweth that he himself also is about to be judged before God; while those also who are under his hand shall be withheld by the fear of God from acting wrongly towards their sovereign, and shall also be withheld by fear from doing what is wrong to each other. And by this knowledge and fear of God all wickedness may be removed from the realm. For if the sovereign abstain from injuring those who are under his hand, and they abstain from doing wrong against him, and against each other, it is evident that the whole country will dwell in peace. And many advantages will be there, because amongst them all the name of God will be glorified. For what advantage is greater than this, that a sovereign should deliver the people which is under his hand from error, and by this good deed obtain the favour of God? For from error all those evils arise. But the chief of error is this: that while a man is ignorant of God, he should worship in God's stead that which is not God.

But there are men who say, that it is for God's own honour we make the idol;—that forsooth, they may worship the image of the hidden God! And they are ignorant that God is in every country, and in every place, and is never absent, and that there is not any thing done, and He knoweth it not. But thou, feeble man, within whom He is, and without whom He is, and above whom He is, hast gone and bought for thyself wood from the carpenter's house, which is graven and made into an abomination of God. To this same thing thou offerest sacrifices, and knowest not that the all-seeing eye beholdeth thee, and the word of truth reproacheth thee, and saith to thee, The invisible God, how can He be sculptured? But it is the likeness of thyself that thou makest, and then worshippest it. Because the wood has been graven, dost thou not perceive that it is wood, or that it is stone? And the gold one taketh by weight, how much it weigheth: and when thou hast made it, why dost thou weigh it? Therefore thou art a lover of gold, and not a lover of God. And art not thou

ashamed, perchance it should be deficient, to demand of him who
made it, why he has stolen some of it? And although thou hast eyes,
dost thou not see? and although thou hast a heart, dost thou not understand? Why rollest thou thyself upon the earth, and offerest
5 supplication to things which are without perception? Fear Him
who shaketh the earth, and maketh the heavens to revolve, and
quelleth the sea, and removeth the mountains from their place;
Him who can make himself like fire,[30] and burn up every thing.
And if thou be not able to justify thyself, yet add not to thy sins;
10 and if thou be unable to know God, yet think that He exists.

Again, there are men that say, Whatsoever our fathers
bequeathed to us, that we reverence. Therefore, forsooth, those to
whom their fathers bequeathed poverty, strive to become rich!
and those whom their fathers did not instruct, desire to be in-
15 structed and to learn what their fathers knew not! And why,
forsooth, do the children of the blind see, and the children of
the lame walk? For it is not well for a man to follow after such
as have gone before that walked badly; but that we should turn
from the same path, lest that which befel those who have gone
20 before should also bring injury upon us. Wherefore, inquire if
thy father walked well; *if so*, do thou also follow after him: but if
thy father walked ill, walk thou well, and let thy children also
follow after thee. Be solicitous too respecting thy father, because he
walketh ill, so long as thy solicitude may be of avail to help
25 him. But as for thy children, say to them thus, That there
does exist a God, the Father of all, who never was brought into
being, neither was He made, and every thing subsisteth by his
will; and He made the lights that *his* works may behold one
another, and He concealeth himself in his might from all his
30 works; for it is not possible for any mutable thing to see Him
who is immutable. But such as have been admonished and
admitted into that covenant which is immutable, they see God so
far as it is possible for them to see him. These same will be
able to escape from being consumed when the flood of fire shall
35 come upon all the world. For there was once a flood and wind,
and the chosen men were destroyed by a mighty north wind,

and the just were left for demonstration of the truth; but again, at another time there was a flood of waters, and all men and living creatures were destroyed by the multitude of waters, and the just were preserved in an ark of wood, by the ordinance of God. So also it will be at the last time; there shall 5 be a flood of fire, and the earth shall be burnt up together with its mountains, and men shall be burnt up together with the idols which they have made, and with the graven images which they have worshipped; and the sea, together with its isles, shall be burnt; and the just shall be delivered from the 10 fury, like their fellows in the ark from the waters of the deluge. And then those who have not known God, and those who have made idols for themselves, shall lament, when they behold the same idols on fire together with themselves,(31) and nothing shall be found to help them.   15

But when thou, O Antonius (Antoninus) Cæsar shalt learn these things thyself, and thy children also with thee, thou wilt bequeath to them an eternal inheritance which fadeth not away; and thou wilt deliver thine own soul, and also the soul of thy children from that which is about to befal the whole earth in the judgment of truth and righteousness. Because, as thou hast 20 acknowledged him here, He will acknowledge thee there; and if thou esteem him great here, He esteemeth not thee more than those who have known him and confessed him. Sufficient be these for thy majesty; and if they be too many,—as thou wilt.

HERE ENDETH MELITON.

BY MELITON, BISHOP OF SARDIS,

From the Discourse On the Soul and Body.

FOR this reason the Father sent his Son from heaven incorporeal, that when He was become incarnate through the womb of the Virgin and was born man, He might save man, and collect those members of his which death had scattered when
5 he divided man. *And further on.* The earth quaked, and its foundations were shaken; the sun fled, and the elements turned back, and the day was changed; for they endured not that their Lord should hang upon a tree; and the *whole* creation was wonderstruck, marvelling, and saying, " What new mystery, then, is
10 this? The judge is judged, and holds his peace; the invisible is seen, and is not ashamed; the incomprehensible is seized and is not indignant; the immeasurable is measured, and doth not resist; the impassible suffereth, and doth not avenge; the immortal dieth, and answereth not a word; the celestial is
15 interred, and endureth! What new mystery is this?" The *whole* creation was astonished. But when our Lord arose from the dead, and trode death under foot, and bound the strong one, and loosed man,—then the whole creation perceived, that for man's sake the judge was condemned, and the invisible was seen, and the
20 immeasurable was measured, and the impassible suffered, and the immortal died, and the celestial was interred: for our Lord, when he was born man, was condemned in order that He might shew mercy;[32] was bound in order that He might loose; was seized upon in order that He might let go; suffered in order
25 that He might have compassion; died that He might save; was buried that He might raise up.

By the same, from the Discourse On the Cross.

For the sake of these things He came to us; for the sake of these things, while He was incorporeal, He formed for himself a body of our construction; while He appeared as a sheep, He still
30 still remained the shepherd; while He was esteemed a servant, He denied not the sonship; while He was borne of Mary, He

also was invested with his Father; while He trode upon the earth,
He also filled the heaven; while He appeared as an infant,
He belied not the eternity of his nature; while He was clad
with a body, He also bound not the singleness of his Godhead;
while He was esteemed poor, He also was not divested of his 5
riches; while, inasmuch as He was man, He needed food; still,
inasmuch as He was God, He ceased not to feed the universe;
while He was clad in the likeness of servant, He also changed not
the likeness of the Father. He was every thing in an immutable nature. He was standing before Pilate, and yet was 10
sitting with the Father. He was nailed upon the tree, and yet
was upholding every thing.

From Meliton the Bishop; On Faith.

We have made collections from the Law and the Prophets relative
to those things which have been declared respecting our Lord Jesus
Christ, that we may prove to your love, that He is perfect rea- 15
son, the Word of God; who was begotten before the light; who
was Creator together with the Father; who was the fashioner of
man; who was all in all; who among the Patriarchs was Patriarch; who in the law was the Law; among the priests Chief priest;
amongst kings Governor; among prophets the Prophet; among the 20
angels Archangel; in the Voice the Word; among spirits Spirit; in
the Father the Son; in God God—the king for ever and ever. For
this was He who was pilot to Noah; who conducted Abraham;
who was bound with Isaac, who was in exile with Jacob, who was sold
with Joseph, who was captain with Moses, who was the divider 25
of the inheritance with Jesus the Son of Nun, who in David and the
prophets foretold his own sufferings, who was incarnate in the
Virgin, who was born at Bethlehem,[33] who was wrapped in swad-
dling clothes in the manger, who was seen of the shepherds, who
was glorified of the angels, who was worshipped of the Magi, 30
who was pointed out by John, who assembled the Apostles, who
preached the kingdom, who healed the maimed, who gave light
to the blind, who raised the dead, who appeared in the temple,
who was not believed on by the people, who was betrayed by

Judas, who was laid hold on by the priests, who was condemned
by Pilate, who was transfixed in the flesh, who was hanged upon the
tree, who was buried in the earth, who rose from the dead, who
appeared to the Apostles, who ascended to heaven, who sitteth on
5 the right hand of the Father, who is the rest of those that are
departed, the recoverer of those who were lost, the light of those
who are in darkness, the deliverer of those who are captives, the
guide of those who have gone astray, the refuge of the afflicted,
the bridegroom of the Church, the charioteer of the Cherubim, the
10 captain of the angels, God who is of God, the Son who is of the
Father, Jesus Christ, the King for ever and ever. Amen.

Of Meliton, Bishop of the city of Attica.[40]

This is he that became incorporate in the Virgin, and was
hanged upon a tree, and was buried in the midst of the earth, and
did not undergo dissolution; he that rose from the dead, and raised
15 up men from the earth, from the nether grave to the height of
heaven. This is the lamb that was slain; this is the lamb that
was dumb. This is He that was born of Mary a fair sheep.
This is he that was taken from the flock, and was led to the
slaughter, and was slain at eventide, and was buried at night; who
20 had no bone in him broken upon the tree; who did not undergo
dissolution in the midst of the earth; who rose from the dead,
and raised up the race of Adam from the nether grave. This is
he that was put to death. And where was he put to death? In
the midst of Jerusalem. By whom? By Israel: because he
25 healed their maimed, and cleansed their lepers, and gave light to
their blind, and raised their dead. For this cause he died. Thou
gavest the command, and he was crucified; thou wast exulting, and
he was buried; thou wast reclining upon a soft bed, and he was
watching in the grave and in the coffin. Oh, Israel, transgressor
30 of the law, why hast thou done this fresh wickedness, in casting
the Lord into fresh sufferings; thine own Lord, who himself
fashioned thee, who made thee, who honoured thee, who called
thee Israel. But thou hast not been found to be Israel; for
thou hast not seen God, nor understood the Lord. For thou

knewest not, oh Israel, that this was the first-born of God, who was begotten before the sun, who made the light to rise, who lighted up the day, who separated the darkness, who fixed the first foundation, who suspended the earth, who collected the ocean, who extended the firmament, who adorned the world. Bitter 5 were thy nails, and keen; bitter was thy tongue, which thou sharpenedst; bitter was that Judas, to whom thou gavest hire; bitter were thy false witnesses whom thou stirredst up; bitter was thy gall which thou preparedst; bitter was thy vinegar which thou madest; bitter were thy hands which were full of blood. Thou 10 slewest thy Lord, and he was lifted upon the tree; and a tablet was fixed up to denote who he was that was put to death. And who was this?—what we would not speak harsh, and what we would speak very terrible, nevertheless still listen while ye tremble:—He, on whose account the earth quaked: he that suspended the earth, was 15 hanged up; he that fixed the heavens was fixed *with nails*; he that supported the earth was supported upon a tree: the Lord was exposed to ignominy with a naked body; God put to death; the king of Israel slain by an Israelitish right hand. Ah! the fresh wickedness of the fresh murder! The Lord was ex- 20 posed with a naked body: he was not deemed worthy even of covering; but in order that he may not be seen, the lights were turned away, and the day became dark, because they were slaying God, who was naked upon the tree. It was not the body of our Lord that the lights darkened when they fled, but men's eyes; 25 for because the people quaked not, the earth quaked: because they feared not the creation feared. Thou smotest thy Lord, thou also has been smitten upon the earth; and thou indeed liest dead, but he is risen from the dead, and gone up to the heights of heaven, having suffered for the sake of those who were suffering, and 30 having been bound for the sake of the race of Adam which was in bondage, having also been judged for the sake of him who was condemned, and been buried for the sake of him who was buried.

And further on. This is he who made the heaven and the earth, and in the beginning together with the Father created 35 man; who was preached by the law and the prophets; who was incarnate in the Virgin; who was hanged upon the tree; who was buried in the earth; who rose from the dead, and ascended to the height of heaven, and sitteth upon the right-hand of the Father.

Of the Holy Meliton, Bishop of Ittica.

5   He that supported the earth was supported upon a tree. The Lord was exposed to ignominy with a naked body; God put to death: the King of Israel slain.

———————

FROM THE FOURTH BOOK OF THE HISTORY OF THE CHURCH: CHAPTER THE TWENTY-FOURTH, CONCERNING THEOPHILUS, BISHOP OF ANTIOCH, AND PHILIP, AND MODESTUS, AND ME-LITON, AND THOSE WHOM HE HAS MENTIONED, AND CON-CERNING APOLLINARIS AND MUSANUS.

BUT as to Theophilus, concerning whom we have said that he was Bishop of Antioch, there are three treatises by him against Auto-
10 lycus, and another which is inscribed " Against the heresy of Hermogenes," in which he uses testimonies from the Revelation of John; and there are other books by him which are suitable for teaching. But those, who pertained to heretical doctrine, even at that time like tares were corrupting the pure seed of the
15 doctrine of the Apostles; but the Pastors which were in the churches in every country, were driving them like beasts of the wilderness away from the flock of Christ; at one time by teaching and exhortation to the Brethren, but at another time [34] openly before their faces they contended with them in discussion, and
20 put them to shame; and again, also, by writing treatises they diligently refuted and exposed their opinions. But Theophi-lus, together with others, contended against them; and he is celebrated for one treatise, which was ably composed by him against Marcion, which, together with the others that I have

already mentioned, is still preserved. And after him Maximinus received the Bishoprick of the Church of Antioch, who was the seventh after the Apostles.

But Philip, respecting whom we have learned from the words of Dionysius, Bishop of Corinth, that he was Bishop of the church of the city of Gortyna, he also composed with accuracy a treatise against Marcion; Irenæus too, and Modestus, who, more than the others, openly exposed the error of this man; and many others whose treatises are preserved in the possession of many Brethren up to this day.

At this time, also, Meliton, Bishop of the church of Sardis, and Apollinaris, Bishop of the church of Hierapolis, flourished with praise; who made, each one of them for himself, a separate apology for the Faith, and presented it to the Emperor of the Romans, who lived at that time. But the treatises by these, with which we have become acquainted, are the following:—by Meliton, On Easter two, and On Polity, and On the Prophets; and another On the Church, and another On the First Day of the Week; and again another On the Faith of Man, and another On his Formation; and again another On the Hearing of the Ear of Faith: and besides these, On the Soul and Body; and again On Baptism, and On the Truth, and On the Faith; and On the Birth of Christ, and On the word of his Prophecy; and again On the Soul and on the Body; and another On the Love of Strangers, and On Satan, and On the Revelation of John; and again another On God who put on the body; and again another which he wrote to the Emperor Antoninus. But when he wrote respecting the time of Easter, at the commencement he gave this information, "In the time of Servilius Paulus, proconsul of Asia, Agaris (Sagaris) suffered martyrdom; and there was much questioning in Laodicea touching Easter, which varied as to the time in those days, and these things were written." But this same tract Clement of Alexandria (35) mentions in a treatise of his own which he wrote on Easter, and says that it was on the occasion of this treatise of Meliton that he himself also wrote. But in that apology, which he presented to the Emperor, he relates that such things were done by him to our people: "That

I

which never before took place;—the race of those who fear
God is now persecuted by new decrees in Asia; for calumniators
and such as covet the possessions of others, who have no shame,
under the pretence of their having a decree, openly plunder
5 and rob by night and by day men who have done no wrong."
And after other things he proceeds to say, " If thou hast ordered
this to be done, well; it is also done; for a righteous sovereign
never purposeth any thing unrighteously. We even gladly endure
the honour of this death; but we present to thee this supplica-
10 tion only, that thou wouldest first inquire respecting those who
are the actors in this contest, and judge righteously, whether they
be deserving of death and punishment, or of life and quietness.
But if this will, and this new decree, be not from thee, which is not
meet to be executed in this manner, not even towards barbarians
15 and enemies,—the more especially do we entreat of thee not to be
unmindful of us in this persecution by the world." But after
this he proceeds—" Because our philosophy first flourished among
the Barbarians; but it also sprung up among thine own people
in the days of Augustus, and it became for the empire of the
20 Romans a great power, and for thine own empire especially a good
education; for from that time the dominion of the Romans increased
and enlarged itself, which thou hast received and augmented, and
thou wilt still strengthen it together with thy son, so long as thou
protectest this philosophy which groweth up together with thy
25 empire, that commenced with Augustus; which thy fathers also
honoured together with the other religions: and this is a
great proof, that for the good of the empire our preaching
also sprang up together with its auspicious commencement, because since the days of Augustus no evil has befallen your
30 empire, but rather in every thing it has acquired glory and
power through the prayers of us all. And of all who have
been Emperors, Nero and Domitian only gave heed to envious
men, and received the accusation against our doctrine; and from
these same, as by some unreasonable custom, it was brought to
35 pass that the violence of falsehood should be directed against us.[36]
But thine own ancestors corrected the error of these; for oftentimes

they rebuked by letters many who were desirous of attempting to cause troubles on this account; and thy grandfather Hadrian wrote to many touching this; and to Fundius (Fundanus) the proconsul of Asia. But thy father wrote respecting us to different cities, that no man should injure us, during the time 5 that thou also together with him wast governing every thing; even to the Pharisæans (Larissæans) and to the Thessalonians, and to Athens, and to all nations. But respecting thyself, we are persuaded that thou, still more than they, hast a good will concerning these things; and we are persuaded that thou wilt the rather 10 order with wisdom whatsoever we entreat of thee." But so far were these things set down.

But in the Extracts which were written by Meliton, at the beginning of them, he has noted down the number of the books of the Old Testament and shewn which are received: and it is 15 right we should enumerate them here. But he wrote after this manner: "Meliton to Onesimus my brother, greeting: Because oftentimes with that earnestness which thou hast touching the Word, thou hast exhorted me to make for thee Extracts from the Law and from the Prophets relating to our Saviour and to the whole 20 of our faith, and moreover hast been desirous to learn accurately respecting the Antient Books, how many they are in number and what they are consecutively, I have given diligence to do this, because I am persuaded through thy earnestness touching the faith and touching the doctrine of the Word, that thou 25 esteemest the love of God above every thing, and art striving for eternal life. When, therefore, I went up to the East, and proceeded even to that country in which they were preached and practised, and had learned accurately respecting the books of the Old Testament, I wrote them down and have sent them to thee. Their names are 30 these—Of Moses five *books*, Genesis, and Exodus, and Numbers, and Of the Priests (Leviticus), and Deuteronomy; and again of Jesus, the Son of Nun; and the Book of Judges, and Ruth, and four Books of Kings, and two Books of Chronicles, and the Psalms of David; and of Solomon, the Proverbs, which is Wisdom, and Koheleth, 35 and the Song of Songs; and Job; and of the Prophets, Isaiah and

Jeremiah, and the twelve Prophets together; and Daniel, and Ezekiel, and Ezra: from which same I have made Extracts, and arranged them in six discourses." All these of Meliton. And again there are also many treatises by Apollinaris which are still pre-
5 served in the possession of many; but those which have been seen by us are the following—One, which is the Apology, that was made to the same Emperor of whom we have spoken above; and Against the Heathen five *books*; and Against the Jews two *books*; and those which he composed afterwards against the heresy of the
10 Phrygians, which had recently sprung up a little time before, because then Montanus, together with the false prophetesses which were attached to him, had begun to turn aside from the truth.

ΠΥΡΟΜΝΕΜΑΤΑ,

WHICH AMBROSE, A CHIEF MAN OF GREECE, WROTE; WHO BE-
CAME A CHRISTIAN: AND ALL HIS FELLOW-SENATORS RAISED
A CLAMOUR AGAINST HIM; AND HE FLED FROM THEM, AND
WROTE AND SHEWED THEM ALL THEIR FOLLY; AND AT THE
BEGINNING OF HIS DISCOURSE HE ANSWERED AND SAID:

Do not suppose, Men and Greeks, that my separation from
your customs has taken place without a befitting and just cause;
for I have investigated the whole of your wisdom of poetry, and
rhetoric, and philosophy; and when I found not any thing right
or worthy of the Deity, I was desirous of investigating the wis- 5
dom of the Christians also, and of learning and seeing who *they*
are, and when, and what is this its recent and strange production,
or on what good things they rely who follow this wisdom, so as
to speak the truth.

Men and Greeks, when I had made the inquiry I found not 10
any folly, as in the famous Homer, who says respecting the
wars of the two trials, "for the sake of Helen many of the
Greeks perished at Troy, far from their beloved home." For first
they say respecting Agamemnon their king, that through the
folly of Menelaus his brother, and the vehemence of his madness, 15
and the incontinence of his lust, he was desirous to go and rescue
Helen from a leprous shepherd: but when the Greeks had been

Μὴ ὑπολάβητε, ὦ ἄνδρες Ἕλληνες, ἄλογον ἢ ἀνεπίκριτον εἶναί
μου τὸν ἐκ τῶν ὑμετέρων ἐθῶν χωρισμόν· οὐδὲν γὰρ ἐν αὐτοῖς εὗρον
ὅσιον ἢ θεοφιλές. Αὐτὰ γὰρ τὰ τῶν ποιητῶν ὑμῶν συνθέματα
λύσσης καὶ ἀκρασίας ἐστί μνημεῖα. Τῷ γὰρ ἐν παιδείᾳ παρ᾽ ὑμῖν
προὔχοντι φοιτῶν τις πάντων ἀνθρώπων ἐστὶν ἀργαλεώτατος.
Πρώτιστα μὲν γάρ φασι τὸν Ἀγαμέμνονα, τῇ τοῦ ἀδελφοῦ ἀκρα-
σίᾳ, ἐπιτεταμένῃ λύσσῃ καὶ ἀκατασχέτῳ ἐπιθυμίᾳ συνεργοῦντα, καὶ
τὴν θυγατέρα πρὸς θυσίαν εὐδοκήσαντα δοῦναι καὶ πᾶσαν ταράξαι
τὴν Ἑλλάδα, ἵνα ῥύσηται τὴν Ἑλένην ἀπὸ λεπροῦ ποιμένος

victorious in the war, and had burnt some cities, and taken some
women and boys captive, and the land was filled with blood, and
the rivers were filled with dead bodies, Agamemnon himself too
was found to be taken captive by passion for Briseis: and Pa-
5 troclus was slain, and Achilles, the son of the goddess Thetis,
lamented over him; and Hector was dragged; and Priam, together
with Hecuba, wept over the loss of their children; and Astyanax,
the son of Hector, was thrown from the walls of Ilium, and his
mother, Andromache, Ajax the great took; and that which had
10 been captured in war after a little while was consumed in lust.

But respecting the perfidy of Ulysses, the son of Laertes,
and his murders, who shall tell? for in one day his house became
the grave for a hundred and ten suitors, and was filled with dead
bodies and blood;[(39)] who also by his vice has gained praises, because
15 through the excess of his cunning he concealed himself: who
also, as ye say, sailed over the sea, and heard not the voice of the
Sirens, because he stopped his ears with wax. But Achilles himself, the son of Peleus, who leaped over the river, and put to
flight the Trojans, and slew Hector, this your champion became
20 the slave of Philoxena, and was vanquished by an Amazon while

---

ἡρπασμένην. Ὁπότε δὲ καὶ τοῦ πολέμου κατασχόντος αἰχμαλώ-
τους ἤγαγον, αὐτὸς Ἀγαμέμνων ὑπὸ Χρυσηΐδος αἰχμάλωτος ἤγετο·
πρὸς τὸν Θέτιδος παῖδα Βρισηΐδος ἕνεκεν ἔχθραν ἤρατο. Αὐτὸς δὲ
Πηληϊάδης, ὁ ποταμὸν πηδήσας, Τροίαν καταστρέψας, Ἕκτορα
χειρωσάμενος, Πολυξένης ὁ ἥρως ὑμῶν δοῦλος ἦν· ὑπὸ Ἀμαζόνος
νεκρᾶς νενίκητο· τὰ θεότευκτα ὅπλα ἀποδυσάμενος, νυμφικὴν στο-
λὴν ἐνδυσάμενος, φίλτρων θῦμα ἐγίνετο ἐν τῷ τοῦ Ἀπόλλωνος
νηῷ. Ὁ γὰρ Ἰθακήσιος Λαερτιάδης ἐκ κακίας ἀρετὴν ἐνεπορεύ-
σατο· ὅτι δὲ ἀγαθῆς φρονήσεως ἄμοιρος ἦν, ὁ κατὰ τὰς Σειρῆνας
διάπλους ἐδήλωσεν, ὅτι μὴ ἠδυνήθη φρονήσει ἐμφράξαι τὴν ἀκοήν.
Ὁ Τελαμώνιος Αἴας, ὁ τὸ ἑπταβόειον φέρων σάκος, διὰ τὴν πρὸς
Ὀδυσσέα περὶ τῶν ὅπλων κρίσιν ἡττηθείς, ὑπὸ μανίας ἡλίσκετο.
Ταῦτα παιδεύεσθαι οὐ θέλω· οὐ γὰρ τοιαύτης ἀρετῆς ἐπιδικάζομαι,

she lay dead: and he stripped off his armour, and put on the bridal dress, and at last was sacrificed to love.

So much, then, with respect to heroes; and I should have been satisfied for Homer to be left to thee, if thy vain words had only proceeded to speak of men, and not concerning the gods, because, 5 touching the gods, I am ashamed even to utter them; for the fabled accounts are very wicked and horrible, and surpassing all belief, and necessarily ridiculous; for a man must laugh when he approaches them, nor will he believe when he hears them: gods, indeed! who have not one of them observed the laws of righteousness, and chas- 10 tity, and modesty, but are adulterers, and have lived in dissipation, and yet have not been condemned to death, as it was just. For the Lord of the gods, that "Father of gods and men," according to what you say, was not only an adulterer, for this would have been too little, but he also slew his own father, and was a pæderast. First, 15 then, I will speak concerning his adultery, although I am ashamed, for he appeared to Antiope like a Satyr; and he dropped down upon Danae like gold; and to Europa he became a bull, and a swan

---

ἵνα τοῖς Ὁμήρου μύθοις πείθωμαι· ἔστι γὰρ ἡ πᾶσα ῥαψωδία, Ἰλιάδος τε καὶ Ὀδυσσείας ἀρχὴ καὶ τέλος, γυνή.

Ἀλλ' ἐπεὶ Ἡσίοδος μεθ' Ὅμηρον Ἔργα τε καὶ Ἡμέρας συνέγραψε, τίς αὐτοῦ τῇ λήρῳ Θεογονίᾳ συνθήσεται; Φασὶ γὰρ Κρόνον, τὸν Οὐρανοῦ παῖδα, τῆς ἀρχῆς καθελεῖν τὸν πατέρα καὶ τῶν σκήπτρων λαβέσθαι, καὶ διευλαβηθέντα τὸ ὅμοιον παθεῖν τεκνοφαγεῖν ἑλέσθαι, τῇ δὲ τῶν Κουρήτων ἐπινοίᾳ τὸν Δία κλαπέντα καὶ λαθόντα δεσμοῖς καθεῖρξαι τὸν πατέρα, καὶ διανείμασθαι, ὡς λόγος, Δία μὲν τὸν αἰθέρα, Ποσειδῶνα δὲ τὸν βυθόν, καὶ Πλουτέα τὴν καθ' ᾅδου μοῖραν λαχεῖν. Ἀλλ' ὁ μὲν Πλουτεὺς τὴν Κόρην ἥρπασε· καὶ ἡ Δήμητρα, ἀλωμένη κατὰ τὰς ἐρήμους, τὸ τέκνον ἐζήτει. Καὶ τοῦτον τὸν μῦθον εἰς ὕψος ἤγαγε τὸ ἐν Ἐλευσῖνι πῦρ. Πάλιν ὁ Ποσειδῶν Μελανίππην μὲν ᾔσχυνεν ὑδρευομένην, ὄχλῳ δὲ Νηρηΐδων οὐκ ὀλίγων κατεχρήσατο, ὧν τὰ ὀνόματα ἐὰν διηγώμεθα, πολὺ πλῆθος λόγων κατατρίψομεν· Ὁ μὲν οὖν Ζεὺς μοιχὸς πολλαχῇ· ἐπ' Ἀντιόπῃ μὲν ὡς σάτυρος καὶ Δανάῃ χρυσὸς καὶ ἐπ' Εὐρώπῃ

to Leda. But the love of Semele, the mother of Bacchus, proved both his own importunity, and also the jealousy of the chaste Juno. And he caught up Ganymede the Phrygian like an eagle, in order that a beautiful and becoming boy might be his cupbearer.   More-
5 over that Lord of the gods slew Saturn his own Father, in order that he might seize upon his kingdom. Oh! of how many censures is the Lord of the gods guilty, and to how many deaths is he obnoxious, as an adulterer, and as a sorcerer, and as a pæderast? Read to the Lord of the gods, oh men and Greeks, the law
10 respecting parricide, and the sentence against adultery, and the shame of the obscenity of pæderastism. For how many adul-terers has the Lord of the gods instructed? For how many pæderasts, and sorcerers, and murderers? for if a man be found to be guilty of lust, he shall not be put to death, because he does
15 this to be like the Lord of the gods; and if he be detected as a murderer, he has an apology in the Lord of the gods; and if a man be a sorcerer, he has learnt it from the Lord of the gods; and if he be (40) a pæderast, the Lord of the gods is his advocate.

ταῦρος ἦν, ἐπτεροῦτο δὲ παρὰ Λήδᾳ. Ὁ γὰρ Σεμέλης ἔρως καὶ αὐτοῦ τὴν ἀκρασίαν ἤλεγξε καὶ τῆς Ἥρας τὸν ζῆλον. Τὸν γὰρ Φρύγα Γανυμήδην, φασίν, εἰς τὸ οἰνοχοεῖν ἀνήρπασε. Καὶ ταῦτα μὲν οἱ Κρονίδαι ἐποίησαν. Ὁ γὰρ μεγαλώνυμος ὑμῶν ὁ Λητοΐδης, ὁ μαντικὴν ἐπαγγειλάμενος, ἑαυτὸν ἤλεγξεν ὅτι ψεύδεται. Δάφνην ἐδίωξεν, ἣν οὐ κατέλαβε· καὶ τῷ ἐρομένῳ αὐτὸν Αἰακίδῃ θρησκεύ-οντι τὸν αὐτοῦ θάνατον οὐκ ἐμαντεύσατο. Ἀθηνᾶς γὰρ τὸ ἀνδρικὸν σιγῶ καὶ Διονύσου τὸ θηλυκὸν καὶ Ἀφροδίτης τὸ πορνικόν. Ἀνά-γνωτε τῷ Διΐ, ἄνδρες Ἕλληνες, τὸν κατὰ πατραλῳῶν νόμον καὶ τὸ μοιχείας πρόστιμον καὶ τὴν παιδεραστίας αἰσχρότητα. Διδάξατε Ἀθηνᾶν καὶ Ἄρτεμιν τὰ τῶν γυναικῶν ἔργα καὶ Διόνυσον τὰ ἀνδρῶν. Τί σεμνὸν ἐπιδείκνυται γυνὴ ὅπλοις κεκοσμημένη, ἀνὴρ δὲ κυμβάλοις καὶ στέμμασι καὶ ἐσθῆτι γυναικείᾳ καλλωπιζόμενος καὶ ὀργιῶν σὺν ἀγέλῃ γυναικῶν;
    Τὸν γὰρ τριέσπερον Ἀλκείδην, τῶν ἀγώνων ἡγήτορα, τὸν δι' ἀνδρείαν ᾀδόμενον, τὸν τοῦ Διὸς υἱόν, ὃς βριαρὸν κατέπεφνε λέοντα

But if a man should speak about courage, Achilles was braver than the Lord of the gods, because he slew him who had slain his friend; but the Lord of the gods wept over Sarpendon, his own son, while he was dying, being very sorry. And Pluto, who also is a god, ravished Proserpine, but the mother of Proserpine was in great trepidation, and searching for her daughter in every desert. And Alexander Paris, when he had carried off Helen, received the judgment of vengeance, as being her lover by force; but Pluto, who was a god, and ravished Proserpine, remained without any disgrace. And Menelaus, who was a man, knew how to go in search of Helen his wife, but Ceres, who was a goddess, knew not where to look for her daughter Proserpine. Let Vulcan pass over his jealousy, and be not envious, for he is forgotten because he is old and lame; but Mars is loved because he is a youth and beautiful in stature. But there was the reproach of adultery because Vulcan was not aware of the love of his wife Venus and Mars; but when he did know, Vulcan said, " Come, see a ridiculous and foolish deed, how me, who am her own, Venus, the daughter of the Lord of the gods, is disgracing me, who am her own, and honouring Mars who is a stranger to her. And is it not a shameful thing for the Lord of the gods, because he loved those which were like these? And Penelope continued as a widow twenty years, because she was expecting her husband Ulysses, and was employed with works, and diligent in occupations during the time that all those suitors were urging her; but Venus, who is a goddess, while her husband Vulcan was present with her, abandoned him because she was overcome by love for Mars.

Hear, men and Greeks, which of you would dare to do this, or

καὶ πολύκρανον ὤλεσεν ὕδραν. Ὗν δ᾿ ἄγριον ἀκάματον ὁ νεκρώσας,
ὄρνιθας δ᾿ ἀνδροβόρους ἱπταμένας καθελεῖν ὁ δυνηθείς, καὶ κύνα
τρικάρηνον ἐξ ᾅδου ἀναγαγών, Αὐγείου δ᾿ ὀχυρὸν τεῖχος σκυβάλων
καθελεῖν ὁ δυνηθείς, ταύρους δὲ καὶ ἔλαφον ἀνελὼν ὧν μυξωτῆρες
ἔπνεον πῦρ, καὶ καρπὸν χρύσεον στελέχους ἔλαβεν, ἑρπετὸν ἰοβό-
λον ἀνελὼν καὶ Ἀχελῷον, τίνος ἕνεκεν ἔκτανεν οὐ θέμις εἰπεῖν,

K

could even bear to behold it. And if one should dare, what torment is reserved for him, or what stripes? Nevertheless, Saturn, who is a god, who ate up all those children, is not even brought before a tribunal. They say, however, that the Lord of the gods, his son,
5 only escaped from him, and the madness of his father Saturn was deceived, because Rhea his wife, the mother of the Lord of the gods, gave him a stone instead of his son the Lord of the gods, to prevent him from devouring him. Hear, men and Greeks, and reflect upon this madness; for the brute beast, that feedeth in
10 the field knoweth its own food, and will not touch strange food; likewise the animals and the reptiles too, and the birds also, know their own food; but respecting men it is not meet[41] for me to say any thing: you know indeed their food, and understand; but Saturn, who is a god, not knowing his proper food, swallowed a stone.
15 Wherefore, oh men and Greeks, if ye be willing to have such gods, do not blame one another whenever ye do such things as these; and be not thou angry against thy son when he purposeth to kill thee, because he is imitating the Lord of the gods. And if a man be guilty of adultery with thy wife, why dost thou
20 reckon him as an enemy, and yet worshippest and servest the Lord of the gods, who resembles him? And why dost thou blame thy wife, when she is guilty of adultery and is without punishment, but honourest Venus and settest her in temples? Persuade Solon to break his own laws, Lycurgus also to abstain from
25 making laws, and let the judges of the Areopagus break theirs and not judge again, nor let there be any more councils for the

---

καὶ τὸν ξενοκτόνον Βούσιριν, καὶ ὄρη πηδήσας ἵνα λάβη ὕδωρ ἔναρθρον φωνὴν ἀποδιδόν, ὡς λόγος· ὁ τὰ τοσαῦτα καὶ τοιαῦτα καὶ τηλικαῦτα δρᾶσαι δυνηθείς, ὡς νήπιος ὑπὸ σατύρων κατακυμβαλισθεὶς καὶ ὑπὸ γυναικείου ἔρωτος ἡττηθεὶς ὑπὸ Λυδῆς γελώσης κατὰ γλουτῶν τυπτόμενος ἥδετο· καὶ τέλος, τὸν Νέσσειον χιτῶνα ἀποδύσασθαι μὴ δυνηθείς, πυρὰν κατ᾽ αὐτοῦ αὐτὸς ποιήσας τέλος ἔλαβε τοῦ βίου. Θέτω τὸν ζῆλον Ἥφαιστος, καὶ μὴ φθονείτω εἰ πρεσβύτης ὢν καὶ κυλλὸς τὸν πόδα μεμίσητο, Ἄρης δὲ πεφίλητο νέος ὢν καὶ ὡραῖος. Ἐπεὶ οὖν, ἄνδρες Ἕλληνες, οἱ μὲν θεοὶ ὑμῶν

Athenians. Let the Athenians dismiss Socrates, for no one re-
sembling Saturn has ever been brought before him. Neither let
.them put Orestes, who slew his own mother, to death; for, lo!
the Lord of the gods has done worse things than these to his
father. Œdipus also too hastily inflicted injury upon himself, 5
who put out his eyes because he had slain his father unawares,
because he did not look to the Lord of the gods, who killed his
father, and remained without any punishment. The Corinthians
also expelled Medæa, because she had slain her children, but they
serve and honour Saturn, who ate up his own children. And as for 10
Alexander Paris, he did right in ravishing Helen in order that he
might imitate the god Pluto, who carried off Proserpine.

Let men be freed from the laws, and let cities belong to lascivious women, and be the abode of sorcerers; for this reason, oh
men and Greeks, because your gods are debased like yourselves, 15
but your warriors are brave as your dramas relate, and your
histories proclaim; respecting the furies of Orestes, and the
bed of Thyestes, and the pollution of Pelops; and concerning
Danaus, who through his jealousy slew and cut off some of his
sons in their banqueting; and also the feasting of Thyestes upon 25
a corpse in vengeance, and Procne up to this time crying as she
flies, and also her sister piping with her tongue cut out. But
what is it fit to say respecting the murder of Œdipus, who
married his own mother, and whose brothers, who were also his
own sons, slew one another?
30
And I hate also your festivals, for there is no moderation there

---

ὑπὸ ἀκρασίας ἠλέγχθησαν, ἄνανδροι δὲ οἱ ἥρωες ὑμῶν, ὡς αἱ παρ'
ὑμῖν δραματουργοὶ ἱστορίαι ἐδήλωσαν, τὰ μὲν Ἀτρέως ἄγη, Θυέ-
στου λέχη, καὶ Πελοπιδῶν μύση, καὶ Δαναὸν φθόνῳ φονεύοντα,
καὶ ἀτεκνοῦντα μεμεθυσμένον, καὶ τὰ Θυέστεια δεῖπνα ἃ Ἐριννύες
ἤρτυον. Καὶ Πρόκνη μέχρι νῦν ἐπτερωμένη γοᾷ, καὶ ταύτης
ἀδελφὴ γλωσσοτόμητος τέτριγεν ἡ Κεκροπίς. Τὰ γὰρ Οἰδίποδος
κέντρα τί δεῖ καὶ λέγειν, καὶ τὸν Λαΐου φόνον καὶ μητρὸς γάμον,
καὶ τὴν τῶν ἀδελφῶν αὐτοῦ καὶ τέκνων ἅμα ἀλληλοκτονίαν;

Καὶ τὰς πανηγύρεις ὑμῶν μεμίσηκα· ἄμετροι γὰρ ἐκεῖ πλησμο-

to the sweet pipes that drive away care, which play with a
tremulous motion, and the preparation of the unguents with which
ye anoint yourselves,[42] and the garlands which ye put on.
And in the abundance of your wickedness ye have forgotten
5 shame, your understandings also are blinded, ye have been tempted
too by importunity, and have loved the bed of lying. And if
these things had been said by another, perhaps they would have
brought an accusation against him that they are not true; but
your own poets declare them, and your songs and dramas proclaim
10 them.   Come, then, and be instructed by the Word of God, and by
consoling wisdom: rejoice and partake of it: know too the King
incorruptible, and become acquainted with his servants, which
boast not in armour, neither make slaughter: because our Captain
delighteth not in the multitude of an army, neither in the horse-
15 men and in their beauty, nor in the illustriousness of family;
but he delighteth in the pure soul, which a wall of justice sur-

---

ναί, καὶ αὐλοὶ γλαφυροὶ ἐκκαλούμενοι πρὸς οἰστρώδεις κινήσεις, καὶ
μύρων περίεργοι χρίσεις, καὶ στεφάνων περιθέσεις.   Καὶ τῷ το-
σούτῳ σωρῷ τῶν κακῶν τὴν αἰδῶ περιγράφετε, καὶ νοῦν πληροῦσθε,
ὑπὸ ἀκρασίας ἐκβακχευόμενοι· καὶ ταῖς ἀνοσίαις καὶ λυσσώδεσι
χρᾶσθαι εἰώθατε μίξεσιν.   Εἴποιμι δ᾽ ἂν ὑμῖν ἔτι καὶ τοῦτο·   Τί
ἀγανακτεῖς, Ἕλλην ὤν, πρὸς τὸ τέκνον σοῦ, εἰ τὸν Δία μιμούμενος
ἐπιβουλεύει σοὶ καὶ ἐπ᾽ ἴσου τὸν γάμον σεσύληκε;   Τί τοῦτον
ἐχθρὸν ἡγῇ, τὸν δὲ ὅμοιον αὐτῷ σέβῃ;   Τί δὲ μέμφῃ σοῦ τὴν γυναῖκα ἀκολάστως ζῶσαν, τὴν δὲ Ἀφροδίτην ναοῖς τετίμηκας;   Καὶ
εἰ μὲν ταῦτα ὑφ᾽ ἑτέρων ἦν εἰρημένα, κατηγορία ἔδοξεν εἶναι ψιλὴ
καὶ οὐκ ἀλήθεια· νῦν δὲ ταῦτα οἱ ὑμέτεροι ἄδουσι ποιηταί, καὶ αἱ
παρ᾽ ὑμῖν κεκράγασιν ἱστορίαι.

Ἔλθετε λοιπόν, ἄνδρες Ἕλληνες, καὶ σοφίᾳ ἀπαραμιλλήτῳ
κοινωνήσατε, καὶ θείῳ λόγῳ παιδεύθητε, καὶ μάθετε βασιλέα
ἄφθαρτον· καὶ τοὺς τούτου ἥρωας ἐπίγνωτε οὔποτε λαοῖς φόνον
ἐργαζομένους.   Αὐτὸς γὰρ ἡμῶν ὁ στρατηγὸς οὐ βούλεται σωμάτων
ἀλκὴν καὶ τύπων εὐμορφίαν οὐδ᾽ εὐγενίας φρύαγμα, ἀλλὰ ψυχήν
τε καθαράν, ὁσιότητι τετειχισμένην, ἤδη δὲ διηνεκῶς ἐπιστατῶν

rounds. But the Word of God is always instructing us, and the promises of our good King and the works of God. Oh the soul that is purchased by the power of the Word! oh the trumpet of peace without war! oh the doctrine quenching the natural fire of the soul, which maketh not poets, nor produceth philosophers, nor the crowd-followed orator; but goeth and maketh the dead pass over that he die not, and raiseth men from earth as Gods, to the region which is above the firmament. Come, be instructed, and be like me, for I also have been like you.

ἡμῖν ὁ θεῖος λόγος, καὶ τὰ τοῦ βασιλέως ἡμῶν συνθήματα, πράξεις θείας, ὡς διὰ λόγου δυνάμεως εἰς ψυχὴν διϊκνουμένης. ὦ σάλπιγξ εἰρηνικὴ ψυχῆς πολεμουμένης, ὦ παθῶν δεινῶν φυγαδευτήριον, ὦ πυρὸς ἐμψύχου σβεστικὸν διδασκάλιον! ἥτις οὐ ποιητὰς ποιεῖ, οὐ φιλοσόφους κατασκευάζει οὐδὲ ῥήτορας δεινούς, ἀλλὰ παιδεύουσα ποιεῖ τοὺς θνητοὺς ἀθανάτους, τοὺς βροτοὺς θεούς· ἐκ γῆς δὲ μετάγει εἰς τοὺς ὑπὲρ Ὄλυμπον ὅρους. Ἔλθετε, παιδεύθητε· γίνεσθε ὡς ἐγώ, ὅτι κἀγὼ ἤμην ὡς ὑμεῖς. Ταῦτά με εἷλε, τό τε τῆς παιδείας ἔνθεον καὶ τὸ τοῦ λόγου δυνατόν· ὅτι καθάπερ ἐπαοιδὸς ἀγαθὸς ἐκ φωλεοῦ ἐξερπύσαι ποιήσας φυγαδεύει δεινὸν ἑρπετόν, οὕτως ὁ λόγος ἐξ αὐτῶν τῶν τῆς ψυχῆς μυχῶν τὰ δεινὰ τῆς αἰσθήσεως ἀπελαύνει πάθη· πρῶτον ἐπιθυμίαν, δι᾽ ἧς πᾶν δεινὸν φύεται, ἔχθραι, ἔρεις ζῆλος, ἐριθεῖαι, θυμοί, καὶ τὰ ὅμοια τούτοις. Ἐπιθυμίας οὖν ἀπελαθείσης εὔδιος ἡ ψυχὴ καὶ γαληνιῶσα γίνεται. Παραλυθεῖσα δὲ τῶν περὶ τὸν τράχλον αὐτῆς κακῶν περιρρεόντων ἀπέρχεται πρὸς τὸν ποιήσαντα αὐτήν· δεῖ γὰρ ἀποκατασταθῆναι ὅθεν ἀπέστη, ἵθεν τις ἐγένετο ἢ ἐστιν.

THE EPISTLE OF MARA, SON OF SERAPION.

MARA, SON OF SERAPION, TO SERAPION MY SON, GREETING.

WHEN thy master and tutor wrote to me a letter, and informed
me that thou art very dililgent in learning for a child of few years,
I blessed God, that thou, being a little boy without one to guide
thee, hast begun with a good intention; and as for me myself this
5 has been a consolation to me, that respecting thee, a little boy
I have heard, of this greatness of mind and good conscience, such
as does not readily remain in many. On this account, lo! I have
written to thee this memorial of what I have experienced in the
world; for the manner of men's living has been experienced by me,
10 and I have walked in instruction, and all those things of the instruction of the Greeks I have found them wrecked together with the
birth of life. Be careful, therefore, my son, of those things which are
suitable for such as be free, to meditate upon learning, and to pursue after wisdom: and in this manner reckon to be confirmed in that
15 with which thou hast begun; and remember my injunctions with
diligence, as a quiet man, who loveth discipline: and although it
appear to thee to be very bitter, when thou shalt experience it for
a little while, it will be very pleasant to thee, because so also it hath
happened to me. But a man when he shall be departed from among
20 his family, and shall be able to retain his own habit, and shall
do with justice whatsoever is proper for him, he is that chosen man
who is called the Blessing of God, and with whose liberty nothing
else can be compared. For such men as are called to discipline,
seek to disentangle themselves from the struggle of the time; and
25 such as lay hold upon wisdom are elevated by the hope of righteousness; and those that stand in the truth exhibit the standard
of their virtue; and those that devote themselves to philosophy
look to escape from the miseries of the world. But thou, too,
my son, conduct thyself so wisely in these things, as a wise
30 man who endeavoureth to spend a pure life: and beware lest the
acquisition of wealth, which the many thirst after, subdue thee, and

thy mind be turned to desire riches which are not real; for neither when *men* obtain their desire do they abide, not even while they continue in righteousness: and all these things which are seen by thee in the world, as of one who is for a short[44] time, are to be dissolved like a dream; for they are the ups and downs of the times. 5

And as to vain glory, which occupies the life of men, thou considerest not that it is one of those things which give us joy: speedily it becometh an injury to us: and especially the birth of beloved children. For in both these things the contest of feelings hurts us: for as to the good, love for them torments us, and 10 we are attracted by their manners; and as to the vicious, we labour for their correction, and grieve over their vices.

For I have heard respecting our companions, that when they were departing from Samosta it grieved them; and like those who blame the time, they also spake after this manner: " Henceforth we 15 are driven far away from the habitation of men, and we are not allowed to return to our city, and to behold our men, and to embrace our gods with praise." It is meet that that should be called a day of lamentation, because one heavy grief laid hold upon them all equally. For with tears they remembered their 20 fathers, and with sighs their mothers, and they grieved over their brethren, and sorrowed over their betrothed whom they left behind: and when we heard the report of their former companions, that they were going to Seleucia, we went secretly on the way towards them, and joined our trouble with theirs. Then was 25 our sorrow very vehement, and justly was our weeping augmented by our loss, and the dark cloud collected our sighs, and our trouble was increased from the mountain, for not one among us was able to quell the miseries which were upon him. For the love of life was retained together with the pains of death, and our misfor- 30 tunes drove us out of the way; for we beheld our brethren and our children as captives, and we remembered our companions that were dead, who were laid in a country not their own: and each of us was also anxious about himself, lest affliction should be added to affliction, or another grief should overtake the one which preceded it. 35

What advantage do men that are imprisoned gain from having

experienced these things! But as for thee, my beloved, let it not
grieve thee that thy loneliness has been driven from place to place;
because men are born for this end, to receive the accidents of the
time. But thus reckon thou, that for wise men every place is equally
5 the same; and for the virtuous, fathers and mothers abound in
every city. Even indeed from thine own self take the trial. How
many men, who know thee not, love thee as their own children,
and a multitude of women receive thee like their own beloved
ones. Verily as a stranger thou hast been successful, verily for
10 thy little love many men have desired thee.

What, then, have we to say [15] touching the error which has come
into the world? Both the progress in it is with heavy labour, and we
are shaken by its commotions like a reed by the wind. For I have
wondered at many that cast away their children, and I have mar-
15 velled at others that brought up those which were not their own:
there are some that acquire the riches in the world, and I have also
marvelled at others who inherit that which is not their own. Thus
understand and see that it is in the path of error we are walking.

A sage among men once began to say to us: On which of *all*
20 possessions can a man rely? Or respecting what things can we
speak as if they are enduring? On abundance of riches? they
are snatched away. On fortresses? they are plundered. On
cities? they are laid waste. On greatness? it is brought low.
On splendour? it is overthrown. On beauty? it withereth. On
25 laws? they pass away. On poverty? it is despised. On children? they die. On friends? they become false. On honours?
envy goeth before them.

Let a man therefore rejoice in his empire like Darius, and in
his prosperity like Polycrates, or in his valour like Achilles, or in
30 his wife like Agamemnon, or in his offspring like Priam, or in his
skill like Archimedes, or in his wisdom like Socrates, or in his
learning like Pythagoras, or in his enlightenment like Palamedes—
the life of men, my son, departs from the world, but their praises
and their virtues continue for ever.

35 But thou, my little son, choose for thyself that which fadeth not
away, because they that occupy themselves in such things are called

modest and beloved, and lovers of a good name : but whenever any evil thing opposeth thee, blame not man, nor be angry against God, neither murmur against thy time. If thou continue in this mind, thy gift is not a small one which thou hast received from God, which standeth not in need of riches, nor is brought near to po- 5 verty, because thou wilt perform thy part in the world without fear, and with rejoicing : for fear and excuse of that which cometh naturally is not for the sake of the wise, but for the sake of those who walk without law ; because a man has never been stripped of his wisdom in the same manner as of his wealth. Be careful for know- 10 ledge rather than for riches, for by how much the more possessions increase, by so much the more does evil abound. For I have seen that where good things abound, so also (40) misfortunes oppose ; and where honours are brought, there also sorrows collect themselves ; and where riches are multiplied, there is the bitterness of many 15 years. If, therefore, thou art wise, and diligently keepest watch, God will not cease from helping thee, nor men from loving thee. Whatsoever thou art able to acquire, let that be sufficient for thee ; and if indeed thou be able to do without possessions, then shalt thou be called blessed, because no one will even envy thee. 20 And remember this too, that nothing troubles thy life very greatly except possessions, that no man after his death is called master of possessions : because weak men are led captive by the lust of them, and know not that a man dwells like a stranger in his pos- sessions : and they are fearful because they are not secured for 25 them ; for they have forsaken that which is their own, and seek that which is not theirs.

For what else have we to say, when wise men are forcibly dragged by the hands of tyrants, and their wisdom is taken captive by calumny, and they are oppressed in their intelligence without 30 defence ? For what advantage did the Athenians gain by the murder of Socrates, the recompense of which they received in famine and pestilence ? Or the people of Samos by the burning of Pythagoras, because in one hour their country was entirely covered with sand ? Or the Jews *by the death* of their wise 35 king, because from that same time their kingdom was taken away ?

L

For with justice did God make recompense to the wisdom of these three: for the Athenians died of famine; and the Samians were overwhelmed by the sea without remedy; and the Jews, desolate and driven from their own kingdom, are scattered through every country. Socrates is not dead, because of Plato; neither Pythagoras, because of the statue of Juno; nor the Wise King, because of the laws which he promulgated.

But I, my son, have experienced in what wretched misery men stand; and I have wondered that they are not overwhelmed by the evils which surround them. Not even wars are sufficient for them, nor griefs, nor sicknesses, nor death, nor poverty; but like vicious beasts they attack one another in hatred, which of them shall inflict the greater evil upon his fellow. For they have gone beyond the limits of truth, and transgress all good laws, because they hang upon their own lust: for so long as a man coveteth that which he lusteth after, how is he able to do with justice that which is befitting him? And they acknowledge no moderation, and seldom do they stretch forth their hands towards truth[47] and virtue, but conduct themselves in their manner of living like the dumb and the blind. The wicked rejoice, and the righteous are troubled: he that hath denieth, and he that hath not striveth to acquire: the poor beg, and the rich conceal: and every one laugheth at his neighbour: the drunken are crazy, and those that have recovered themselves repent: some of them weep, and some sing, and others laugh; others, care has seized upon them: they rejoice in evil things; and they reject the man who speaketh the truth. A man may then wonder, while the world consumes in derision, while they have not one manner of living, they are anxious about these things; and one of them is looking when he shall acquire the name of victory in battle; and the brave look not to how many foolish lusts a man is led captive in the world. But I could wish also that repentance had recurred to them a little, who conquer by their might, and are condemned by their cupidity. For I have tried men; and thus have I tried them, that they look to this one thing—to abundance of riches; and on this account they have no firm counsel, but by the change of their minds each is

speedily cast down to be absorbed in grief; and they regard not
the vast riches of the world, that whatever there be of trouble it
brings us all equally to the same time; for they depend upon the
majesty of the belly, that great disgrace of the corrupt.

But this which comes into my mind to write to thee, it is not 5
enough to read it, but it should also proceed to practise. For I
know too, that when thou shalt experience this manner of living,
it will please thee much, and thou wilt be free from evil indignation,
that on children's account we endure riches. Separate henceforth
from thee the cherished grief of men, a thing which never profits at 10
all; and drive away from thee that care which produceth no advantage, for we have no means and discretion except *in* magnanimity,
to be equal to the misfortunes and to endure the griefs, which we
are always receiving at the hands of the times; for it behoveth us
to look to these things, and not to those which pertain to joy and 15
a good name. Apply thyself to wisdom, the fountain of all good
things, and the treasure which fadeth not, and there shalt thou lay
thine head and rest, for she will be to thee a father and a mother,
and a good companion for life. Have all familiarity with perse-
verance and patience, which are able to meet all the tribu- 20
lations of weak men; for in this manner is their power great,
because they can bear hunger,[18] and endure thirst, and they
refresh every grief. But of labour and death they also declare. Attend to these, and thou shalt pass a tranquil life,
and thou wilt be to me a consolation, while thou shalt be 25
called the Ornament of his parents. For at that former time,
while our city was standing in its magnificence, thou mayst know
that against many men abominable words were uttered. But we
also acknowledged from the Time, that we fully received from
its majesty appropriate love and beauty; but the Time forbade 30
us to complete those things which were resolved upon in our
mind. And here, too, in prison we give thanks to God that
we have obtained the love of many; for we essayed our soul to
continue in wisdom and in rejoicing. But if any drive us by
force, he will proclaim the witness against himself, that he is far 35
removed from all good things, and will receive disgrace and

shame from the vile object of shame.   For we have shewn our
truth, that we have no vice in an empire.   But if the Romans will
permit us to return to our country in justice and righteousness,
let them act like humane men, and they will be called good
5 and righteous, and the country in which they abide will also
be in tranquillity.   For let them shew their own greatness by
leaving us free.   Let us be obedient to that dominion which the
Time has assigned to us, and let them not, like tyrants, treat us
as slaves; and whatever may be decreed to take place, we shall
10 not receive any thing more than the tranquil death which is
reserved for us.

But thou, my little son, if thou desirest diligently to know
these things, first govern lust, and apply moderation to that in
which thou abidest, be satisfied, and beware lest thou be angry:
15 and instead of rage be obedient to virtue.   For I now am meditating
upon this, that, as I recollect, I may leave for myself a book, and
with a prudent mind may accomplish the path to which I am condemned, and may escape without sorrow from the evil destruction
of the world.   For I pray to receive dissolution, and what death,
20 it matters not to me.   But and if any grieve or be anxious, I
counsel him not: for there in the way of life of the whole world
he will find us before him.

One of his friends asked Mara, the son of Serapion, when he
was in bonds by his side, "On thy life, Mara, I pray thee tell
25 me what laughable thing has appeared to thee that thou laughedst?"
Mara said to him, "I was laughing at the Time, because, without
having borrowed any evil from me, it repays me."

HERE ENDETH THE EPISTLE OF MARA, SON OF SERAPION.

NOTES.

BARDESAN.

P. 1. *Book of the Laws of Countries.* The title of this treatise is given by Eusebius, *Ec. Hist.* b. iv. c. 30, Ὁ περὶ εἱμαρμένης διάλογος; by Epiphanius, Κατὰ εἱμαρμένης, *Panarium adversus Hæres.;* 36, p. 477.

L. 1. *Shemashgram.* This is the pronunciation according to the vowels which have been added by a later hand. In Greek it is written Σαμψιγέραμος. There was a king of Emesa so called, whose daughter was married to Aristobulus: See Josephus, *Antiq. Jud.* b. 18, c. 6, and b. 19, c. 8. A Priest of Venus at Emesa of this name went out to meet Sapor, king of Persia, when he advanced against that city in the reign of the Emperor Valerian. See Johannes Malela, *Chronograph.* vol. i. p. 391, edit. Oxon. 1691. In Strabo the name is written Σαμψικέραμος. *Geog.* b. 16. p. 753, edit. Casaubon, 1620. M. Renan has mistaken this for the name of a place, and supposed the particle and verb ⌐Z⌐ which follow to be the name of a person. It is hardly possible to commit a greater number of errors in the same space than M. Renan has fallen into in translating the first lines of this treatise. " Il y a quelques jours, en allant visiter à Schemsgarm notre frère Évéthès, nous y rencontrames Bardesane, qui, après s'être assuré de notre santé," &c. See " Lettre à M. Reinaud sur quelques manuscrits Syriaques du Musée Britannique," in Journal Asiatique. 1852.

L. 8. *Avida.* This name is given by Epiphanius Ἀβειδὰ, the *vau* being sounded like β, as in Ǐ𝚘𝚘 *Sibylla,* p. ⌐𝚘, L. 5. M. Renan has again fallen into an error here, and translated this man's name " un de nos compagnons," adding, in a note, " Je suppose que le traducteur a lu συνήθεια (⌐𝚘𝚜) au lieu συνήθης." Apparently he was ignorant of the account given by Epiphanius, and has assumed against all authority that Bardesan wrote this treatise in Greek.

P. 3. L. 20. Compare what is here said about man's free agency with Justin Martyr. *Apol.* i. c. 7, 43 ; Origen, *De Princip.* iii. c. 1 ; *Philocalia* c. xxvi.

P. 4. L. 14. *Being.* The Syriac word is ⌐Z⌐, which is often used for Æon. See Hahn, *Bardesanes Gnosticus,* p. 58, et seq.

L. 15. *Established.* The original word is ܩܐܝܡ from ܩܘܡ, which corresponds with the Greek term δημιουργέω.

L. 16. *Image of Elohim* ܨܠܡܐ ܕܐܠܗܐ, the Hebrew בצלם אלהים, retained by Bardesan : the Peshito renders ܨܠܡܐ ܕܐܠܗܐ. Gen. i. 27.

L. 36. *The Angels.* Bardesan takes here בני אלהים, Pesh. ܒܢܝ ܐܠܗܐ, Sept. υἱοὶ τοῦ Θεοῦ, Gen. vi. 2, to be 'angels.' So Josephus : Πολλοὶ γὰρ ἄγγελοι Θεοῦ, γυναιξὶ συμμιγέντες, ὑβριστὰς ἐγέννησαν παῖδας, καὶ παντὸς ὑπερόπτας καλοῦ: *Antiq. Jud.* b. 1. c. 3. Justin Martyr : Ὁι δὲ ἄγγελοι παραβάντες τήνδε τὴν τάξιν, γυναικῶν μίξεσιν ἡττήθησαν, καὶ παῖδας ἐτέκνωσαν, οἵ εἰσιν οἳ λεγόμενοι δαίμονες. *Apol.* ii. c. 5. Clemens Alexandrinus : Ἄγγελοί τινες ἀκρατεῖς γενόμενοι, ἐπιθυμίᾳ ἁλόντες, οὐρανόθεν δεῦρο καταπεπτώκασιν: *Strom.* b. 3. And again, Οἱ ἄγγελοι ἐκεῖνοι οἱ τὸν ἄνω κλῆρον εἰληχότες, κατολισθήσαντες εἰς ἡδονὰς, ἐξεῖπον τὰ ἀπόρρητα ταῖς γυναιξὶν, b. 5. Edit. Potter. pp. 538, 650. Tertullian. "Nam et illi, qui ea constituerunt, damnati in pœnam mortes deputantur, illi scilicet angeli, qui ad filias hominum de cœlo ruerunt.——Utrumne mulieres sine materiis splendoris et sine ingeniis decoris placere non possent hominibus, quæ, adhuc incultæ et incompostæ et ut ita dixerim, crudæ ac rudes angelos, moverant?" See *De Cultu fœminarum,* i. c. 2. See also *De Idolatria,* c. ix. Sulpitius Severus : "Angeli, quibus cœlum sedes erat, speciosarum forma virginum capti, illicitas cupiditates appetierunt: ac naturæ suæ originisque degeneres, relictis Superioribus, quorum incolæ erant, matrimoniis se mortalibus miscuerunt:' *De Sacra Historia,* b. i. p. 7. Lactantius : "Misit angelos ad tutelam cultumque generis humanii——. Itaque illos cum hominibus commorantes dominator ille terræ fallacissinus consuetudine ipsa paulatim ad vitia pellexit, et mulierum congressibus inquinavit." *Institut. Divin.* lib. ii. c. 14. The author of the *Testaments of the* XII *Patriarchs.* Ἔθελξαν τοὺς Ἐγρηγόρους πρὸ τοῦ κατακλυσμοῦ, κἀκεῖνοι συνεχῶς ὁρῶντες αὐτὰς, ἐγένοντο ἐν ἐπιθυμίᾳ ἀλλήλων κ.τ.λ. *Test. Reuben,* c. 5. Grabe, *Spicilegium.* Vol. 1. p. 150. This opinion of the more antient Christian writers Chrysostom refutes, *Homil.* 22 *in Genes.* Edit. Paris, 1614, p. 249 ; Theodoretus, *Quæst. in Genesin,* 47 ; and Augustin : although in the copies of Genesis, which he used, the term 'angels' was found, "Nam et Canonica Scriptura sic loquitur, in quo libro hæc legimus, cujus verba ista sunt. *Et factum est postquam cœperunt homines multi fieri super terram et filiæ natæ sunt illis, videntes Angeli Dei filias hominum, quia bonæ sunt, sumpserunt sibi uxores ex omnibus quas elegerunt.*

De Civitate Dei b. xv. c. 23. The opinion generally held is this of
Augustin and others, that the בְּנֵי אֱלֹהִים, the "Sons of God," were
the descendants of Seth. In this the *Book of Adam*, lately translated from
the Ethiopic by Dillman, concurs : " Die kinder Seths aber, die oben auf
dem berge waren, hatten gepflegt zu beten and God zu lobpreisen anstatt
der schaaren (der engel) die gefallen waren, und Gott hatte ihnen den
namen "engel" gegeben und sich sehr über sie gefreut:" *Das christliche
Adambuch des Morgenlandes*, in Ewald's " Jahrbucher der Biblichen
wissenschaft," 1853. p. 93. I find the same notion in the ܡܥܪܬ ܓܙ̈ܐ
Cave of Treasures, ܘ، ، ، ، ، ، ، ، ، ، ، ، ، ، ، ، ، ،
ܐ، ،
ܘ، ،
، ،
، ،
، ، ، ، ، ، ، ، ، ، ، ، ، ، " And they were not willing to give ear to
the commandment of Jared and to the words of Enoch, and they dared to
transgress the commandment, and went down an hundred men mighty in
valour, and when they beheld the daughters of Cain, that they were fair to
look upon, and that without modesty they were unveiled, the sons of Seth
were inflamed with the fire of lust ; and when the daughters of Cain beheld
their beauty they flew upon them like corrupt beasts, and defiled their
bodies, and the sons of Seth lost themselves in fornication with the daughters
of Cain." fol. 11. Respecting the ܡܥܪܬ ܓܙ̈ܐ see my Corpus Ignatianum,
pp. 286, 360.

P. 5, L. 13. *Beings when they are set in order,* ܐܟܬܐ ܘܟܬܐ̈،،،،،،،،،
i.e. by the Demiurgus. See note above, p. 78.

P. 6, L. 25. *Tares,* I have rendered as in our English version : properly ܙܝܙܢܐ *ζιζάνια*.

L. 31. *Governors,* ܡܕܒܪ̈ܢܐ.

P. 8, L. 1. *The nature of man,* &c. It will be seen, upon comparing the
passage comprised in this and the following pages with that cited by
Eusebius, *Præpar. Evan.* vi. c. 10, printed below, that the Greek varies
considerably from the Syriac : there are many interpolations which are not
found in the original ; and again several sentences of the Syriac have been
omitted in the Greek.

P. 11, L. 2. *Fortune* ܓܕܐ. The corresponding Greek term is γένεσις.

L. 4. *O Philip and Baryama.* I am not sure respecting this latter word, whether it be a proper name or not: perhaps ܒܪ ܝܡܐ may be rendered " even profoundly," *literally,* " even a son of the sea." The book of Chronicles is called in the Peshito ܣܦܪ ܕܝ ܝܡܐ, that is ܣܦܪ ܝܡܐ ܕܝ ܬܪܬܝܢ. I do not know whether by my fault or the compositor's, the word is spelled wrongly *Phillip* in this place.

L. 7. *In another place.* Probably referring to some of his former works.

P. 15, L. 26. *Associations.* ܟܘܢܫܐ. Julius Firmicus Maternus calls this "radiationis societas." See *Ad Mavortium Lollian. Astron.* b. ii. c. 26. Edit. 1551, p. 36.

L. 30. *The doctrine of both countries is the same.* The Chaldæans, according to Diodorus Siculus, were a colony from Egypt, *Bibl. Hist.* b. i, p. 73. Edit. Hanoviæ, 1604. Clemens Alexandrinus writes Αἰγύπτιοι γοῦν πρῶτοι Ἀστρολογίαν εἰς ἀνθρώπους ἐξήνεγκαν ὁμοίως δὲ Χαλδαῖοι: *Stromat.* i. p. 361. Cited also by Euseb. *Præp. Evang.* x. 6. See also Gallæus, *De Sibyllis,* p. 484. Julius Firmicus says that he has embodied in his treatise on Astrology all that the Egyptians and Babylonians had said on this head. " Hæc cum omnia mihi a te, Mavorti, ornamentum bonorum, facili demonstrationis magisterio traderentur, ausus sum etiam ipse aliquid inconsulti sermonis temeritate proferre, ut promitterem me tibi editurum, quicquid Ægyptii veteres, sapientes ac divini viri, Babyloniique prudentes, de vi stellarum ac potestatibus divinæ nobis doctrinæ magisterio tradiderunt." See Præfat. The reader who is desirous of further information as to many astrological questions alluded to by Bardesan will find them stated fully by Julius Firmicus.

P. 16, L. 7. *Seres.* Respecting these see Pliny, *Hist. Nat.* vi. c. 17; Solinus c. 53; Pomponius Mela i. c. 2; *Vetus orbis descriptio Græci Scriptoris sub Constantio.* Ed. J. Gothofred. Genevæ, 1628, p. 1.

L. 11. *The fierce,* Syr. ܐܙܝܙܐ, Ἄζιζος, as Julian has it. Eusebius renders πυριλαμπέος; and so also Cæsarius, whose version is independent of that used by Eusebius. See p. 35, L. 30. Ruffinus in the *Recognitions:* "stella Martis ignita."

P. 17, L. 1. *Of the Brahmins.* For the account of the Brahmins amongst the ancients, see Palladius, *De Gentibus Indiæ et Bragmanibus;* and two other writers edited in the same volume by Ed. Bisse, 4to. Lond. 1665. Strabo: *Geog.* x. p. 712. Origen; *Contra Celsum,* p. 19. Edit. Spencer. Cantab. 1658. Jerome in his Second Book, *Adversus Jovinianum,* refers to this matter: "Bardesanes, vir Babylonius, in duo dogmata apud Indos gymnosophistas dividit, quorum alterum appellat Brachmanas, alterum

Samanæos, qui tantæ continentiæ sunt, ut vel pomis arborum juxta Gangen fluvium, vel publico orizæ, vel farinæ alantur cibo, et cum rex ad eos venerit, adorare illos solitus sit, pacemque suæ provinciæ in illorum precibus arbitrari sitam." Edit. Erasmi, tom. ii. p. 55. There is no mention of the name *Samanæi*, either in the original Syriac, or by Eusebius, Cæsarius, or Ruffinus in his version of the Recognitions. They are named, however, by Porphyry, referring to Bardesan, *De abstinentia*, lib. 4. § 17. Ἰδὼν γὰρ τῆς πολιτείας εἰς πολλὰ νενεμεμένης, ἐστί τι γένος παρ' αὐτοῖς τὸ τῶν θεοσόφων· οὓς Γυμνοσοφιστὰς καλεῖν εἰώθασιν Ἕλληνες. τούτων δὲ δύο αἱρέσεις, ὧν τῆς μὲν Βραχμᾶνες προΐστανται, τῆς δὲ Σαμαναῖοι· ἀλλ' οἱ μὲν Βραχμᾶνες ἐκ γένους διαδέχονται, ὥσπερ ἱερατείαν, τὴν τοιαύτην θεοσοφίαν. Σαμαναῖοι δὲ λογάδες εἰσὶν, κᾀκ τῶν βουληθέντων θεοσοφεῖν συμπληρούμενοι. ἔχει δὲ τὰ κατ' αὐτοὺς τοῦτον τὸν τρόπον, ὡς Βαρδησάνης, ἀνὴρ Βαβυλώνιος, ἐπὶ τῶν πατέρων ἡμῶν γεγονὼς, καὶ ἐντυχὼν τοῖς περὶ Δαμάδαμιν πεμπομένοις Ἰνδοῖς πρὸς τὸν Καίσαρα ἀνεγραψεν. Origen also speaks of the Samanæi in conjunction with the Brahmins, τῶν παρ' Ἰνδοῖς φιλοσοφούντων Βραχμᾶνες, ἢ Σαμαναῖοι : *Contra Celsum*, lib. 1, p. 19. Clemens Alexandrinus too mentions them. Προέστησαν δὲ αὐτῆς Αἰγυπτίων τε οἱ Προφῆται, καὶ Ἀσσυρίων οἱ Χαλδαῖοι, καὶ Γαλατᾶν οἱ Δρυΐδαι, καὶ Σαμαναῖοι Βάκτρων.—Ἰνδῶν τε οἱ Γυμνοσοφισταί· ἄλλοι τὲ φιλόσοφοι βάρβαροι. διττὸν δὲ τούτων τὸ γένος, οἱ μὲν Σαρμᾶναι, αὐτῶν, οἱ δὲ Βραχμᾶνοι καλούμενοι. *Stromat.* lib. 1, p. 359. Edit. Potter.

P. 18. L. 1. *By custom*, ‏ܪܒܝܕܐ‎. The Greek of Eusebius has ἀγρευόντες, as if he had read ‏ܪܨܝܕܐ‎; an error which might easily have arisen if the words were written in the antient square character רביידא and רבצידא respectively.

L. 10. This abominable law of the antient Persians is frequently referred to by the early Christian writers. Tertullian, " Plane Persæ, Ctesias edit, tam scientes quam non horrentes cum matribus libere vivunt. *Ad Nationes* 1. c. 18. edit. Fr. Oehler, p. 338. See also Clemens. *Hom.* xix. c. 19 : Origen, *Contra Celsum*, p. 248. 331. See *Vetus orbis descriptio*, p. 9. The author of this law is stated by Theodoretus to be Zaradas. Ἀλλὰ κατὰ τοὺς Ζαράδου πάλαι Πέρσαι πολιτευόμενοι νόμους, καὶ μητράσι καὶ ἀδελφαῖς ἀδεῶς καὶ μέντοι καὶ θυγατράσι μιγνύμενοι, καὶ ἔννομον τὴν παρανομίαν νομίζοντες : *Græc. Affec. Curat.* De legibus : edit. Gaisford, p. 351. In the ‏ܟܬܒܐ‎, f. 22. b., it is stated that Idashir ‏ܐܪܕܫܝܪ‎, the Magus received the following instruction : ‏ܐܥܠ ܠܟ ܕܢܝ ܐܣܐ ܥܣ ܕܪܟܣܬܐ ܕܪܡ ܠܟ ܣܪ‎ ‏ܕܐܙܠ ܕܥܣܝ ܕܬܟܣܣ ܐܠ ܪܟ ܥܣܝ ܐܢܬ ܟܠܘܣܐܐ ܟܟ ܐܥܪ ܘܣܟ‎ ‏.ܣܘܢ ܕܬܟܣܣ ܐܪܕܫܝܪ ܟܣܕ ܘܟܣ ܟܣܪ ܥܠܝ ܘܣܟ ܣܪܝܟ‎ "The Dæmon said to that priest, that a man cannot become a priest and a Magus until he shall have had connexion with his mother, and with his daughter, and with his sister; and he made Idashir priest in this manner."

P. 19, L. 1. *Called Magi.* Eusebius has Μαγουσαῖοι, and so the Recognitions ' Magusæi,' and Epiphanius, *Panarium adv. Hæres.* p. 1094.

P. 20, L. 1. Epiphanius makes a blunder, and attributes what is said here of the Geli to the Seres. See *Panar. adv. Hæres.* p. 1091.

L. 12. *Lascivious.* The Syriac is ܥܠܝܡܬܐ, which I have not found in any Lexicon. Both Eusebius and Cæsarius have σπατάλους. Ruffinus seems to have read the preceding word ἄνανδρους in rendering ' effeminatos.'

P. 21, L. 1. *Bactrians which are called Cashani.* Eusebius has Βάκτροις only; Cæsarius Σούσοις τῆς Βαβυλῶνος; and Ruffinus " in Susis." I have written *Cashani*, but am ignorant of the true way of enunciating ܩܫܝܢܐ. We may compare كشانية and كاسان. See Abulfeda تقويم البلدان, edit. Reinaud et De Slane, ٢٩٢. ٥٠٠. Strabo has, *Geog.* xv. p. 728, Λέγονται δὲ καὶ Κίσσιοι οἱ Σούσιοι. There are two countries, ἡ Κίσσια and οἱ Κόσσαι, bordering on Susiana, the latter on the side of Assyria, the former towards the Elymites. See Ptolemy, *Geogr.* vi. 3.

L. 7. *With their slaves.* These characteristics of the Bactrian women are attributed to the Liburni by Scylax, *Periplus*, edit. Vossius, Amstel. 1639, p. 7. The same things are also said of the women of the Geli. See above, p. 19.

L. 15. *The Racami, and of the Edesseans and the Arabians.* Eusebius has only ἐν δὲ τῇ Ἀραβίᾳ καὶ τῇ Ὀσροηνῇ. The whole is omitted by Cæsarius and the Recognitions. In the Peshito, Jud. vi. 3, we find ܟܢܒ ܪܩܡ for the Arabians. There is a town of Syria called Racim near Balca, all the houses of which are hewn out of the rock, as if they were one stone. الرقيم وهو بليدة صغيرة بقرب البلقاء وبيوتها كلها منحوتة من صخر كانها حجر واحد. See Abulfeda, *loc. cit.* p. ٢٢٧.

P. 22, L. 1. *Hatra.* ܚܛܪܐ. At p. 20 this is written ܚܣܛܪܐ. This was the town the seige of which Trajan was compelled to raise shortly before his death. See Tillemont, *Histoire des Empereurs*, vol. ii. p. 209.

L. 2. *Even of little value.* ܕܥܠܝ ܩܠܝܠ. Eusebius has ὀβολοῦ ἄξιον, as if he had read ܕܥܠܡܐ ܩܠܝܠ.

L. 10. *Laws of* * * * The rest has been purposely erased. Eusebius, however, gives Παρ' Ἕλλησι, which is also omitted by Cæsarius and the Recognitions.

L. 15. *Laws of the Orientals.* The context seems to shew that this is an error of the transcriber. Eusebius has Παρὰ δὲ Γάλλοις, and the Recognitions 'apud Gallos,' which agrees here with the sequel better than the Syriac.

P. 24, L. 7. Book of the Chaldæans. M. Renan has cited a few lines from this place; but he has erred in stating " Le dernier paragraphe est donné sous le titre spécial de ܠܡܝܕ؟ ܟܠܕ, *Livre de Chaldéens.*" It will be seen that this is not the last paragraph of the treatise of Bardesan. The heading is only given in distinctive red letters, like ܠܡܝܝ؟ ܬܥܟܠ, and the others above.

L. 11. *And dancers* ܐܪܘܨܐ. M. Renan has transcribed erroneously ܐܪܘܨܐ, and omitted to translate it.

L. 12. *Tayites* ܛܝܝ؟. The name of a race of Arabs, and often used for Arabs generally. Eusebius, probably not understanding the word, has Ταïοῖς. Cæsarius, who also does not appear to have understood it, has Ἡλείοις; and the author of the Recognitions, or Ruffinus the translator, has avoided the difficulty by omitting it altogether. M. Renan has printed ܛܝܝ؟ to agree with the Greek of Eusebius, but has translated 'le pays des Tay.'

L. 14. *Nomades.* The Syriac has ܢܘܣܪܘܡܣ, evidently an error of the scribe for ܢܘܣܪܘܡܣ, and Νομάσι of Eusebius.

L. 15. *Hispania.* Eusebius and Cæsarius both have ἐν τῇ Σκυθίᾳ, and the Recognitions 'Scythas.'

P. 25, L. 3. The Zazi, and in Brusa, which is beyond the Duro. Eusebius has Ὠτανῇ καὶ Σαυνίᾳ καὶ ἐν Χρυσῇ; the Recognitions 'in Chrysea insula' only; and Cæsarius omits the passage altogether. Epiphanius, who evidently had this treatise of Bardesan before him, has ἢ Γερμανῶν χώρᾳ, ἢ Σαρματίᾳ, ἢ ὁπόσοι ἐν τοῖς Δαύνισιν, ἢ παρὰ Ζιχοῖς, p. 1091. It is plain that the text of Bardesan was not clearly understood by the translators, and, as is often the case in obscure passages, it has suffered further corruption in the transcription. This may be the reason why it is omitted by Cæsarius. I find it not an unusual thing for translators to omit what they do not understand, and to take no notice of it whatever. We may trace the connexion of Hispania, or Spania, with Σαυνίᾳ and Δαύνισιν, and of Zazi with Ζιχοῖς. The difference between Brusa and Χρυσῇ must have arisen from the similarity between ב and כ in ברוסא and ברוכא. As it is difficult to pronounce with any degree of certainty what are the precise places meant by Bardesan; I have not thought it expedient to waste my own and the readers' time by offering uncertain conjectures.

P. 28, L. 10. Decani. The twelve signs of the zodiac were each divided into three parts, making thirty-six, which, being again each subdivided into ten portions, were called Decani. " Singula signa in tres partes dividuntur: singulæ autem partes singulos habent decanos ut sint in singulis signis terni decani." See Julius Firmicus, *Ad Mavort. Loll. Astron.* p. 17. Manilius, *Astronomicon*, B. 4. L. 298, gives the following account of them :

> " Quapropter Grajæ dixere Decania gentes ?
>
> A numero nomen positum est, quod partibus astra
>
> Condita tricenis triplici sub sorte feruntur,
>
> Et tribuunt denas in se coeuntibus astris,
>
> Inque vicem ternis habitantur singula signis."

P. 29, L. 17. *Of their establishing* ܏ܘܣ‍‍ܩ‍ܩ‍. Eusebius has τοὺς πρὸ αὐτῶν, as if he had read ܏ܘܣ‍‍ܩ‍ܩ‍; as it is found three lines below, 'abrogated all their *ancient* laws,' where, however, he has τοὺς τῶν βαρβαρων νομόυς ἤλλαξαν.

P. 31, L. 14. *Tharatha.* This is the same as the goddess Rhea. Justin Martyr mentions this practice καὶ φανερῶς εἰς κιναιδίαν ἀποκόπτονταί τινες καὶ εἰς μητέρα θεῶν τὰ μυστήρια ἀνάφερουσι, *Apol.* 1. c. 27, edit. Otto, p. 72. Itane propterea Galli abscissi huic Magnæ Deæ serviunt, ut signifiant, qui semine indigeant, terram sequi oportere? See Augustin, *De Civit. Dei*, b. 7, c. 24. See also Epiphanius, *Panar.* p. 1092. *Abgar* was a general title borne by the Kings or Toparchs of Edessa. See Assemani, *Bibl. Orient.* tom. i. p. 261. Bayer thinks the king especially alluded to here was Abgar, son of Maanes, who began to reign about A.D. 200. *Historia Osrhoena et Edessena ex numis illustrata*, p. 169; but this does not accord with the accounts given by other writers. It seems much more probable that this was Abgar, the son of Maanes, who began his reign A.D. 152. See Hahn. *Bardesan. Gnost.* p. 14.

P. 32, L. 9. *On the appointed days.* The Syriac is ܒ‍ܘܣ‍ܩܐ ܕܡ‍ܩ‍ܝ‍ܡ‍. I do not know what the precise meaning of ܕܡ‍ܩ‍ܝ‍ܡ‍ here is, and Eusebius gives no aid, for he has omitted this passage, and the Greek also otherwise varies considerably from the original to the end of the treatise. Compare what Bardesan says here relative to the change effected by Christianity, with Eusebius, *Præp. Evang.* lib. 4, and Theodoret, *Græc. Affec. Curat.* edit. Gaisford, p. 349.

P. 40, L. 16. *150 circuits of Mercury 60 years.* This will not agree with the calculation a few lines below, *12 thousand circuits of Mercury 6 thousand years.* There is therefore an error in the manuscript in the first instance reading 150 for 120, or in the latter 12 for 15.

ON MELITON.

P. 41. *Who was in the presence.* M. Renan translates "qui factus est coram," referring to " sermo " before. The writer in the "Journal of Sacred Literature," 1855, who signs his initials B. H. C., whom I shall henceforth designate by these letters, has " before Antoninus Cæsar," omitting altogether to translate ܠܘܗܝ. It does not, however, seem probable that the oration was made in the Emperor's presence, because the author speaks of *writing* it. " But touching Nebo, which is in Mabug, why should I *write* to you." See p. 44, L. 34 above. Meliton appears to have seen and conversed with the Emperor, and afterwards to have written this oration. An active verb relating to the *author*, ܐܡܪ ܠܗ, B.H.C. has made passive, and referred it to the *Oration*, " and it was addressed."

L. 1. *It is not an easy matter,* &c. There is a sentence so exactly like this in Justin Martyr, that it would almost seem as if the one were copied from the other. Ἀλλ' ἐπεὶ γνωρίζομεν οὐ ῥᾷον ἀγνοίᾳ κατεχομένην ψυχὴν συντόμως μεταβάλλειν. *Apol.* i. 12, p. 32, edit. Otto.

L. 2. *Has been pre-occupied by error.* B.H.C. having before made an active verb passive, here makes a passive verb active, and translates " apprehends him." As there are so many grammatical blunders committed by this translator, it would be a waste of time to mention them all. I shall therefore only notice some of the other errors that he has fallen into, which may mislead such as would depend upon his translation, as exhibiting the real meaning of the Syriac.

L. 9. *Like passion and sleep,* ܐܝܟ ܚܫܐ ܘܫܢܬܐ, M. Renan has translated " morbo vel dementiæ." ܫܢܬܐ, indeed, signifies *madness* as well as *sleep*; but the words immediately following shew that the latter is meant here.

L. 10. *Using the word as a stimulus, and smiting such as are asleep also awaketh them.* M. Renan has wrongly translated " Veritas vero utitur verbo sicut clavi (ad liberandum eos.) Ipsa vivificat eos qui dormiebant," mistaking the meaning of the word ܣܘܟܣܐ, and supposing ܡܚܐ to be from the root ܚܝܐ instead of ܡܚܐ.

L. 15. *And so then they suppose that this is righteousness.* B.H.C. wrongly " inasmuch as they think thus—that this is righteousness." M. Renan, surely by an oversight, has translated ' et existimant justitiam salvam esse.'

L. 18. *A good excuse that a man be in error with the many.* Justin Martyr writes, παραιτουμένους δόξαις π α λ α ι ω ν ἐξακολουθεῖν, which, however, is cited by Johannes Damascenus with the reading of πολλῶν as here instead of παλαιῶν : *Apol.* i. 2, p. 4, edit. Otto.

ʟ. 27.   *While all things are changed.* This is omitted by B.H.C.

P. 42, ʟ. 4.   *It is found from his own words,* ܥܒ ܟܐ ܘܐܓܒܪ̈ ܟܚܐ̈ܠ ܣ݁ܟܒ ܝ݁ , or literally, *from what he saith the thing is found.* B.H.C. translates, absurdly enough, " when he has so said the thing is possible," evidently not knowing the difference between ܟܚܐ̈ܠ ܣ and ܟܚ̈ܣ. M. Renan, also, does not seem to have understood the passage in rendering it " de quacumque re id dicat."

ʟ. 11.   *Are not these things that we use as we please,* ܠܐ ܗܘܐ ܗܠܝܢ ܐܢܘܢ ܕܐܦ : literally, *Is it not these are they which we use according to our pleasure.* B.H.C. has translated, without any apparent meaning, " they are not such which we use as we will ;" and M. Renan, with too much liberty, ' non sunt Dii, quando quidem utimur illis secundum voluntatem nostram.'

ʟ. 17.   *That so long as a man not having heard, neither discerneth nor understands,* ܟܒܣܐ̈ ܐܝܢܐ ܕܠܐ ܫ݁ܡܥ ܘܠܐ ܡ݁ܦܪܫ ܘܠܐ ܡ݁ܣܬܟܠ . It is difficult to see how B.H.C. could have so misunderstood this plain sentence, and have translated it, " however many the men who do not hear, nor discern, nor understand."

ʟ. 25.   *That a voice has been heard in all the earth.* Rom. x. 18.

ʟ. 31.   *Light without envy is given to all of us, that we may see thereby; and if, when light has arisen upon us, any one closeth his eyes that he may not see, his course is to the ditch.* B.H.C. gives the following extraordinary translation : " Behold, light has arisen unto us ! Man shuts his eyes that he may not see the pit to which he is journeying." M. Renan has wrongly translated ܘܠܐ ܢܚܙܐ " quæ not fascinat." *To the ditch,* alluding to our Lord's words, Matt. xv. 14, who himself probably had reference to some proverb current amongst the Jews. In the *Testaments of the Twelve Patriarchs, Test. Reuben,* c. 2, we have the following similar passage : ὅτι ἀγνοίας πεπλήρωται, καὶ αὐτὴ τὸν νεώτερον ὁδηγεῖ ὡς τυφλὸν ἐπὶ βόθρον. See Grabe *Spicilegium,* vol. i. p. 147.

P. 43, ʟ. 10.   *That also the Sybil has said respecting them.* B.H.C. has rendered this in a marvellous manner—" Now I say that rejection is denounced against those." Not knowing that ܣܒܠ meant Sybil, he has invented a word, and translated it " rejection," apparently deriving it from the root ܣܒܠ ; from which, however, it could not have been derived. But had that been the case, in its present form as an abstract noun, it would be in the masculine gender: this translator, however, has had no difficulty in making it agree with a verb in the feminine, nor, again, in turning an active verb into a passive to suit his convenience. M. Renan, also, apparently ignorant of the meaning of ܡܟܒ, has omitted it altogether in his translation, and rendered the passage "quod jam dixi." See note above p. 77. Every one conversant with the early Christian writers Justin Martyr, Theophilus, Tertullian, Origen, Clemens Alexandrinus, Lactantius, &c., is aware that they often refer to the prophecies of the Sibyls. The passage to which Meliton seems especially to allude here is the following: See *Sibyllina Oracula*, edit. Gale, p. 467:

’Ημεῖς δ’ ἀθανάτοιο τρίβου πεπλανημένοι ἦμεν
’Εργά τε χειροποίητα σεβάσμεθα ἄφρονι θυμῷ
Εἰδώλων ξοάνων τε καταφθιμένων ἀνθρώπων.

This is also quoted, with two slight variations in the first verse, in the *Cohortatio ad Gentiles*, attributed to Justin Martyr. See edit. Oehler, p. 62.

Again, ’Αθάνατον γενετῆρα θεῶν, πάντων τ’ ἀνθρώπων
Οὐκ ἔθελες τιμᾶν, θνητῶν εἴδωλα δ’ ἐτίμας.

See Gale, *ibid.* p. 385. Read G. J. Vossius, *De Theolog. Gentil.*, lib. 1, c. 11—13.

l. 13. *More than the former gods.* Tertullian writes to the same effect." Immo jam per deos dejerandi periculum evanuit, potiore habita religione per Cæsarem dejerandi, quod et ipsum ad offuscationem pertinet deorum vestrorum; facilius enim per Cæsarem pejerantes punirentur quam per ullum Jovem: *Ad Nationes*, lib. i, c. 10, p. 328, edit. Oehler. And again in his *Apology*, c. 28, p. 228: Ventum est igitur ad secundum titulum læsæ augustioris majestatis, siquidem majore formidine et callidiore timiditate Cæsarem observatis quam ipsum de Olympo Jovem. Et merito, si sciatis: Quis enim ex viventibus quilibet non mortuo potior?—Citius denique apud vos per omnes deos quam per unum genium Cæsaris pejeratur. Justin Martyr writes: Καὶ τί γὰρ τοὺς ἀποθνήσκοντας παρ’ ὑμῖν αὐτοκράτορας, οὓς ἀεὶ ἀπαθανατίζεσθαι ἀξιοῦντες καὶ ὀμνύντα τινὰ προάγατε ἑωρακέναι ἐκ τῆς πυρᾶς ἀνερχόμενον εἰς τὸν οὐρανὸν τὸν κατακαέντα Καίσαρα: *Apol.* 1, c. 21, p. 56. Tertullian also expresses the same opinion as Melito respecting the origin of the heathen gods: Recogitemus omnem idolatrian in homines esse culturam, cum ipsos deos nationum homines retro fuisse etiam apud suos constet: *De Idolatria*, c. 15, p. 93. Respecting the divine honours paid to Julius Cæsar, see Suetonus, *Jul. Cæs.* c. 76: Valerius Maximus, lib. i. c. 6. § 13. Touching divine honours paid by the Emperor Hadrian to the wretch Antoninus, see Justin Martyr, *Apol.* i. c. 29, p. 76; Eusebius, *Præpar. Evan.* b. ii. c. 6; *Hist. Eccl.* iv. 8; and Valesius' notes ad locum; and Tillemont, *Hist. des Empereurs,* vol. ii. p. 267.

L. 16. *And diminish the revenue of Cæsar,* B.H.C. renders " and fail to accomplish the decrees of Cæsar." M. Renan translates no better, " et decretis Cæsaris non obtemperant." The error of both has arisen from confounding ܩܘܡܣ, the Latin " fiscum," with the Syriac ܦܘܡܣܩ. Compare what Meliton says here with Tertullian, *Apol.* c. 13, and *Ad Nationes,* lib. i. c. 10.

L. 20. *Of such as worship,* ܃ ܘܢܪܓܣܐ ܕܐܝܠܝܢ, B.H.C. translates " that they go in and worship." He has evidently mistaken ܕܐܝܠܝܢ, and read as if it were ܐܝܠܝܢ; but even then his version would be erroneous. M. Renan has not been much more felicitous in his rendering of this passage.

L. 23. *Instigate the deficient in understanding to worship that which hath no perception.* M. Renan, very erroneously, " impediunt et dehortantur imbecilles corde ne adorent ea quæ sensibus non capiuntur.' Compare ܡܣܬܟܠ ܠܐ, " which hath no perception," with the expression, λίθων οὐδεμίαν αἴσθησιν ἐχόντων, in the passage from Meliton's *Apology,* cited by the author of the *Chronicon Paschale,* edit. Dindorf, p. 483: Routh. *Reliq. Sacra.* vol. i. p. 118.

L. 30. *The wives of many.* See respecting the wives of Hercules, Diodorus Siculus, *Biblioth.* b. 4; and Eusebius, *Præpar. Evang.* lib. ii. c. 2.

L. 31. *Zuradi.* That is, Zaradas the Persian, said to be the author of the abominable law of the Persians: see note above, p. 81. Photius speaking of the work of Theodorus on Persian Magic, writes, καὶ ἐν μὲν τῷ πρώτῳ λόγῳ προτίθεται τὸ μιαρὸν Περσῶν δόγμα, ὃ Ζαράδης εἰσηγήσατο: *Biblioth.* Cod. 81, edit. Bekker, p. 63. B.H.C. has given the name ' Urdi,' adding the following note: " Manuscript ܐܘܪܕܝ. Who is meant is not apparent, but probably he was known to the Greeks and Romans by another name." Now the manuscript certainly reads ܐܘܪܕܝ, and the blunder has arisen from his confounding ܐ and ܠ of his own transcript. In the manuscript written in the old character these very dissimilar letters could not be confounded.

L. 34. *Acte.* B.H.C. has again erred here, and written " Ecate," adding the following note: " Manuscript ܐܩܛܐ, perhaps Thebes, which was called *Hecatompolis,* from its hundred gates." *Acte* is the same as *Attica:* " Sunt ergo Athenæ, ut ego accepi, prope litus maris sitæ, unde et regio adjacens ab ἀκτή, quod litus interpretatur, *Acte* vel *Attica,* ipsique Athenienses *Attici* nuncupantur." See *Scriptores Rerum Mythicarum:* Mythog. iii. 4, p. 172:

edit. G. H. Bode. See also Stephanus Byzant. *De Urbibus*, ad verbum 'Ακτὴ: edit. Th. de Pinedo, p. 55: Strabo, *Geograph.* lib. ix. : edit. Casaubon, p. 391. Augustin speaks to the same fact as Meliton : " His temporibus Dionysium, qui etiam Liber Pater dictus est et post mortem deus habitus est, vitem ferunt ostendisse in Attica terra hospite suo :" see *Civitat. Dei*, lib. xviii. c. 12. Compare Tertullian, "Ceterum si propterea Liber deus, quod vitem demonstravit, male cum Lucullo actum est, qui primus cerasia ex Ponto Italiæ promulgavit, quod non est propterea consecratus ut frugis novæ auctor, qui ostensor :" *Apol.* c. 11, p. 158.

L. 35. *Joseph, a Hebrew, who is called Serapis.* Meliton is not singular in this view. Tertullian, "Nam Serapis iste quidem olim Joseph dictus fuit, de genere sanctorum :" *Ad Nationes* ii. c. 8, p. 366. Julius Firmicus Maternus, *De Errore profan. relig.* c. 9 : " Joseph, qui ob pudicitiam in carcerem missus, ereptus post interpretationem somnii, fuit particeps regni. Nam septem annorum collectis et servatis frugibus, alterius septennii egestatem divinæ manus providentia mitigavit. Huic post mortem Ægyptii patrio gentis instituto templa fecerunt ——. Nomen etiam, ut sanctus coleretur, ex primo auctore generis accepit. Nam quia Saræ pronepos fuerat, ex qua nonagenaria Abraham indulgentia Dei susceperat filium, Serapis dictus est græco sermone, hoc est Σαρᾶς ἄπο." Ruffinus states, b. xi. c. 22, " Quidam in honorem nostri Josephi formatum perhibent simulachrum, ob dimensionem frumenti, qua famis tempore subvenit Ægyptiis. Alii repertum in historiis Græcorum veteribus ferunt, Apin quendam patremfamilias seu regem in Ægypto Memphis positum, cum famis tempore frumenta apud Alexandriam defecissent ex proprio affatim civibus alimenta præbuisse. Quo defuncto, in honorem ejus instituerunt apud Memphis templum, in quo bos quasi indicium optimi agricolæ nutritur, habens quædam coloris insignia, qui ex nomine ejus Apis appelletur: σορὸν vero, id est, sepulchrum, in quo corpus ejus inerat, Alexandriam deduxerint, et soron Apis primo ex compositione Sorapin, post vero per corruptionem Serapin nominarint." See *Auctores Hist. Eccl.* edit. Basil. 1528, p. 256. Suidas has evidently followed Ruffinus : Σάραπις: τούτου ἐν 'Αλεξανδρείᾳ καθεῖλε Θεόφιλος ὁ 'Αρχιεπίσκοπος τὸ ξόανον, ἐπὶ Θεοδοσίου τοῦ Μεγάλου : τοῦτον δὲ οἱ μὲν Δία ἔφασαν εἶναι· οἱ δὲ τὸν Νεῖλον, διὰ τὸ μόδιον ἔχειν ἐν τῇ κεφαλῇ, καὶ τὸν πῆχον, ἤγουν τὸ τοῦ ὕδατος μέτρον· ἄλλοι δὲ τὸν Ἰωσῆφ ἀπὸ τῆς σοροῦ καὶ τοῦ Ἄπιδος σύνθετον ὄνομα πεποιηκότες ἐκάλουν αὐτὸν Σόραπιν, οἱ δὲ μετὰ ταῦτα Σάραπιν : see ad Σάραπις.

P. 44, L. 5. *Erecthippus,* ܡܣܠܘܐܝ. Evidently an error for *Erethonius* or *Erectheus.* Augustin writes, " Erechthoni regis Atheniensium, cujus novissimis annis Jesus nave mortuus reperitur, Vulcanus et Minerva parentes fuisse dicuntur :" see *Civitat. Dei*, b. 18. c. 12.

L. 12. *Balthi* is the Syriac name of Venus, *Tamuz* of Adonis ; and *Cuthar* is the Κινύρας of the Greeks : see Nork, *Die Gotter Syriens*, p. 79 : Selden, *De Diis Syris* Synt. ii. c. 2, 3 : Vossius, *De Theol. Gent.* b. i. c. 22, 23.

L. 20. *While he was hunting wild boars*, ܒ݁ܟ݂ܶܕ݂ ܡܶܢ ܨܰܝܕܳܐ ܕ݂ܚܰܙܺܝܪ̈ܐ. There is no such word as ܨܰܝܕܐ. It is evidently an error of the copyist for ܢܳܨܶܕ or ܢܳܨܕܝܢ, "hunting :" written in Persian شکار. B.H.C. has translated it, without noticing the difficulty, "where he was wounded by a boar;" and M. Renan altogether wanders from the meaning. " Cyniram (?) vero vertit in Aprum."

L. 21. Respecting the temple of Venus in Apheca : ἐν ἀκρωρείας μέρει τοῦ Λιβάνου ἐν Ἀφάκοις : see Eusebius, *De Vita Constant.* b. iii. c. 55 ; and *De Laud. Constant.* c. viii. edit. Zimmermann, pp. 959, 1159; Zosimus, cited by Selden, *De Diis Syr.* p. 278, writes, Ἄφακα χωρίον ἐστι μέσον Ἡλιουπόλεώς τε καὶ Βύβλου, καθ᾽ ὃ ναὸς Ἀφροδίτης Ἀφακίτιδος ἵδρυται. Lucian says that it was founded by Cinyras: see *De Syria Dea*, c. 9.

L. 23. *Nuh.* The manuscript reads plainly ܢܘܚ. B.H.C. has read otherwise, and translated ' Hai :' M. Renan ' Noe.' It is apparently a blunder of the copyist, probably for ܢܝ, ' Nai ;' or 'Anai,' ܐܢܝ, the goddess Anais, or Anaitis. M. Renan has also suggested this name.

L. 26. *Athi a Hadibite.* I do not know what ܚܕܝܒܝܐ refers to. Nor am I able to offer any satisfactory explanation respecting this account of Meliton. The story seems to have originated in that of the little maid who was brought away captive out of the land of Israel, and waited upon Naaman's wife, and of the cure of Naaman's leprosy by Elisha. 2 Kings c. 5. Perhaps *Athi* may have some connection with the name Ἄττης or Ἄττις, who is said to have instituted the orgies for Rhea. See Lucian, *De Syria Dea*, c. 13. Vossius: *ibid.* c. 20. The account by Damascius of his visiting Hierapolis and sleeping there—as Photius has related it, and of the pestilential and deadly vapours which were emitted from a cavern under the temple of Apollo—taken in reference to what Meliton says respecting the unclean spirit in the sacred wood of Mabug, called also Hierapolis, and the way in which this was remedied by the daughter of Hadad, would seem to shew some connection between the stories and the names; but there is so much uncertainty in all this, that it would be needless to waste my own and the reader's time in offering conjectures. The passage alluded to in Photius is this : Λέγει δὲ ὁ συγγραφεὺς ὅτι τότε τῇ Ἱεραπόλει ἐγκαθευδήσας ἐδόκουν ὄναρ ὁ Ἄττης γενέσθαι, καί μοι ἐπιτελεῖσθαι παρὰ τῆς μητρὸς τῶν Θεῶν τὴν τῶν ἱλαρίων καλουμένων ἑορτὴν. See *Bibliotheca*, cod. 242, edit. Bekker, p. 345.

ι. 32. *Bacru, the patrician of Edessa.* B.H.C. has translated "prince," and M. Renan "regem." The word ܡܪܐ is used in the Syriac version of the Theophania of Eusebius ܡܠܘ̈ܝܢܘ ܡܠܐ̈ܐ ܡܕ̈ܝܪܐ ܡܪܐ ܗܘܐ ܒܠ, where Dr. Lee translates ' rulers,' adding in a note, " ܡܪܐ, by mistake perhaps for ܐܒ̈ܐ, rulers being styled fathers." The recurrence of the word, how-ever, here shews that it is not a mistake: see Book iii. c. 1. There were two kings of Edessa named Bacru, of whom an account has reached us: see *Chronicon Edessenum* in Assemani *Bibl. Or.* tom. i. p. 418, and Bayer, *Historia Orshoena*, p. 67.

ι. 31. *Cuthbi.* The manuscript reads most plainly ܟܘܬܒܝ. B.H.C. has given " Cutheb," and says that the manuscript reads ܟܘܬܒ.

ι. 34. *Mabug,* more generally known as Hierapolis. Pliny: "Bambyce quæ alio nomine Hierapolis vocatur Syris vero Magog. Ibi prodigiosa Atargatis, Græcis autem Derceto dicta coletur :" b. v, c. 33.

ι. 36. *A Thracian Magus.* B.H.C., I know not why, "the Magian, an enchanter." In the next line he has turned the proper name, ܗܕܪܢ, " Hadran," into a verb, and then translated it " *they* honour.' Had it been a verb, it could only have been rendered " *we* honored." Eusebius also intimates some connexion between Zoroaster, or Zaradusht, and Orpheus the Thracian, in the following passage of his *Præpar. Evang.* v. c. 4: εἴτε μάγων τῶν περὶ Ζωροάστρην ὁ λόγος οἶτός ἐστιν, εἴτε Θράκιος ἀπὸ Ὀρφέως. The author of the Clementine Homilies, ix. 4, says that Zoroaster was indentical with Nimrod! See also Recognitions iv. 27.

P. 45, ι. 4. *The passage* B.H.C. translates " *the secret parts* ;" apparently confounding ܠܘܒܠ with the Hebrew עֶרְוָה. The unclean spirit probably meant, the exhalation of pestilential vapours, see note above.

ι. 6. *That she should draw water from the sea, and cast it into the well.* B.H.C., wrongly, " that water should be drawn ;" and M. Renan, not less erroneously, " ut aqua e mari allata inpleret hanc planitiem." Both have referred to the passage of Lucian *De Syria Dea*, c. 13, which I transcribe here : Τὰ δὲ ἀπὸ τούτου, λέγεται λόγος ὑπὸ τῶν ἐν τῇ ἱρῇ πόλει, μεγάλως ἄξιος θωυμάσαι, ὅτι ἐν τῇ σφετέρῃ χώρῃ, χάσμα μέγα ἐγένετο, καὶ τὸ σύμπαν ὕδωρ κατεδέξατο. Δευκαλίων δὲ, ἐπεὶ τάδε ἐγένετο, βωμούς τε ἔθετο, καὶ νηὸν ἐπὶ τῷ χάσματι Ἥρης ἅγιον ἐστήσατο. ἐγὼ δὲ τὸ χάσμα εἶδον, καὶ ἔστι ὑπὸ τῷ νηῷ κάρτα μικρόν· εἰ μὲν ὦν, πάλαι καὶ μέγα ἐὸν, νῦν τοιόσδε ἐγένετο, οὐκ οἶδα. τὸ δὲ ἐγὼ εἶδον, μικρόν ἐστι. σῆμα δὲ τῆς ἱστορίης τόδε πρήσσουσι. δὶς ἑκάστου ἔτεος ἐκ θαλάσσης ὕδωρ εἰς τὸν νηὸν ἀπικνέεται· φερουσι δὲ οὐκ ἱρέες μοῦνον, ἀλλὰ πᾶσα Συρίη, καὶ Ἀραβίη, καὶ πέρηθεν τοῦ Εὐφρήτεω, πολλοὶ ἄνθρωποι εἰς θάλασσαν ἔρχονται, καὶ πάντες ὕδωρ φέρουσι· τὸ πρῶτα μεν ἐν τῷ νηῷ ἐκχέουσι, μετὰ δὲ εἰς τὸ χάσμα κατέρχεται, καὶ δέκεται τὸ χάσμα, μικρὸν ἐὸν, ὕδατος χρῆμα πολλόν· τὰ δε ποιέοντες, Δευκαλίωνα ἐν τῷ ἱρῷ τόνδε νόμον θέσθαι λέγουσι, συμφορῆς τε καὶ εὐεργεσίας μνῆμα ἔμμεναι.

L. 8. *According to that which was a mystery in their Magism.* B.H.C., erroneously, " as if there was some mystery in their enchantments."

L. 12. *But thou, a free intelligence, and cognizant of the truth, enter into thyself, and if they clothe thee in the fashion of a woman.* B.H.C. translates absurdly, " Now, the understanding is free, and a knower of truth : whether it is in these things consider with thyself. And if they dress up for thee the figure of a woman." M. Renan, less faulty, but not correctly, " Tu vero, mens libera et cognitor veri si reputaris, stude ut talis sis in anima tua, etsi ornatu muliebri indueris."

L. 23. *Impalpable.* ⳬⳬⳬ by transposition for ⳬⳬⳬ from the root ⳬⳬⳬ, and not from ⳬⳬⳬ as M. Renan has taken it in translating " nec commovetur." He also has mistaken in the next line ⳬⳬⳬ for ⳬⳬⳬ, and rendered " nec capitur." It is difficult to conceive how B.H.C. ever arrived at such a meaning as " is endowed with consciousness " for the former word. He has also strangely rendered the next sentences.

L. 32. *He needeth nothing,* ⳬⳬⳬ. B.H.C. has translated this passage, " and know that he asketh nothing which is needless." And M. Renan, scarcely better, " Et scias eum nihil quærere a te de iis quæ non sunt necessaria (cognitu)."

L. 36. *But what is truth?* B.H.C. has omitted this altogether, and consequently made nonsense.

P. 46. L. 3. *Touching this matter,* ⳬⳬⳬ. M. Renan rightly, " de hac re ;" but B.H.C., not knowing the difference between ⳬⳬⳬ as a masculine and as a feminine noun, has translated absurdly, " against this generation," and consequently continues his error in the following passage.

L. 9. *And what disgrace can be greater than this?* B.H.C., apparently ignorant of the force of ⳬⳬⳬ, " and the reproach from this is great.' The following sentence is equally wrong; but it would be tedious to notice all this translator's numerous errors.

L. 28. *But perchance thou mayest say, Why did not God create me so that I should then have served him and not idols?* Compare Bardesan, p. 1, l. 10, and p. 3, l. 19 above. B.H.C. has translated this most absurdly, " But perhaps thou wilt say, How is my work not the God whom thou worshippest, and not an image ?"

P. 48, L. 3. *And of it be careful,* B.H.C. translates, "and his solicitude."

L. 19. *Is that God which is bought and sold?* Compare Tertullian : " Status Dei cujusque in senatus æstimatione pendebat. Deus non erat quem homo consultus noluisset et nolendo damnasset. Domesticos Deos, quos Lares dicitis, domestica potestate tractatis, pignerando, venditando, demutando aliquando in cacabulum de Saturno, aliquando in trullam de Minerva, ut quisque contritus atque contusus, dum diu colitur, ut quisque dominus sanctiorem expertus est domesticam necessitatem. Publicos æque publico jure fœdatis, quos hastario vectigales habetis. —— Dei vero qui magis tributarii, magis sancti, immo qui magis sancti, magis tributarii. Majestas quæstuaria efficitur. Circuit cauponas religio mendicans. Exigitis mercedem pro solo templi, pro aditu sacri. Non licet Deos gratis nosse: venales sunt: *Apol.* c. xiii. p. 164: see also *Ad Nationes* i. c. x. p. 326, where the same things are repeated almost in the same words.

L. 26. *I am not able to conduct myself well,* &c. B.H.C. has sadly distorted this, and translated, " Am I not able, to govern well, because I am a king? And is it not mine to influence the will of many? He who thus speaks is truly fitted for sport. For wherefore is he a king?"

L. 35. *Those who go wrong,* ܣܛܝܢ. B.H.C., ignorant of the difference between this and ܣܟܠܝܢ, has translated " those who walk wisely." In the next sentence he has committed as great an error, and translated, " and shall reverence Him, so as to observe among men those who are obedient to Him." The true meaning is as I have given it: *and through fear of Him shall be withheld from injuring those who are his subjects.*

P.49. L. 13. *For what advantage is greater than this.* B.H.C., ignorant, as I have before observed, of the force of ܐܝܬ ܗܘ, has given the following erroneous version: " For there is this good thing which hence especially arises."

L. 27. *An abomination of God,* ܓܢܝܬܐ ܕܐܠܗܐ. An idol in scripture is frequently called an abomination. B.H.C. has rendered ' fitted to the *form* of a god;' giving ܓܢܝ the signification of ܕܡܘܬܐ. The passage may also bear the meaning of M. Renan, ' in opprobrium Dei.'

L. 36. *And art thou not ashamed perchance it should be deficient to demand of him who made it?* &c. B.H.C., absurdly, " And art thou not ashamed that blood should be required of the maker of it." He has mistaken the particle ܕܠܡܐ " perchance," for ܕܡܐ " blood;" and then, to make the words ܕܠܡܐ ܢܒܥܐ

ܐܠܐ ܕܬܬܒܥ ܠܥܒܘܕܗ agree with this, has given the above translation, violating all grammar and common sense.

P. 50, L. 4. *Why rollest thou thyself upon the earth, and offerest supplication to things which are without perception? Fear Him who shaketh the earth.* This is rendered, if possible, still more absurdly than the preceding passage by B.H.C.: "wherein thou wallowest on the earth, and yet art favoured. For things which are destitute of consciousness are afraid of him who maketh the earth tremble."

L. 35. *A flood of wind.* B. H. C. gives as a note, but without any authority, "The destruction of Sodom and Gomorrah is here alluded to." He is, however, altogether mistaken. *The flood of wind* relates rather to the destruction of the tower of Babel: see Josephus *Antiq.* b. i. c. 4. Περὶ δὲ τοῦ πύργου τούτου, καὶ τῆς ἀλλοφωνίας τῶν ἀνθρώπων, μέμνηται καὶ Σίβυλλα, λέγουσα οὕτως: "πάντων ὁμοφώνων ὄντων τῶν ἀνθρώπων, πύργον ᾠκοδόμησαν τινες ὑψηλοτάτον, ὡς ἐπὶ τὸν οὐρανὸν ἀναβησόμενοι δι' αὐτοῦ. οἱ δὲ θεοὶ, ἀνέμους ἐπιπέμψαντες, ἀνέτρεψαν τὸν πύργον, καὶ ἰδίαν ἑκάστῳ φωνὴν ἔδωκαν.

The passage in the Sibyl, to which Josephus alludes, seems to be this:

Καὶ βούλοντ' ἀναβῆν' εἰς οὐρανὸν ἀστερόεντα
Αὐτίκα ἀθάνατος * * *
Πνεύμασιν. αὐτὰρ ἔπειτ' ἄνεμοι μέγαν ὑψόθι πύργον
Ῥίψαν, καὶ θνητοῖσιν ἐπ' ἀλλήλοις ἔριν ὦρσαν.

See Gale *Sibyll. Orac.* p. 336. Abydenus, cited by Eusebius, *Præp. Evang.* lib. ix. c. 14: Ἐντὶ δ' οἳ λέγουσι τοὺς πρώτους ἐκ γῆς ἀνασχόντας, ῥωμῇ τε καὶ μεγέθει χαυνωθέντας καὶ δὴ θεῶν καταφρονήσαντας ἀμέινονας εἶναι, πύργων τύρσιν ἠλίβατον ἀείρειν, ἵνα νῦν Βαβυλών ἐστιν, ἤδη τε ἆσσον εἶναι τοῦ οὐρανοῦ καὶ τοὺς ἀνέμους θεοῖσι βωθέοντας ἀνατρέψαι περὶ αὐτοῖσι τὸ μηχάνημα· τοῦ δῆτα ἐρείπια λέγεσθαι Βαβυλῶνα. The author of the *Cave of Treasures*, ܡܥܪܬ ܓܙܐ, to which I have already referred, p. 79, gives a nother account of the *Flood of Wind:* to which tradition, indeed, Meliton may refer:—ܘܒܫܢܬ ܡܐܐ ܕܢܚܘܪ ܟܕ ܚܙܐ ܐܠܗܐ ܠܒܢܝ̈ܢܫܐ ܕܡܕܒܚܝܢ ܒܢܝܗܘܢ ܠܫ̈ܐܕܐ ܘܣܓܕܝܢ ܠܦܬܟ̈ܪܐ. ܦܬܚ ܐܠܗܐ ܐܘܨ̈ܪܐ ܕܪܘܚܐ ܘܬܪ̈ܥܐ ܒܟܠܗ ܘܢܫܒܬ ܥܠܥܠܐ ܕܪܘܚܐ ܒܟܠܗ ܐܪܥܐ. ܘܡܚܬ ܠܨܠ̈ܡܐ ܘܡܕܒܚܬ (read ܒܘܣܡܬܐ as below) ܕܟܠܗ̈ܬܐ ܕܫ̈ܐܕܐ. ܘܢܫܒܬ ܐܝܟ ܠܦܬܟ̈ܪܐ ܘܠܓ̈ܠܘܦܐ ܘܠܡܕܒ̈ܚܐ. ܘܥܒܪܬ ܠܟܠܗ ܡܢܗܘܢ ܠܬܠܐ ܪܘܪܒܐ ܕܡܢ ܠܡܘܬܒܐ. ܘܠܗܕܐ ܒܘܣܡܬܐ ܕܪܘܚܐ ܡܬܩܪܝܢ ܠܗ ܡܫܟܢܐ ܠܒܘܣܢܐ ܕܪܘܚܐ., "And in the hundredth year of Nahor, when God saw that men sacrificed their children to devils, and worshipped idols, God opened the storehouse of his wind, and the tempest's door, and a storm of wind went forth through all the earth, and overthrew the images and the temples of the devils, and collected together the idols and the images, and the statues, and made great heaps over them until this day. And this storm of wind the doctors call the *Flood of wind*:" see fol. 22. The same account is also given in the Ethiopic *Book of Adam*, translated by Dr. A. Dillman in Ewald's *Jahrbücher*, 1853, p. 118: "Und im 100stem jahre des Nahor sah Gott auf die menschenkinder, welche ihre kinder den gözen opferten; und er liess die vorraths-kammer der winde öffnen und liess stürme winde und nebel über die ganze oberfläche der erde kommen, bis dass alle die gözen und bilder und figuren zusammengebracht (-geweht) waren, und sehr hohe berge daraus wurden, und die gözen blieben in ihnen begraben bis auf diesen tag. Viele weisen (gelehrte) haben über jenen wind geschrieben: einige von ihnem sagen, dass es eine windfluth gewesen sei."

P. 51. L. 5. *The earth shall be burnt up*, &c. Meliton evidently alludes here to 2 Pet. iii. 10. 12. This may probably be one reason why my friend, the Chevalier Bunsen, to whom I lent the translation of this *Apology*, and who at first did not doubt its authenticity, might have been led afterwards to think that it "bears the stamp of a late and confused composition;" and "for that reason to abstain from giving it a place among the genuine texts:" *Hippolytus and his Age*, vol. i. p. xi. 1854. Mr. Bunsen does not admit the authenticity of the Second Epistle of St. Peter. It is, however, certainly alluded to here by one of the earliest and most learned writers of the Christian Church in the second century, and consequently appears to have been admitted by him as genuine.

L. 12. *Shall lament*, ܢܬܬܙܝܥܘܢ. B.H.C. "shall be made alive." M. Renan, more consistenly with the sense, but altogether erroneously, "evanescent."

L. 20. This last sentence is obscure, and I am not sure that I have given the exact meaning. I believe, however, M. Renan's version, as well as that of B.H.C. to be incorrect.

The four following extracts are taken from one of the Syriac manuscripts brought from Nitria, now in the British Museum, No. 12,156, f. 70. 76, 77, written A.D. 562. As I have already given a description of this manuscript in my *Corpus Ignatianum*, p. 352, it is needless for me to repeat it here.

P. 52. *Of Sardis.* The Syriac has *of Sardeon*, which is the genitive of the Greek retained in the translation.

On the Soul and Body. This treatise is named by Eusebius, see below, p. 98; and by Jerome, " De Anima et Corpore :" and by Ruffinus, " De Anima et Corpore et Mente."

On the Cross. B.H.C. has translated incorrectly " on the crucifixion." This is not one of those works of Meliton mentioned by Eusebius, who, however, speaks as if he had not seen all his writings.

L. 30. *While he was esteemed a servant, he denied not the Sonship.* B.H.C. renders truly absurdly, as well as erroneously, " He was declared a man by the adoption, but he did not deny."

P. 58. *Melito the Bishop*, without any other designation. *On the Faith.* Jerome has " De fide librum unum ;" but in the printed editions of Eusebius we have only ὁ περὶ ὑπακοῆς πίστεως. Respecting this, see note below, p. 98.

L. 15. *That we may prove to your love that he is perfect reason, the Word of God.* B.H.C. " that we may shew to your *condemnation* that the word of God is perfect wisdom." The very tyro in Syriac surely knows that ܚܘܒܐ means " love," from the root ܚܒ. This translator, however, has apparently looked for it under ܚܘܒ, and then rendered it as if it had been ܟܘܚܒܐ.

L. 19. *Who in the law was the law, among the priests Chief priest, among kings Governor.* For this B.H.C. gives " who is a law among the priests, in counsel a leader."

L. 21. *In the Voice the Word.* This confirms the reading of the Syriac in the Epistle of Ignatius to the Romans, c. ii. ܬܘܒ ܗܘܐ ܐܢܐ ܠܝ ܩܠܐ, and of the old Latin, " rursus factus sum vox," against the Greek πάλιν ἔσομαι τρέχων: see my note on this passage, *Corpus Ignatianum*, p. 291.

P. 54. L. 12. *Of Meliton, Bishop of the city of Attica.* This and the following extract were not printed at the same time as the others, because I did not believe them to be by the Bishop of Sardis, which inscription the two first bore. It is plain, however, that this is from the same work as that cited by Anastasius from the tract called Λόγος εἰς τὸ πάθος, because it contains the passage quoted : Ὁ Θεὸς πέπονθεν ὑπὸ δεξίας Ἰσραηλίτιδος : see Routh, *Reliq. Sacr.* vol. i. p. 122. I have therefore printed it subsequently at p. 49. No one who compares this with the preceding can fail, I think, to draw the conclusion that they are by the same hand, although perhaps by a different one from that of the *Apologies.* Neither is there any work attributed by Eusebius to Meliton which has the title Εἰς τὸ πάθος ———. It seems probable that there has arisen some confusion in the transcribers between the names Meliton and Meletius. B.H.C. assumes at once that this is the case. That Meletius of Sebaste in Armenia, and afterwards of Antioch, is the person meant, and consequently he has not hesitated to declare that the name of the city is mis-spelt, and Antioch clearly intended; and therefore has made no difficulty in giving *Antioch* instead of *Attica*. That a Syrian writer should have made any blunder in spelling the name of their great city *Antioch* is as improbable as that an educated Englishman should mis-spell London. There is a considerable difference between the words ܐ‍‍ and ܐ‍. Besides this Meletius was translated to Antioch contrary to the canons of the Church, and was therefore soon expelled, and driven into exile. He would therefore hardly have been generally styled Bishop of *Antioch*, although indeed he afterwards returned, and was again expelled, and again returned. " Apud Antiochiam sane diversis temporibus multa et admodum confuse gesta sunt. Mam defuncto Eudoxio, cum multi diversarum urbium episcopi ad illam sedem summa ambitione niterentur, ad ultimum Meletium de Sebastia, Armeniæ civitate, contra decreta concilii illuc transferunt. Qui tamen ab ipsis rursum in exilium traditur:" see Ruffinus, *Hist. Ecc.* b. x. c. 24. The word *Attica* is unquestionably right, and the error must have arisen from some copyist adding the word *city* to τῆς Ἀττικῆς. There was a Meletius, Bishop of Sebastopolis, in Pontus, who was present at the Council of Nice, and well known to Athanasius, and to Eusebius, who, on account of his great learning and powers of oratory, was called *The honey of Attica*, Τὸ μέλι τῆς Ἀττικῆς: see Eusebius, b. vii. c. 32 ; and Valesius' notes. He could hardly be the same as Meletius, who was made Bishop of Antioch in the year 360, thirty-five years after the Council, although the similarity of their own names and that of their sees, the one being Bishop of Sebastopolis in Pontus, and the other of Sebaste in Armenia, might cause some confusion. The latter, according to Socrates, was translated from Sebaste, first to Berœa, and then to Antioch : see *Hist. Eccl.* b. ii. c. 44; and Sozomen, *Hist. Eccl.* b. iv. c. xxviii. Both Meliton and Meletius were celebrated for their eloquence.

L. 18. *Was taken from the flock.* B.H.C., erroneously, " was seized by the shearer."

L. 24. *In the midst of Jerusalem. By whom? By Israel.* B.H.C. " in the midst of Jerusalem by those who are of Israel."

L. 28. *Thou wast reclining on a soft bed*, B.H.C. translates in an absurd manner, " Thou didst lie down against rectitude of mind ! !" and then explains it thus, " *i.e.* crouch like a wild beast to seize its prey," or, it may be simply " with a guilty conscience."

L. 30. *Why hast thou done this fresh wickedness?* B.H.C. "Wherefore this iniquity ? It is a new crime."

P. 55, L. 34. *The heaven and the earth.* B.H.C. " the *sun* and the earth," mistaking ܠܫܡܐ for ܐܪܥܐ .

P. 56, L. 5. *Meliton, Bishop of Ittica.* This is the same as the preceding, although written ܐܝܛܘܐ : B.H.C., in support of his assertion above, has not hesitated to turn *Meliton* into *Melitus ;* and *Itica,* or *Ittica,* into *Antioch.*

This last extract is taken from a volume procured in Egypt in 1843 by Dr. Tattam, with several leaves added in 1847 from the fragments obtained by M. Pacho. It appears to have been written about the seventh or eighth century, is imperfect both at the beginning and the end, and in its present state consists of 186 leaves written in two columns. It contains numerous extracts from the Fathers of the Church, cited in opposition to various heresies. What the title of the work is, or who is its author, does not appear. Cod. Add. 14,533 (not 14,532 as B.H.C. states).

History of the Church. This chapter of the fourth book of Eusebius is taken from the antient Syriac version, of which I have inserted an account in the *Corpus Ignatianum,* p. 350, which see. I have given the entire chapter as it stands. It comprises the 24, 25, 26, and 27th of the Greek editions. It may be considered a fair specimen of the Syriac version, which future editors of Eusebius should not neglect to consult.

P. 57, L. 5. *Bishop of Corinth,* omitted in the Greek. Ruffinus omits here also all mention of Dionysius.

L. 18. *On the Faith of Man.* So Ruffinus, *De fide hominis ;* and also several Greek manuscripts. The editions have περὶ φύσεως ἀνθρώπου.

L. 20. *On the hearing of the ear of faith.* Gr. Ὁ περὶ ὑπακοῆς πίστεως καὶ ὁ περὶ αἰσθητηρίων. Ruffinus, *De obedientia fide. De sensibus.*

L. 22. *On the faith ;* with several manuscripts. Ruffinus, *De fide.* Some editions have κτίσεως. See Dr. Routh's note on this place, vol. i. p. 139.

L. 23. *And again on the Soul and on the Body.* With several Greek manuscripts, and Ruffinus, *Item de anima et corpore.*

L. 24. The Greek editions add καὶ ἡ κλείς ; and Ruffinus, *Item liber qui dicitur Clavis.*

L. 25. *On God who put on the body.* Gr. Ὁ περὶ ἐνσωμάτου Θεοῦ. Ruffinus, *De Deo corpore induto.* See Dr. Routh's note, p. 143.

L. 29. *Agaris,* an error for Σάγαρις. See b. v. c. 24.

L. 36. *By him,* ܐܣ̈ܟ, as if he had read ἀπ' αὐτοῦ instead of ἐπ': a common occurrence. Ruffinus has "illis temporibus."

P. 59, L. 3. *Fundius,* and below, *Pharisæans:* doubtless errors of the scribe.

AMBROSE.

P. 61. M. Renan has inserted a few lines from this in the *Journal Asiatique.* The text is correctly printed, with the exception of ‖ܠܘܒܣ for ‖ܐܘܠܒܣ; but he has erred greatly in the translation. The first sentence he renders thus: " N'avez-vous point pensé, hommes de la Grèce, qu'il était contra la loi et la justice de me chasser du milieu de vous ?" and the last sentence still more wrongly, " Après l'avoir étudiée, j'ai reconnu tout ce qu'il y a en cette doctrine de nouveau et d'étrange, et quelle confience elle donne à ceux qui la professent pour enseigner la vérite."

P. 61, L. 11. *Wars of the two trials.* I suppose the author means, of the gods as well as the men engaged in it ; to which also reference is made in the *Cohortatio ad Gentiles,* c. ii. edit. Otto, p. 24 ; and the passage of Homer, Il. xx. v. 66—72 cited, beginning,

Τόσσος ἄρα κτύπος ὦρτο θεῶν ἔριδι ξυνιόντων:

Compare Tertullian, *Ad Nationes* i. c. 10, p. 329.

L. 12. *For the sake of Helen,* &c. Homer, Il. ii. v. 177.

Ἀγγείην Ἑλένην, ἧς εἵνεκα πολλοὶ Ἀχαιῶν
Ἐν Τροίῃ ἀπόλοντο, φίλης ἀπὸ πατρίδος αἴης.

L. 16. *A leprous shepherd.* The Syriac proves the antiquity of the Greek reading λεπροῦ, which has been suspected by critics. See Otto's notes.

P. 62, L. 20. *Amazon.* The Syriac has ܐܡܘܙܢ, the ‖ being omitted.

P. 63. Compare what is said here relative to the Gods with Justin Martyr, *Apol.* i, c. 21. See also Augustin, *De Civitate Dei* ii, c. 7, 8 ; and Joh. Ludov. Vives' notes to these chapters : edit. Fancof. 1661.

L. 13. *Father of Gods and men.* The common expression of Homer πατὴρ ἀνδρῶν τε θεῶν τε, which Ennius among the Latins translated " patrum divûmque hominunque." See Cicero, *De Nat. Deor.* p. 104.

L. 15. *Concerning his adultery.* Compare the passage of Homer, Il. xiv. 315—327, in which Jupiter recounts his amours to Juno : cited also in the *Cohortatio ad Gent.* c. 2. p. 22.

P. 64, L. 6. *Of how many censures is the Lord of the gods guilty,* &c.

Compare Tertullian, *Apol.* c. 11, vol. i. p. 159: "Illuc (in Tartarum scilicet) enim abstrudi solent, impii quique in parentes et incesti in sorores, et maritarum adulteri, et virginum raptores, et puerorum contaminatores, et qui sæviunt, et qui occidunt, et qui furantur, et qui decipiunt, et quicumque similes sunt alicujus dei vestri, quem neminem integrum a crimine aut vitio probare poteritis, nisi hominem negaveritis. Atquin ut illos homines fuisse non possitis negare, etiam istæ notæ accedunt quæ nec deos postea factos credi permittunt. Si enim vos talibus puniendis præsidetis, si commercium, colloquium, convictum malorum et turpium probi quique respuitis, horum autem pares deus ille majestatis suæ consortio adscivit, quid ergo damnatis, quorum collegas adoratis? Suggillatio est in cœlo vestra justitia. Deos facite criminosissimos quosque, ut placeatis deis vestris."

P. 65, L. 3. *Wept over Sarpedon.* He alludes to the following lines of Homer, Il. xvi. 433, which Athenagoras also quotes, *Legat.* c. 21

Ὢ μοι ἐγών, ὅτε μοι Σαρπηδόνα φίλτατον ἀνδρῶν

Μοῖρ᾽ ὑπὸ Πατρόκλοιο Μενοιτιάδαο δαμῆναι!

This is also quoted in the *Cohort. ad Gent.* c. 2. p. 20.

L. 7. *Carried off.* The text is ܘܠܡ, which seems to be a blunder for ܘܠܡ.

L. 22. *Penelope.* The manuscript has ܦܢܠܦܐ, evidently an error for ܦܢܠܦܐ.

L. 24. *Employed.* The manuscript reads ܡܬܟܪܟ, which appears to be an error. There is no such root in the Lexicons. Perhaps ܡܬܟܪܟ was intended.

P. 66, c. 6. *Rhea.* The text has ܪܗܝ, evidently an error for ܪܗܐ.

L. 22. *Is guilty of adultery, and is without punishment.* The Greek is ἀκολάστως ζῶσαν: see p. 68, L. 25. The translator did not understand the word ἀκολάστως.

P. 67. L. 14. *Are brave*, ܓܢܒܪܝܢ. The translator must either have read ἀνδρεῖοι instead of ἄνανδροι, or the Syriac copyist have mistaken ܓܢܒܪܝܢ for ܡܚܝܠܝܢ.

L. 15. *Horsemen and their beauty.* The Greek has τύπων εὐμορφίαν. The Syriac translator probably read ἱππέων for τύπων.

P. 69, L. 7. *And make the dead pass over that he die not*, ܕܠܐ ܢܥܒܪ ܠܡܝܬܐ. Although the sense is good, there appears to be an error of the copyist in writing ܠܥܠ for ܠܥܠ when the translation would be simply, 'maketh the dead (or the mortal) that he die not."

MARA, SON OF SERAPION.

P. 70, L. 11. *Wrecked together with the birth of life,* ܡ ܝܕ ܥܬ ܐܟܣܪ ܡ ܕ ܥܘܬ ܠܡ܀. These words are obscure. I suppose they refer to the new birth of a Christian rendering the precepts of Greek philosophy superfluous. Compare what Ambrose says, p. 61 above. There are several very obscure passages in this letter. Although I have endeavoured to give the meaning of them as accurately as I could, I cannot confidently assert that I have in no instances failed. M. Renan has given a short extract from this letter in the *Journal Asiatique*; and has left off in the middle of a sentence omitting the words which I have just mentioned, and consequently destroying the sense of the passage. He has made several mistakes in the texts—ܩܪܒ for ܩܠܒ, and ܩܪܝܒ for ܩܪܝܒ, and ܗܘܐ for ܩܘܗ, and ܩܠܒ for ܩܠܒ. In the translation he has omitted the name Mara, and written only "Bar Sérapion." The last sentence he has rendered altogether wrongly. "C'est pourquoi je l'adresse ce livre comme un mémorial de toutes mes recherches; il a été pour moi l'univers, est c'est lui qui m'a introduit dans la science; car, tout ce que je sais, je l'ai appris de la Grèce."

P. 71, L. 36. *Imprisoned.* The original work ܣܝܪܐ means also, *a recluse,* a monk practising a certain mode of asceticism, concerning which see Assemani *Disser. de Syris Monophysitis.* This would well agree with the meaning here; but at P. 75, L. 32, the writer speaks as if he were actually in prison or bondage at the time.

P. 73, L. 33. *Or the people of Samos.* See respecting the burning of Pythagoras, Diogenes Laertius, *De vitis et dogm. Philosoph.* lib. viii. seg. 39, with Menagius' Notes; and Stanley's *History of Philosophy,* second edit. p. 506. The Sibylline Oracles were said to have foretold the destruction of Samos. Ἔσται καὶ Σάμος ἄμμος, ἐσεῖται δὲ Δῆλος ἄδηλος. See *Sybil. Orac.* p. 405, and Gale's Notes illustrating this matter.

P. 74, L. 6. *Statue of Juno:* This was the statue which the Romans erected in honour of Pythagoras, when they were commanded by the Oracle of Delphi to erect statues to the bravest and the wisest of the Greeks.

L. 23. *His neighbour:* ܫܒܪܗ this is evidently an error of the copyist for ܫܒܪܗ which would easily be made in the square character for the similarity of ה and ה.

P. 75, L. 4. *The majesty of the belly:* Compare Tertullian. "Deus enim tibi venter est, et pulmo templum, et aqualiculus altare, et sacerdos

cocus, et sanctus spiritus nidor, et condimenta charismata et ructus pro-
phetia. *De Jejunio*, c. xvi. vol. i. p. 877.

P. 76 : L. 23. *Mara.* M. Renan here also has omitted this name, and
in the following line misunderstood it, and translated it, "Seigneur."
In the next line he has omitted it again, and translated the reply altogether
wrongly, "Je ris du temps, qui se venge de moi, quand je ne lui ai fait
aucun mal."

Additional Note to page 40.

The extract given here is cited from Add. MS. in the British Museum,
12,154, f. 248, b, respecting which see my *Corpus Ignatianum*, p. 359.
The passage is quoted from a writer known as the Persian Philosopher,
whose real name was Jacob: see subscription to Add. MS. 17,182, transcribed A.G. 785, or A.D. 473. There is another copy of this work of
nearly as early date, Add. MS. 14,619. The author wrote the last of his
treatises in the year of Alexander, 656, or A.D. 342. These treatises, both
from their antiquity and the matter contained in them, are very important;
but as I am preparing them for publication, I abstain at present from any
further observations.

ERRATA.

In the Syriac Text.

Page 5, L. 17,	*for*	‎ܟܘܟܒܐ‎	*read*	‎ܘܟܕܒܐ‎	
,, 7, L. 1,	,,	‎ܘܣܡܠܐ‎	,,	‎ܢܣܡܠܐ‎	
,, 12, L. 24,	,,	‎ܠܟܣܡܘܐ‎	,,	‎ܠܟܣܘܟܣܐ‎	
,, 27, L. 24,	,,	‎ܗܝܡܘ‎	,,	‎ܗܡܘܡ‎	
,, 29, L. 16,	,,	‎ܘܪܗ‎	,,	‎ܘܗܝ‎	
,, 45, L. 1,	,,	‎ܘܟܣܟܣܒ‎	,,	‎ܟܣܟܣܘ‎	
,, L. 27,	,,	‎ܘܐܬܐ‎	,,	‎ܘܐܬܐ‎	

In the Translation.

,, 41, L. 1,	,,	Melito	,,	Meliton.
,, 43, L. 7,	,,	which subject	,,	which are subject.

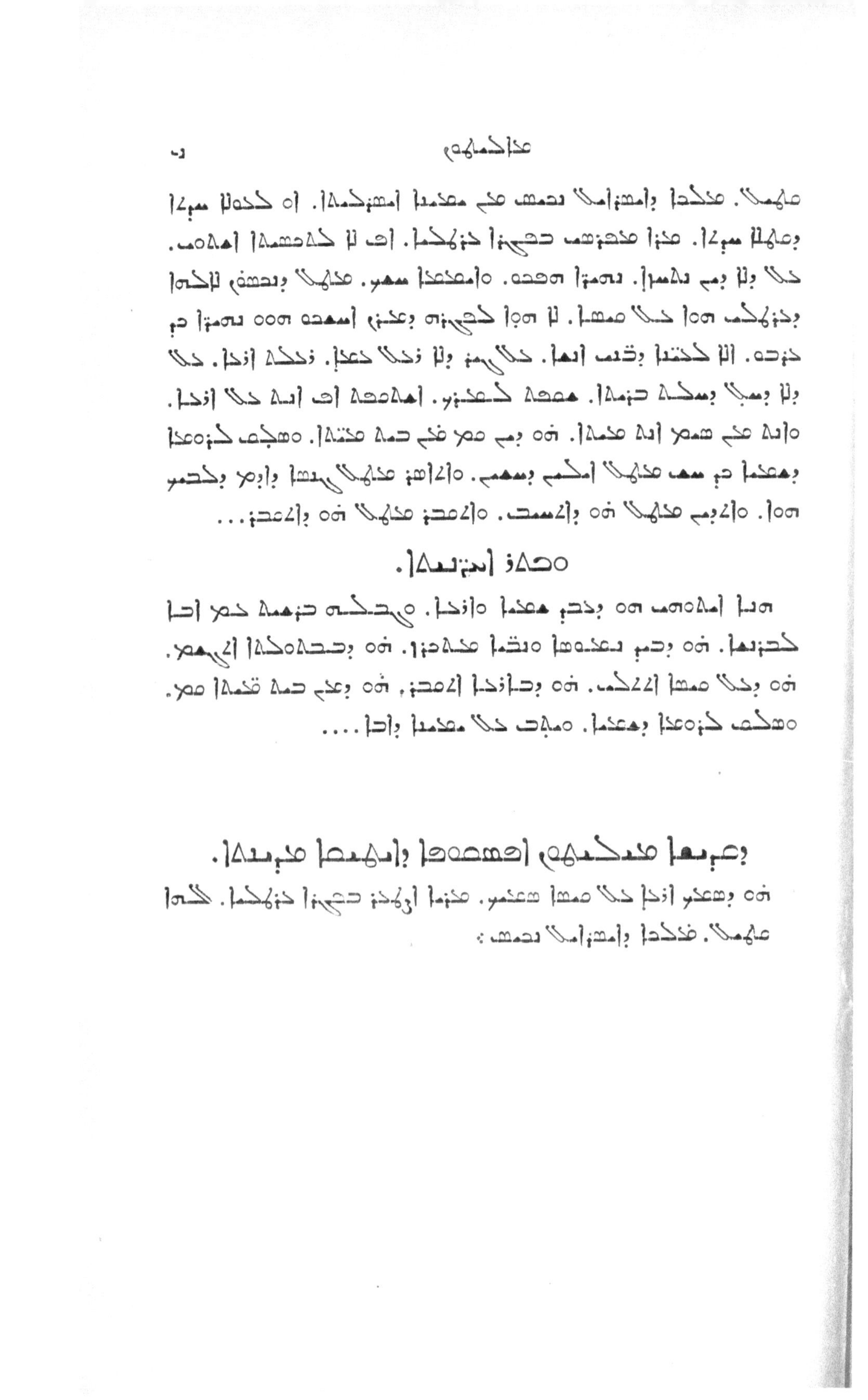

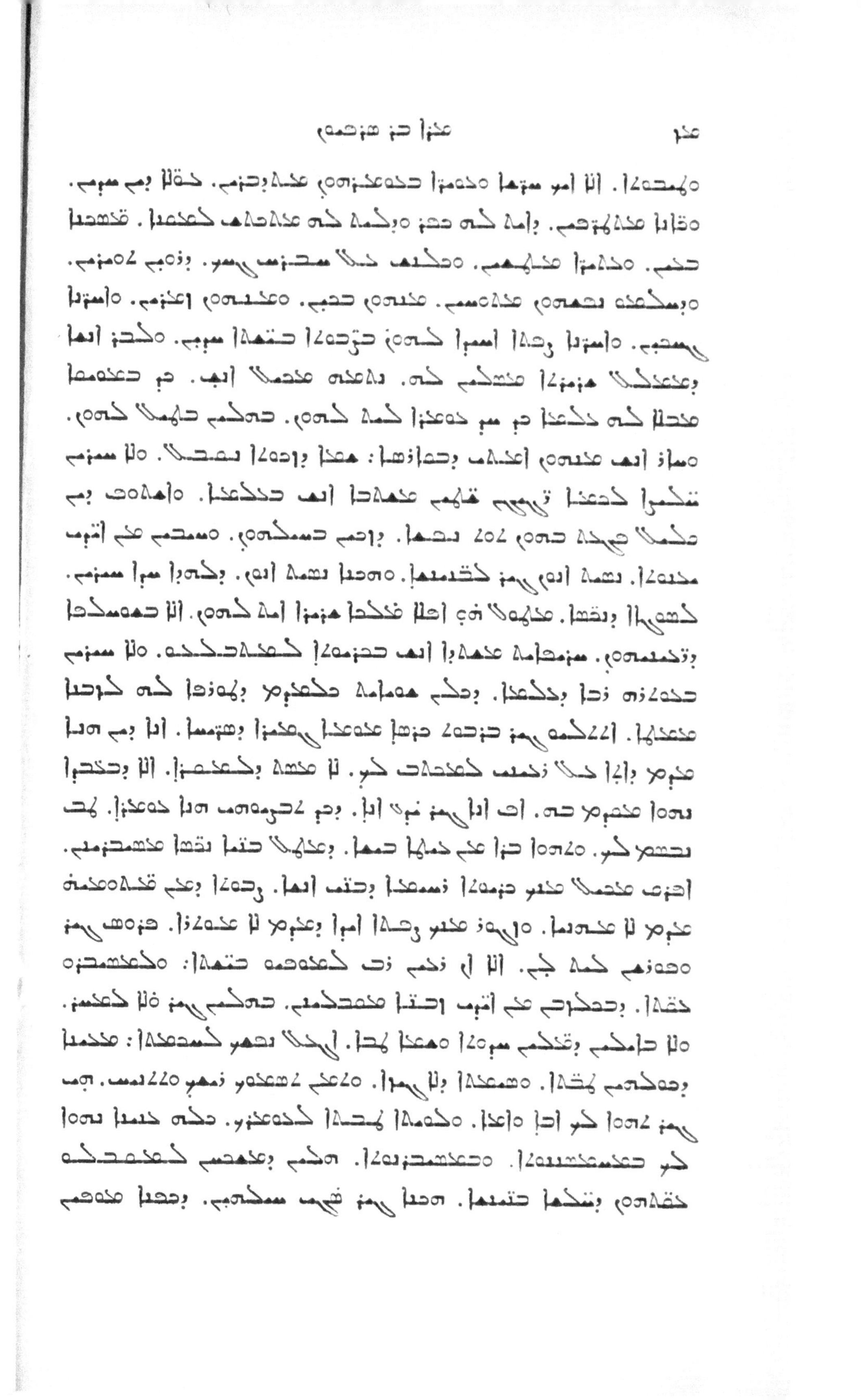

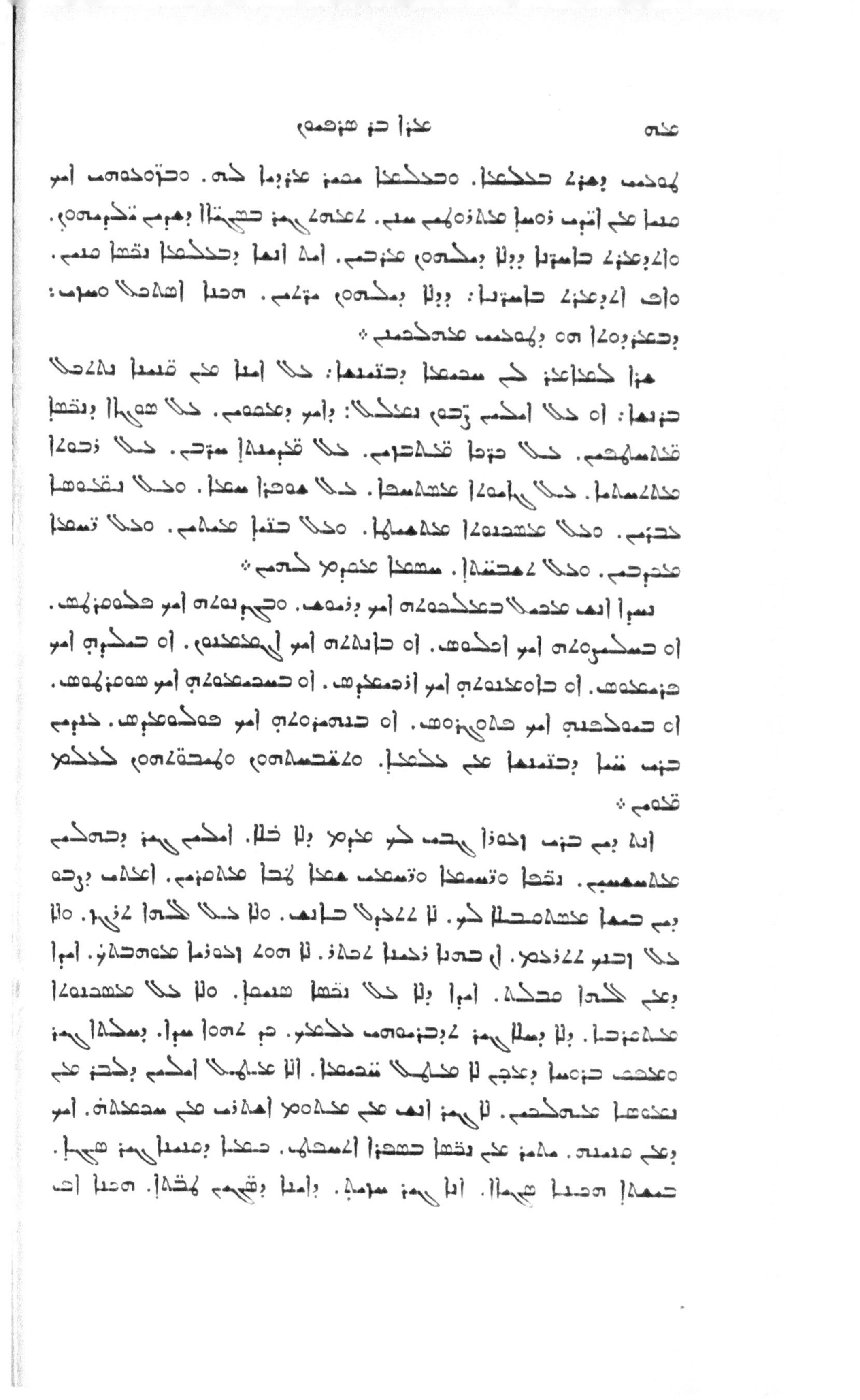

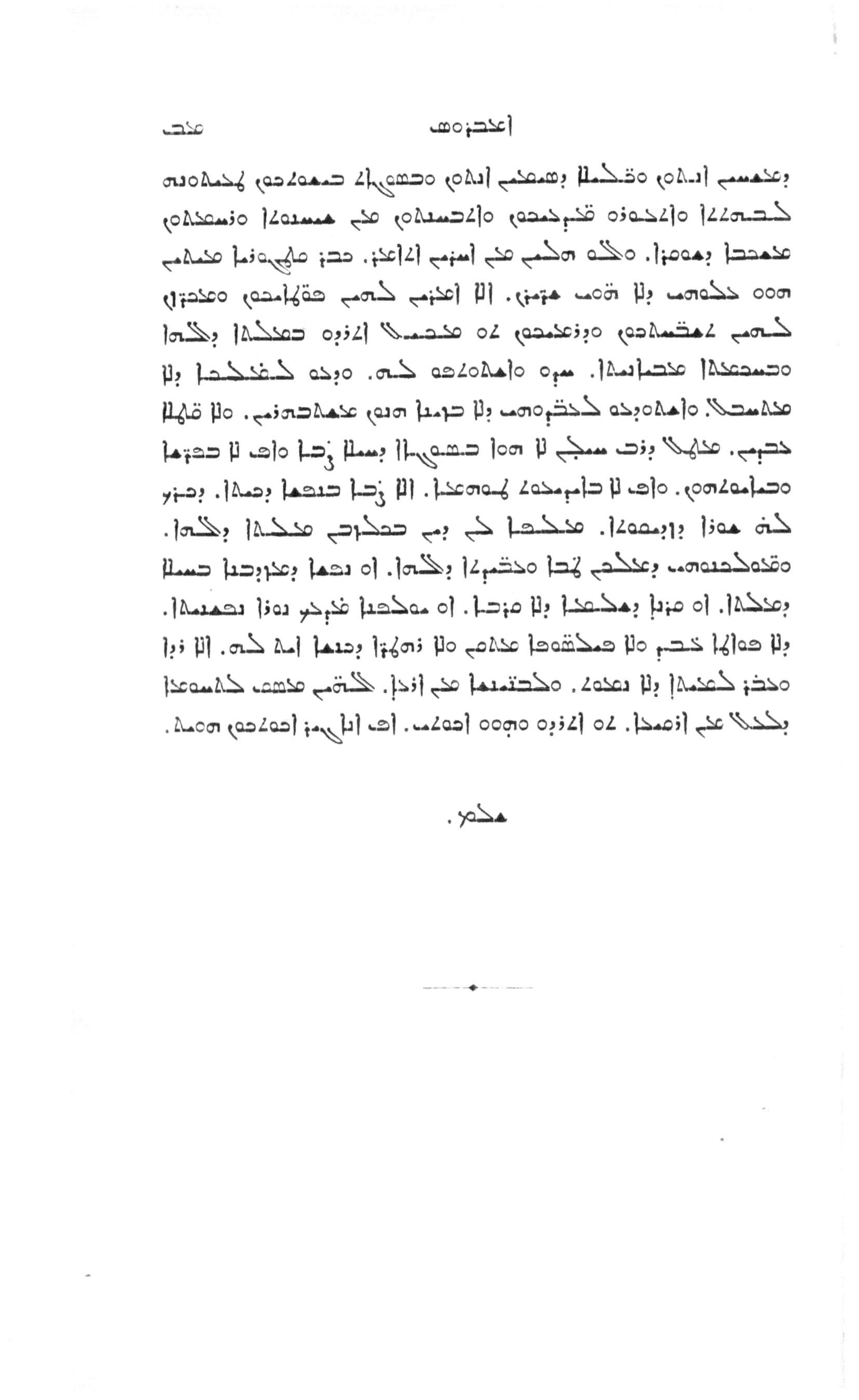

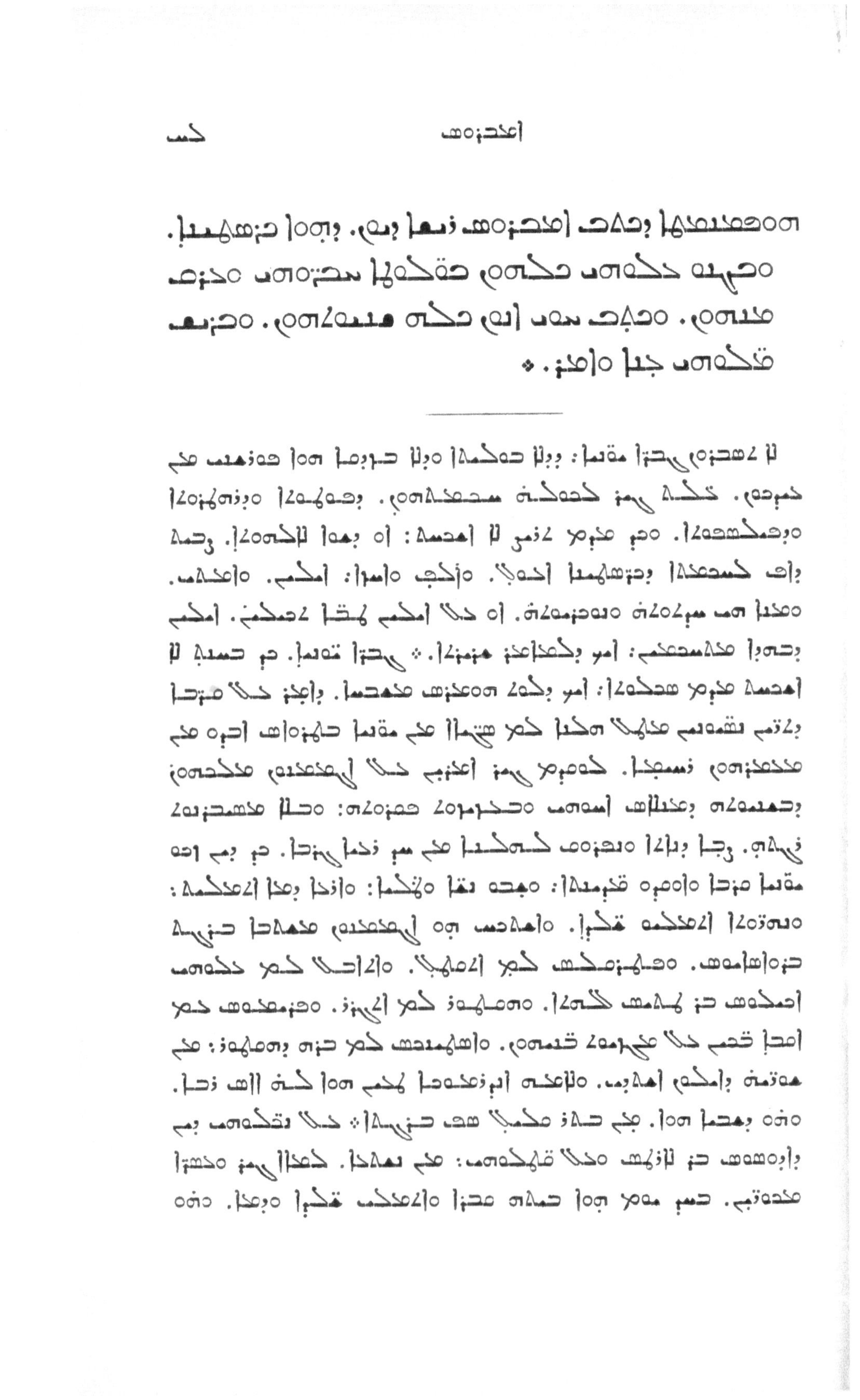

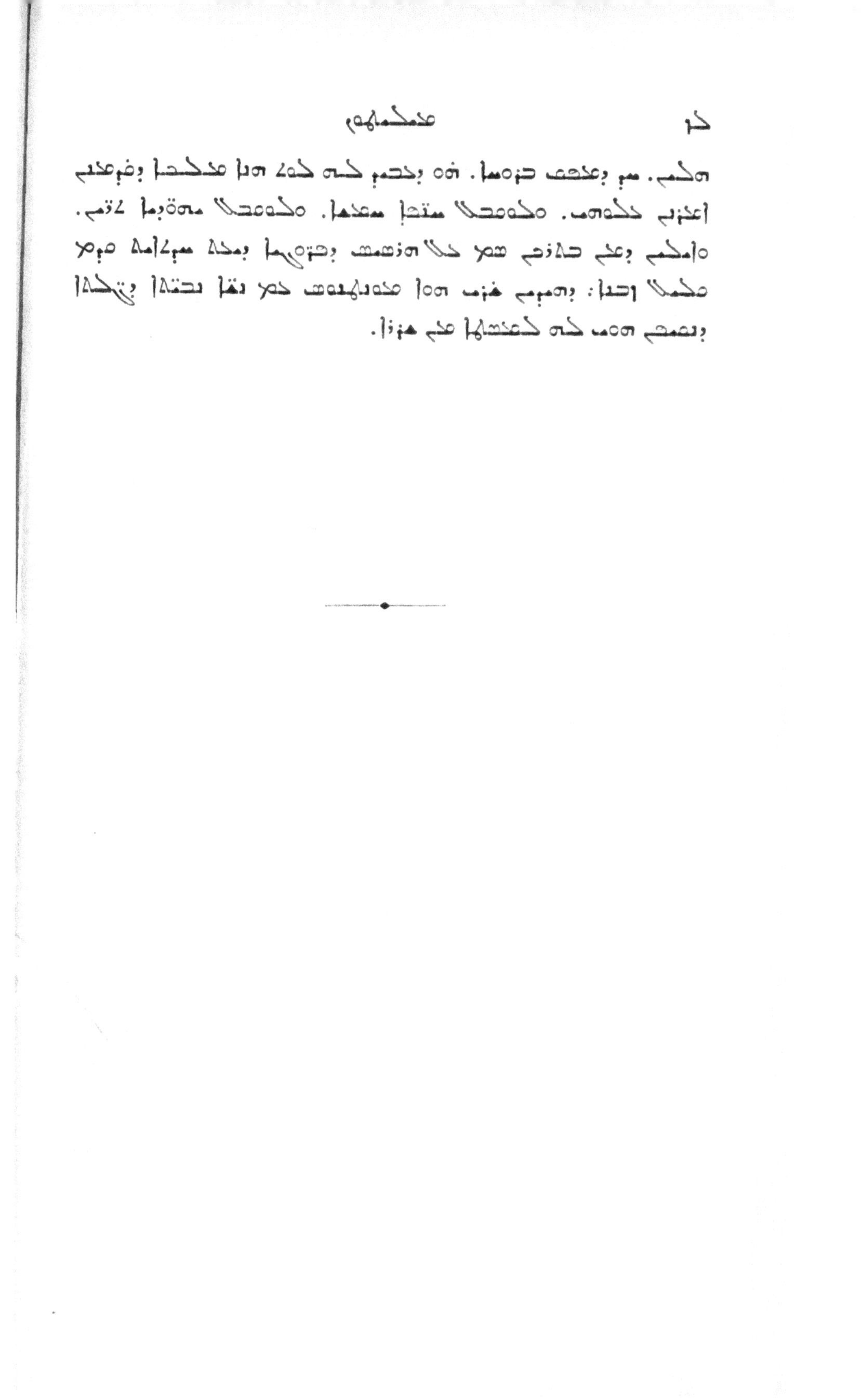

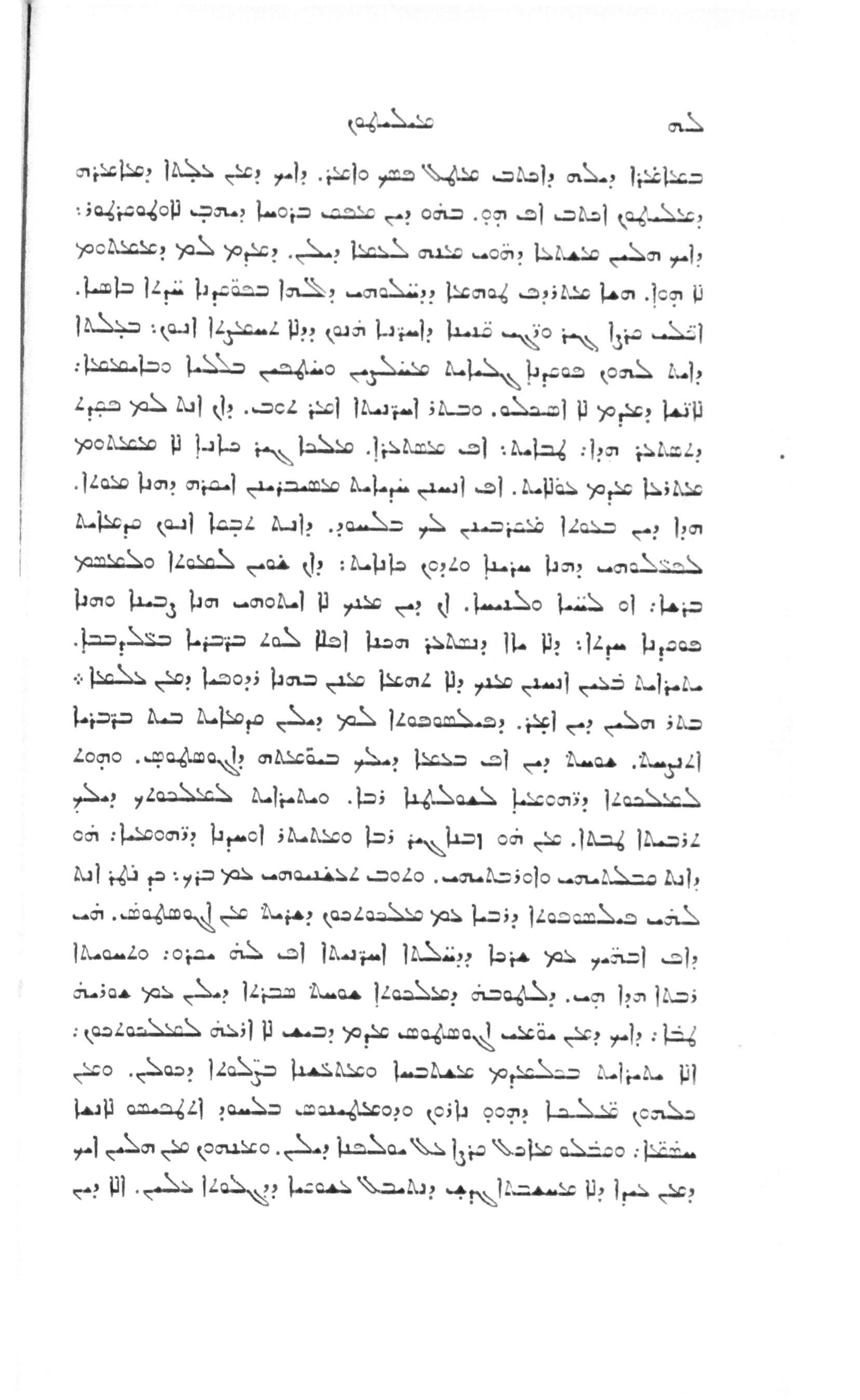

---•---

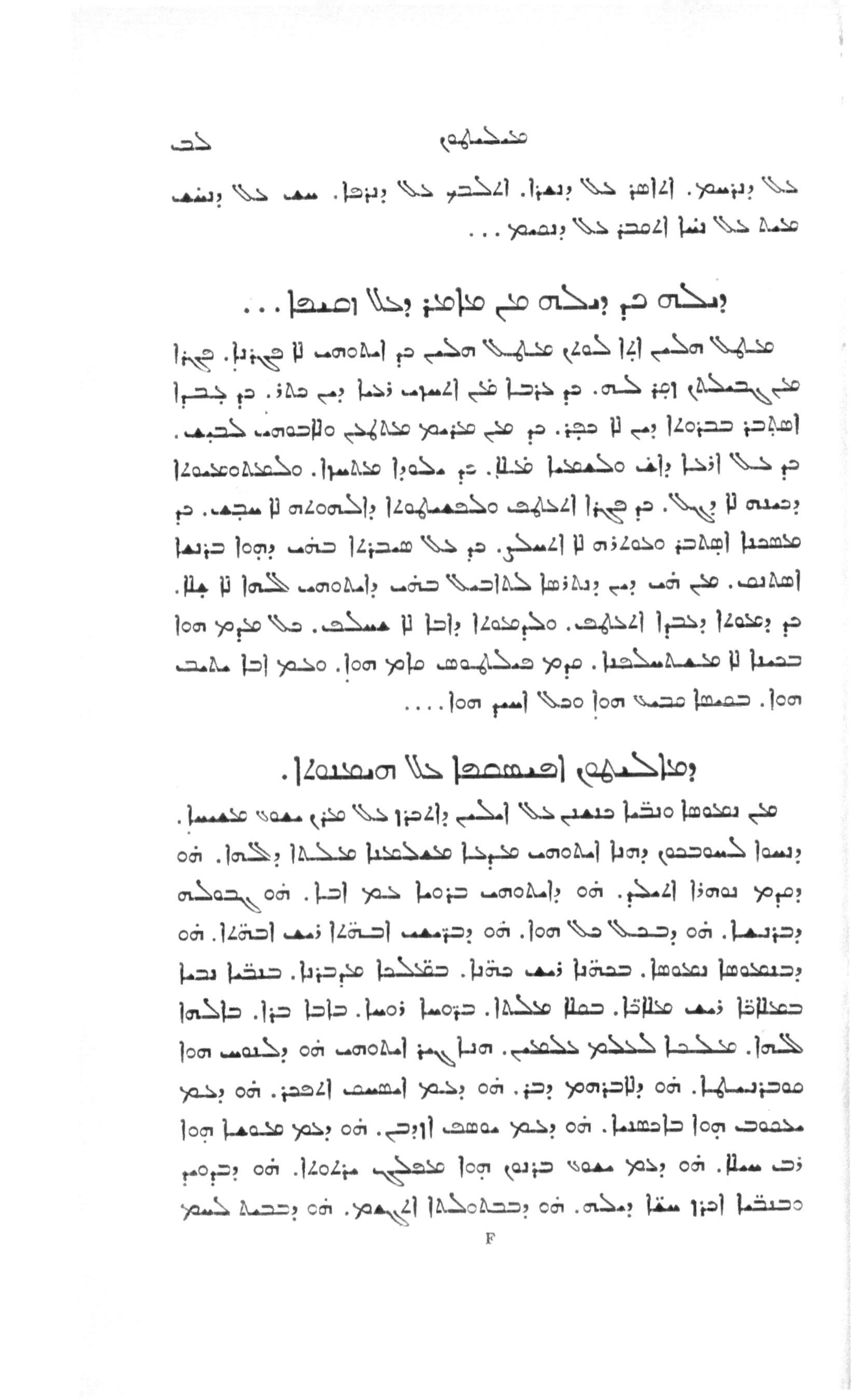

.

...

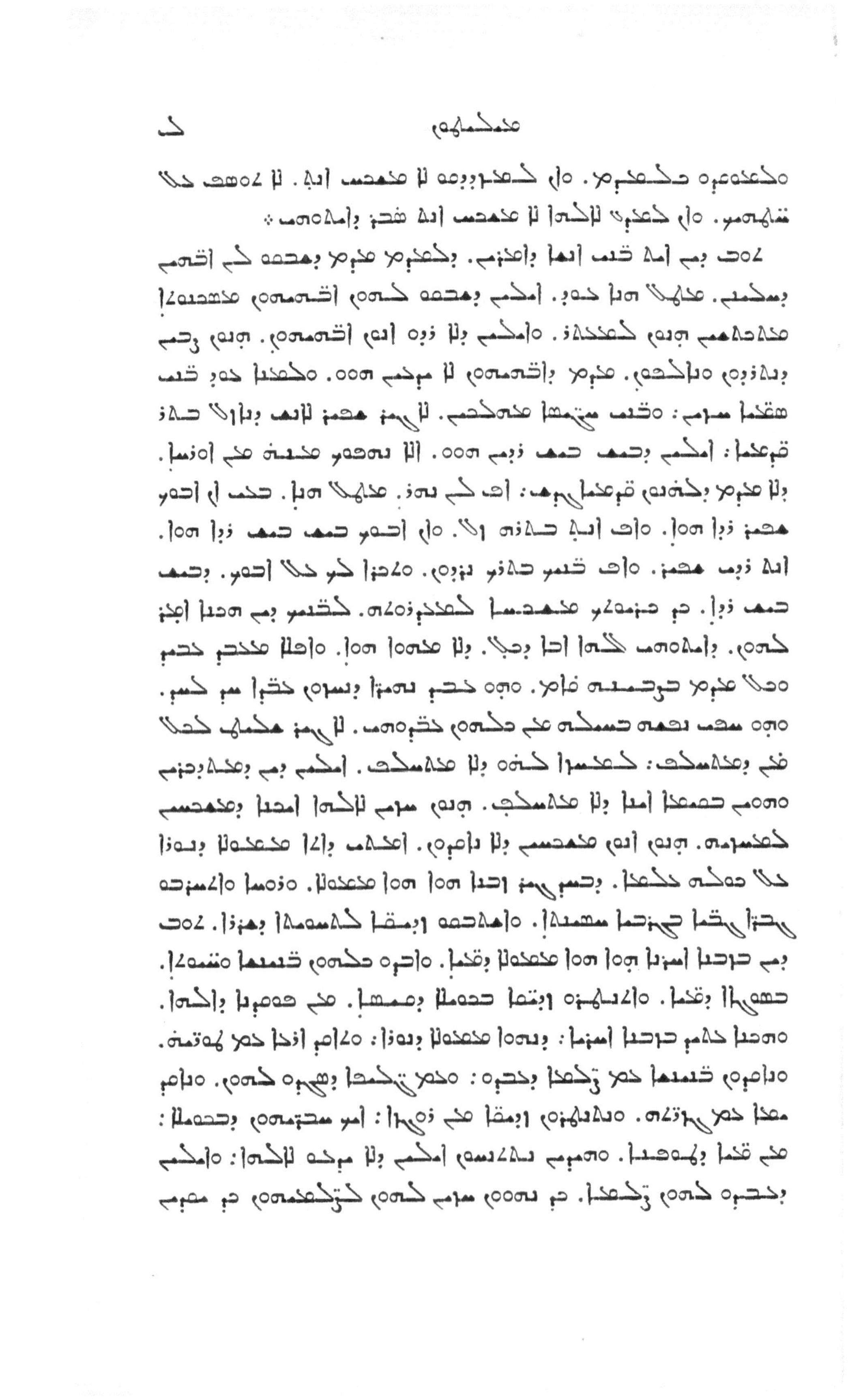

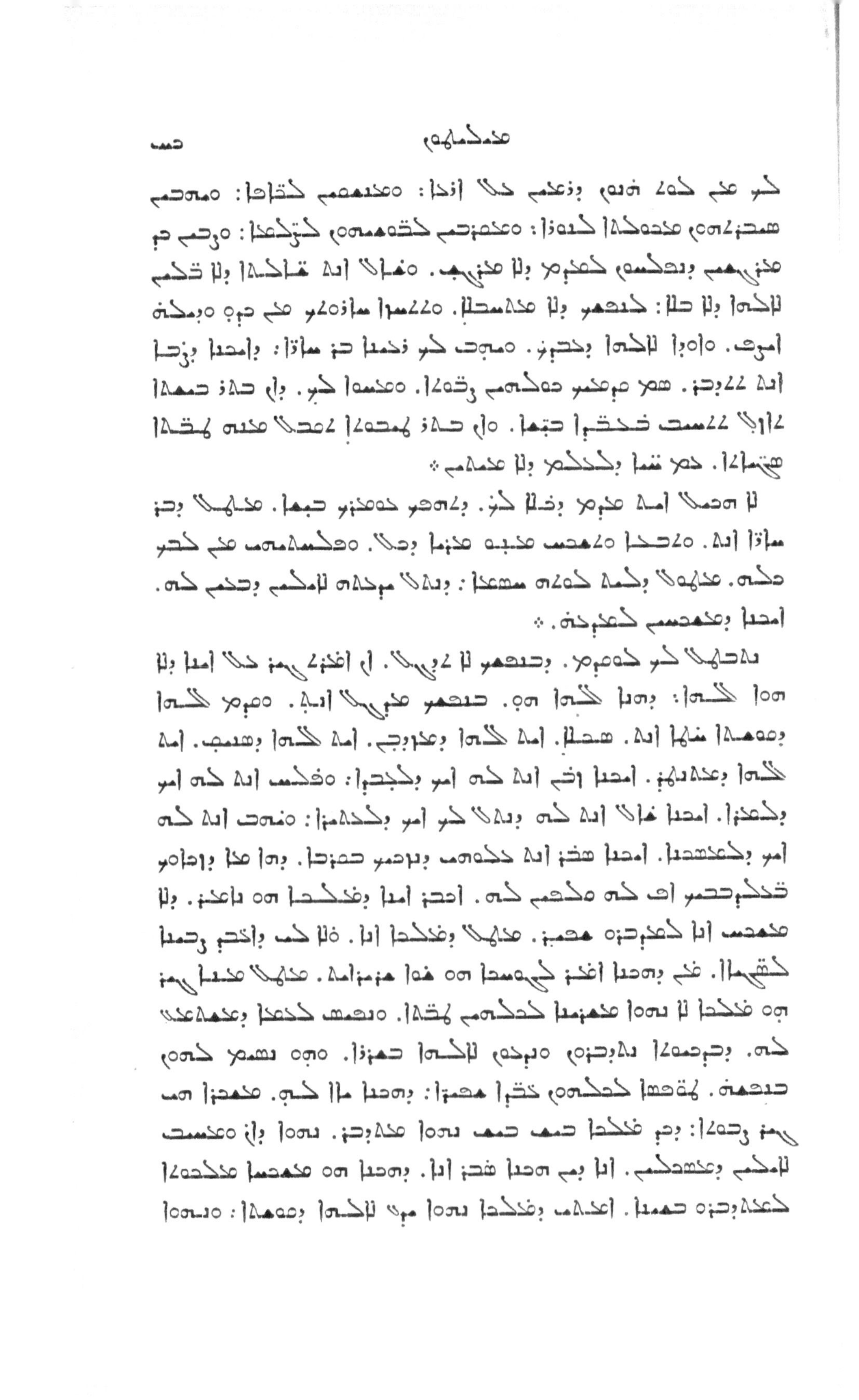

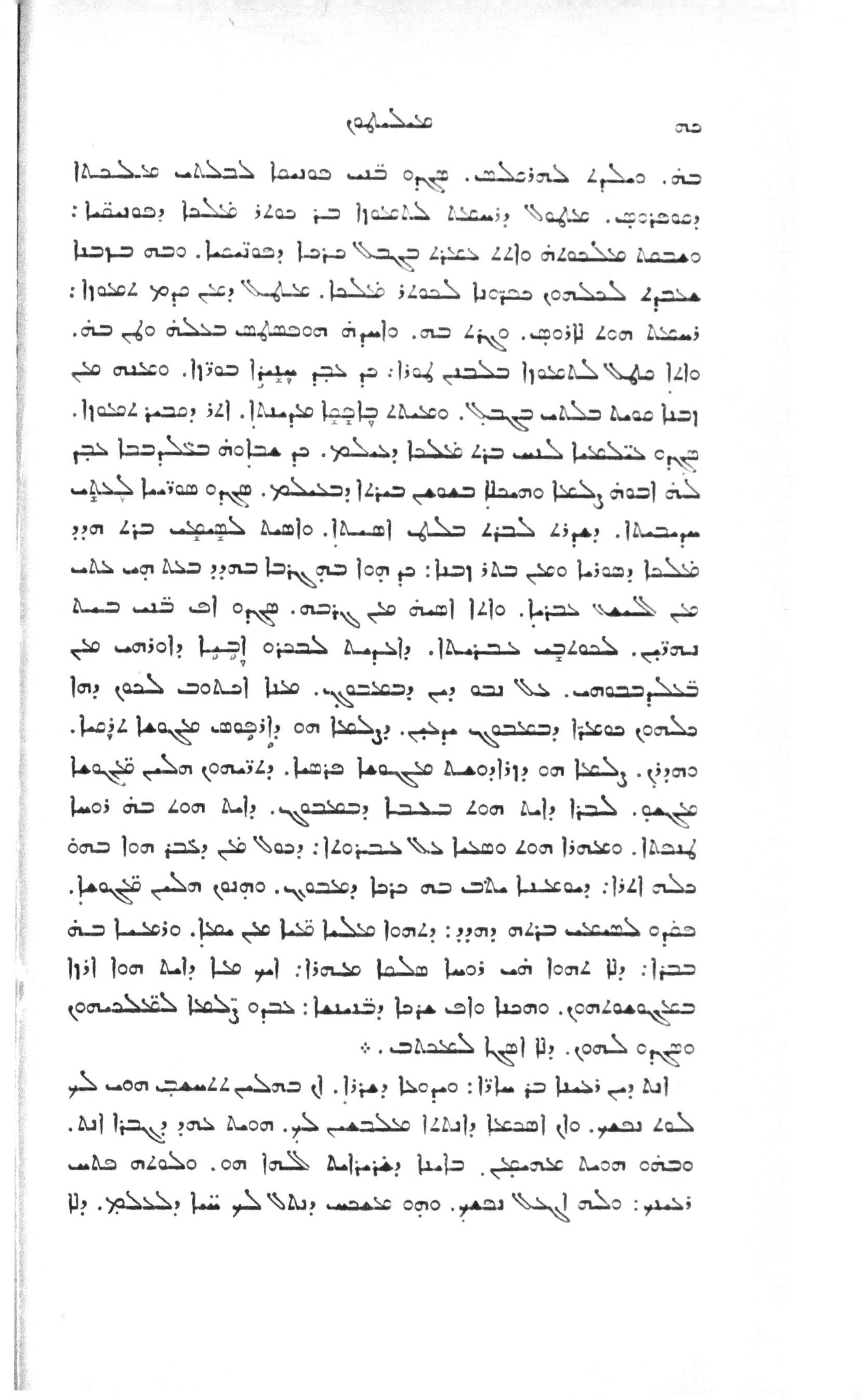

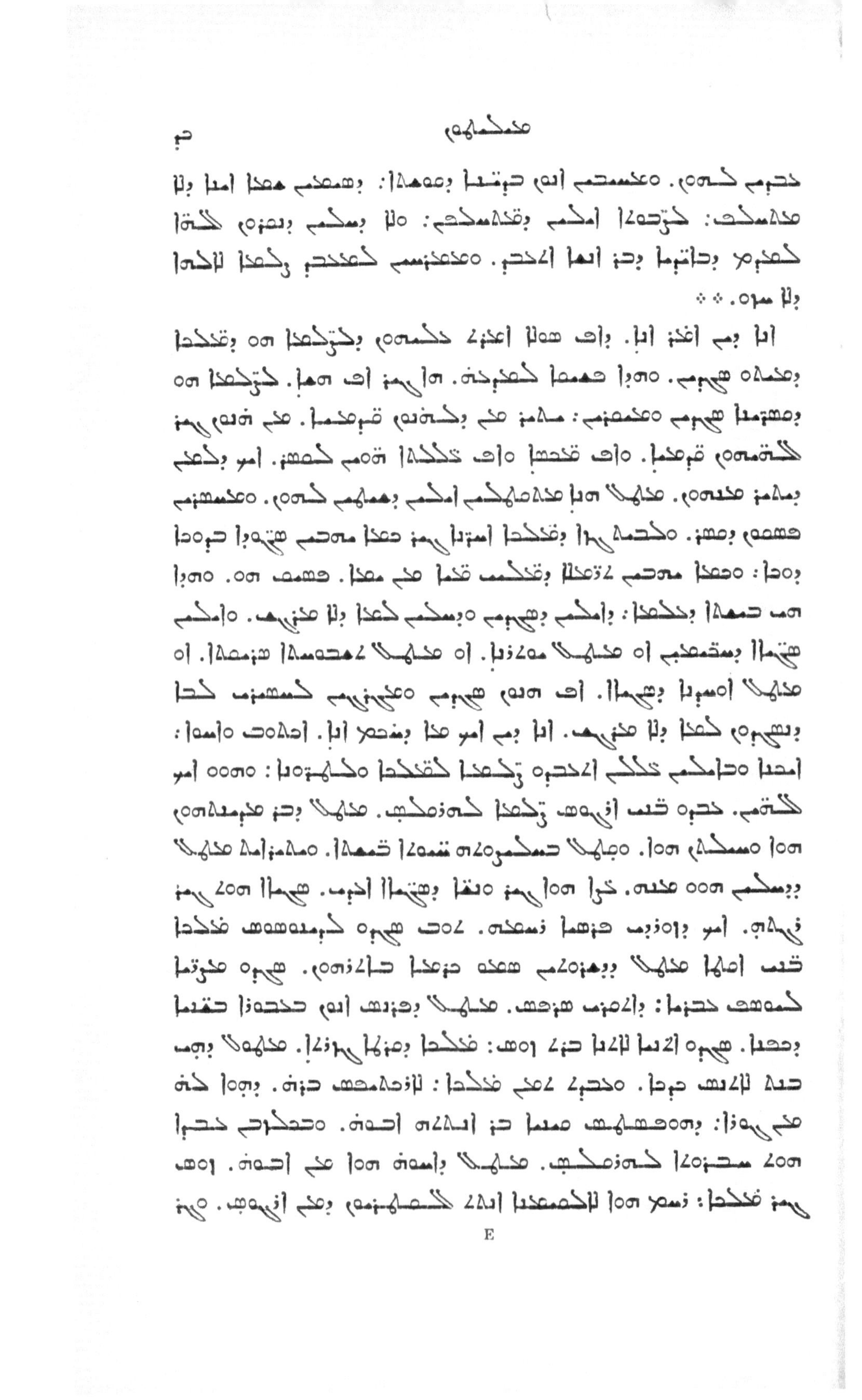

———————————

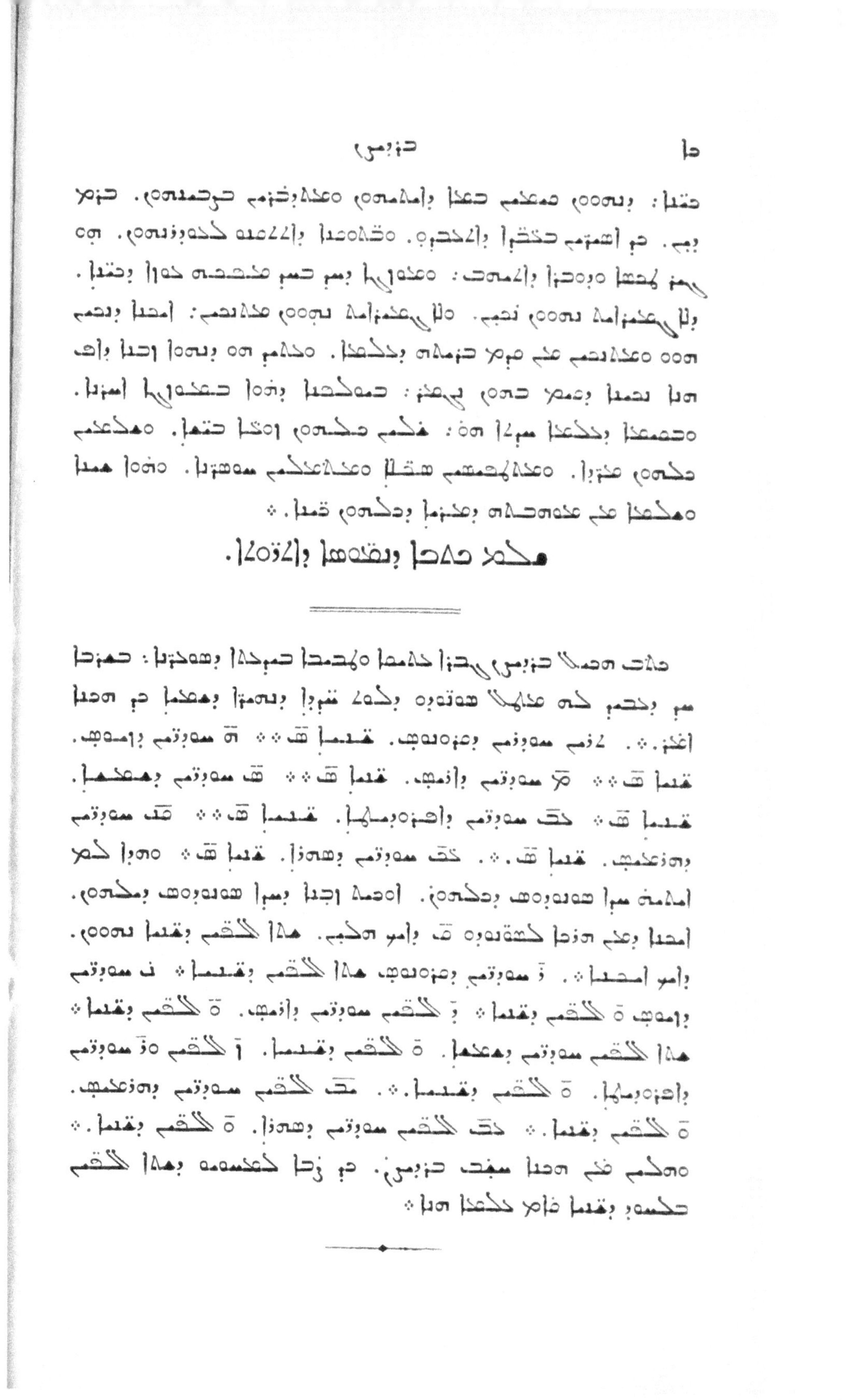

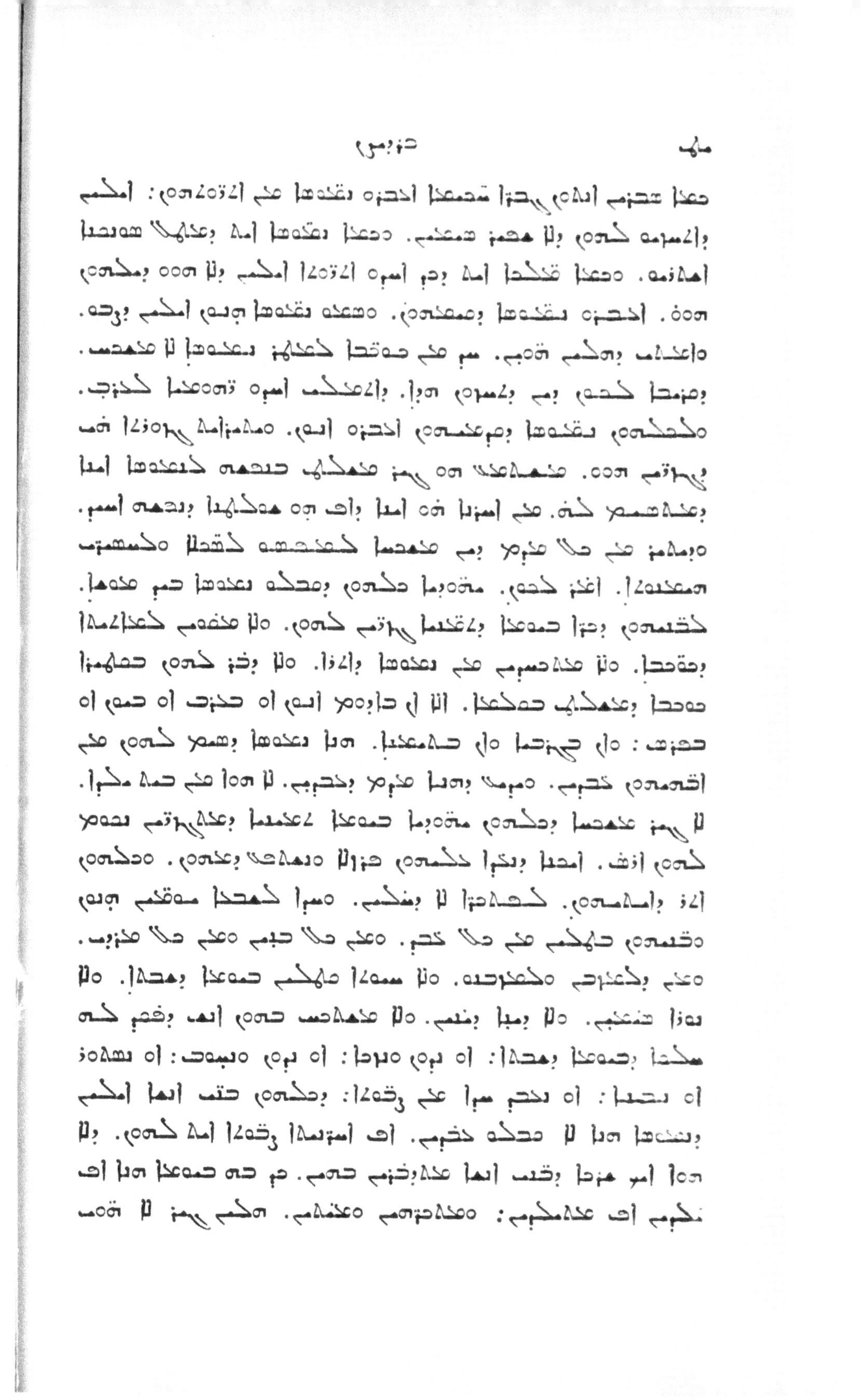

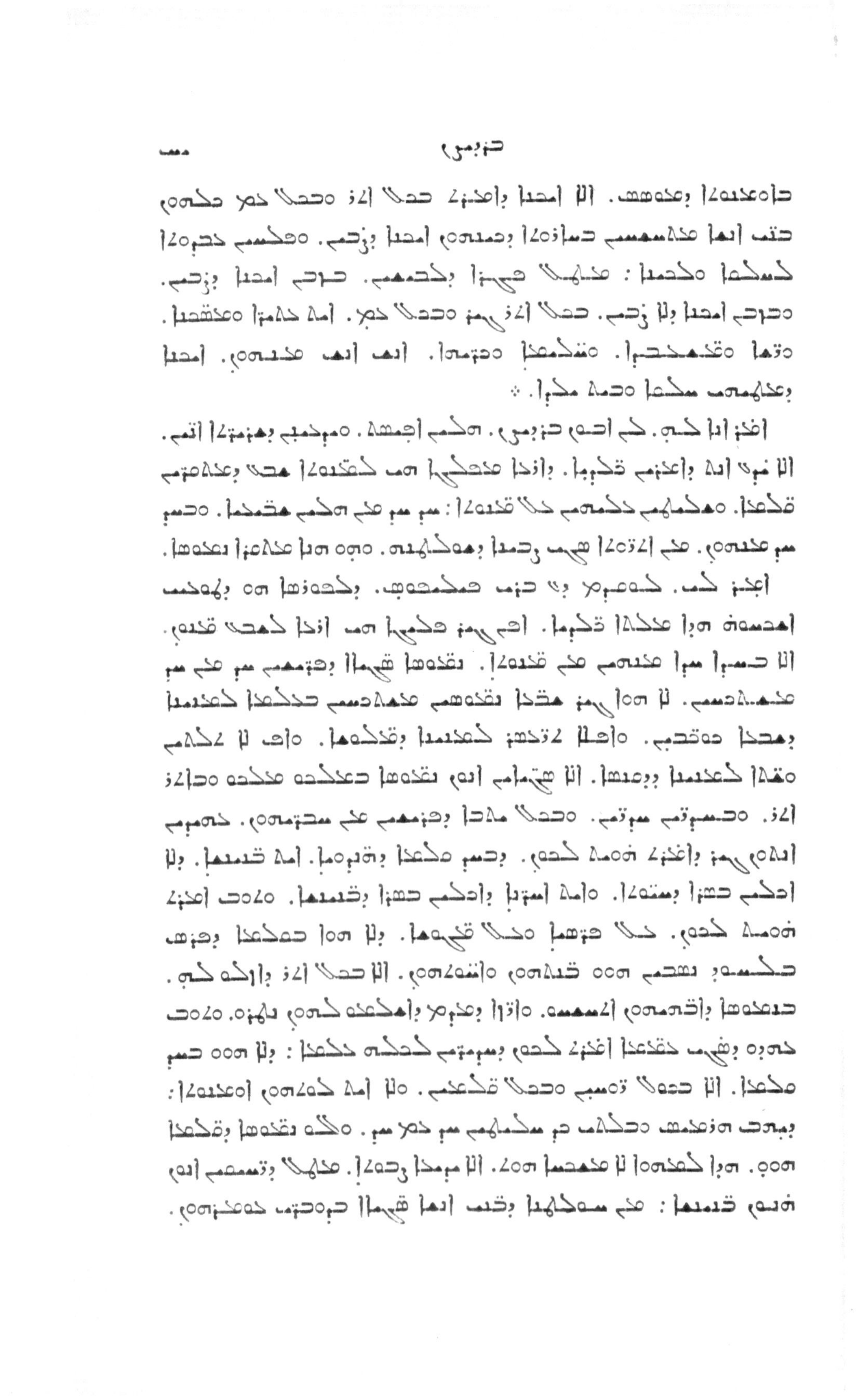

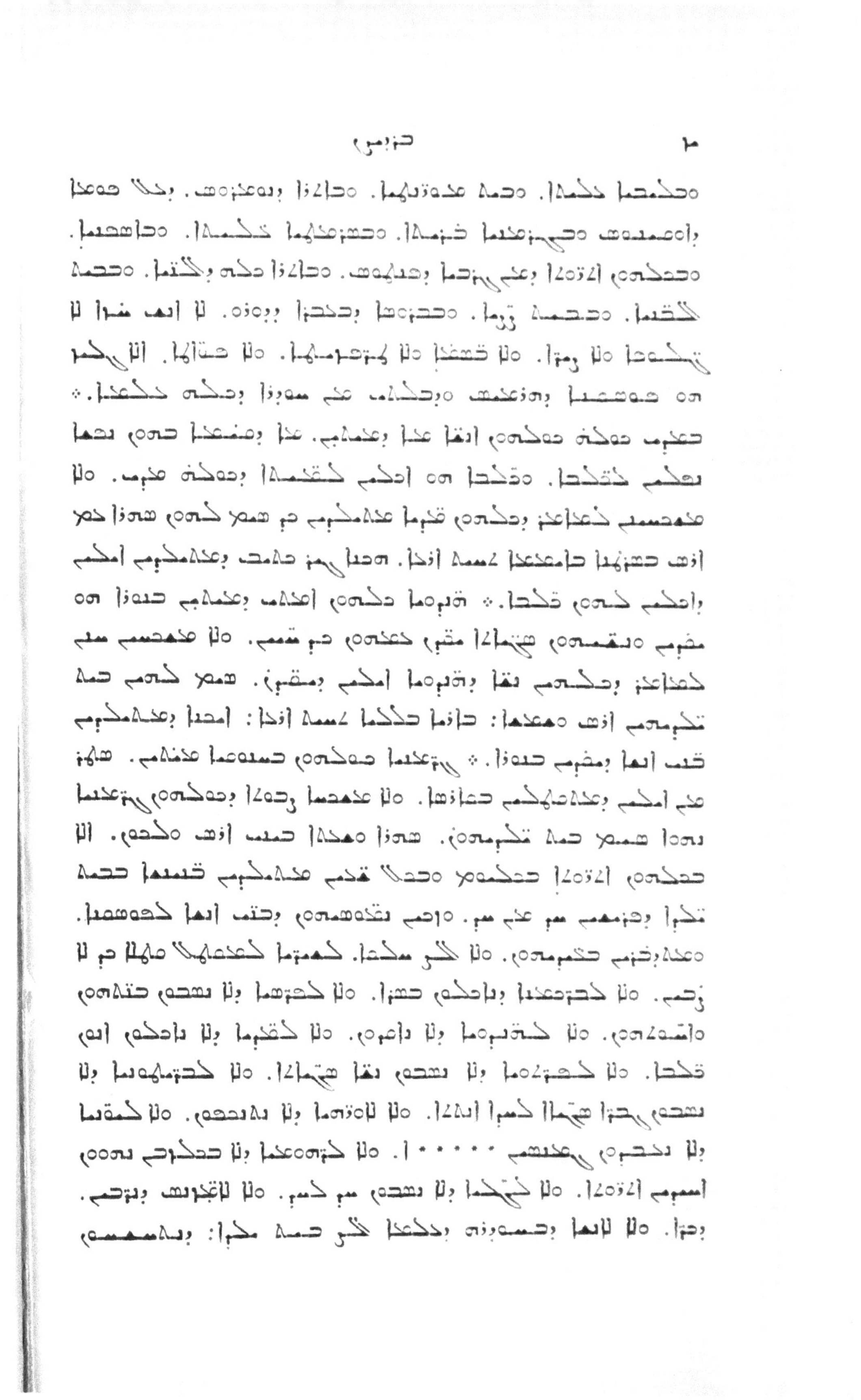

ܟܬܒ

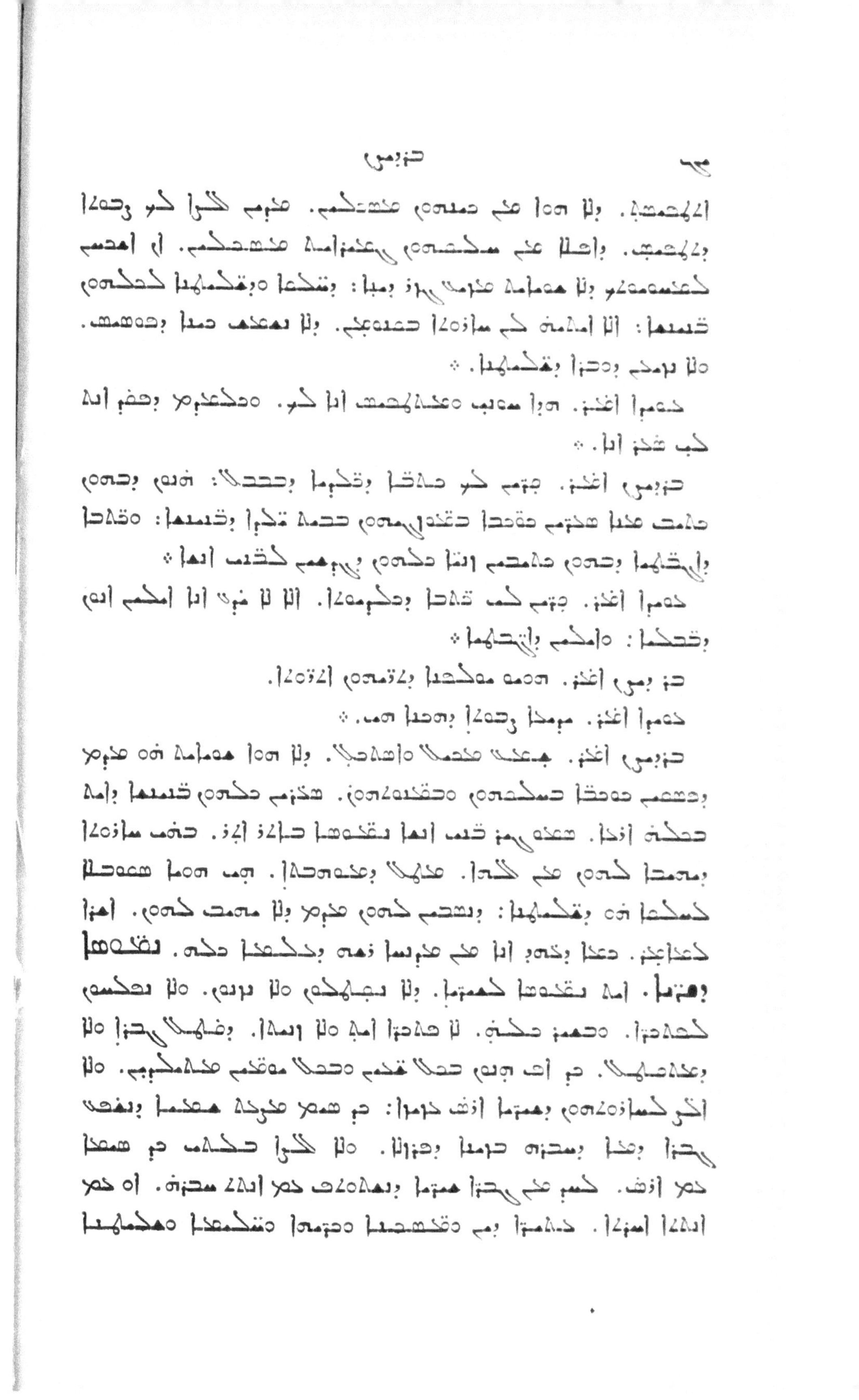

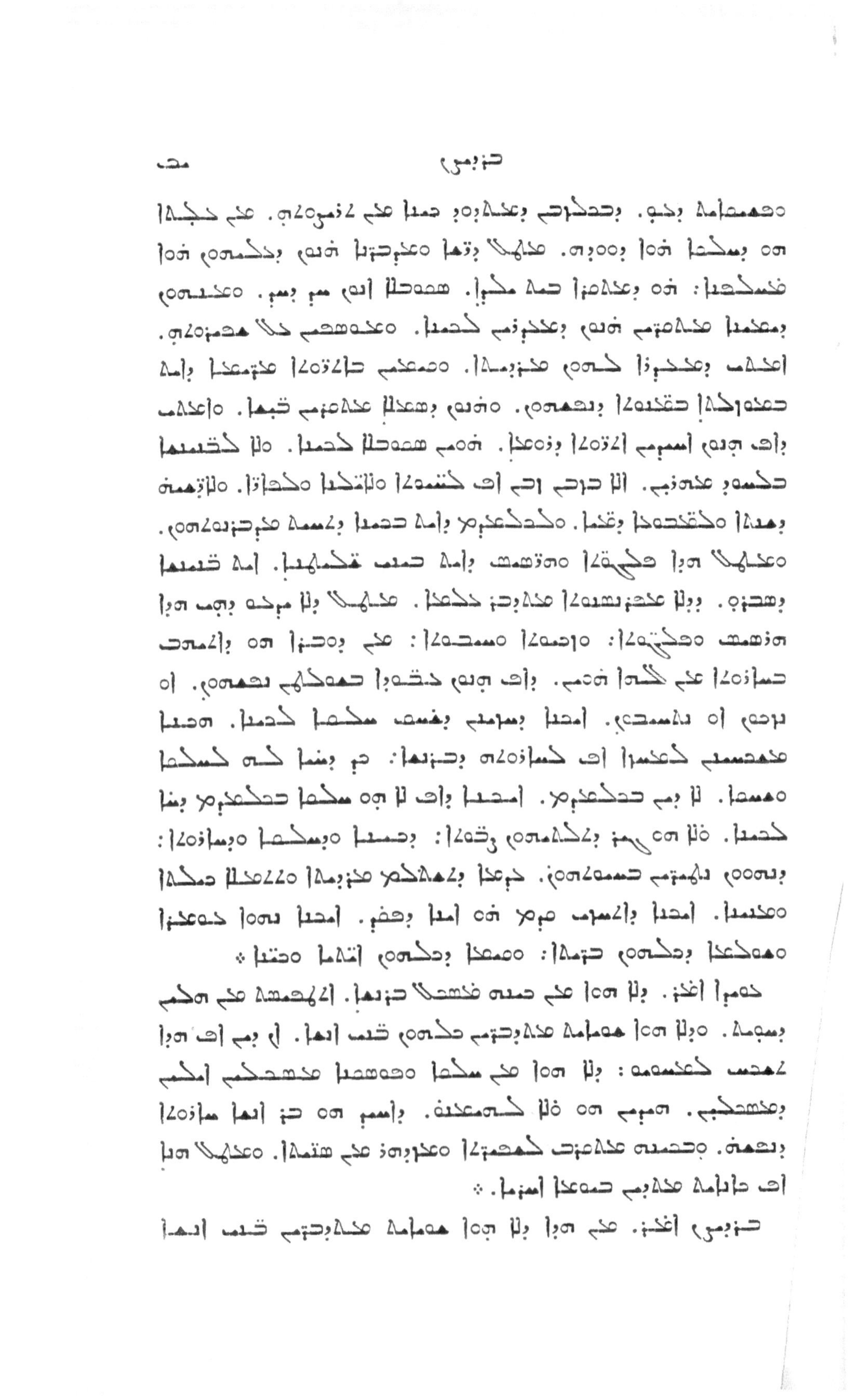

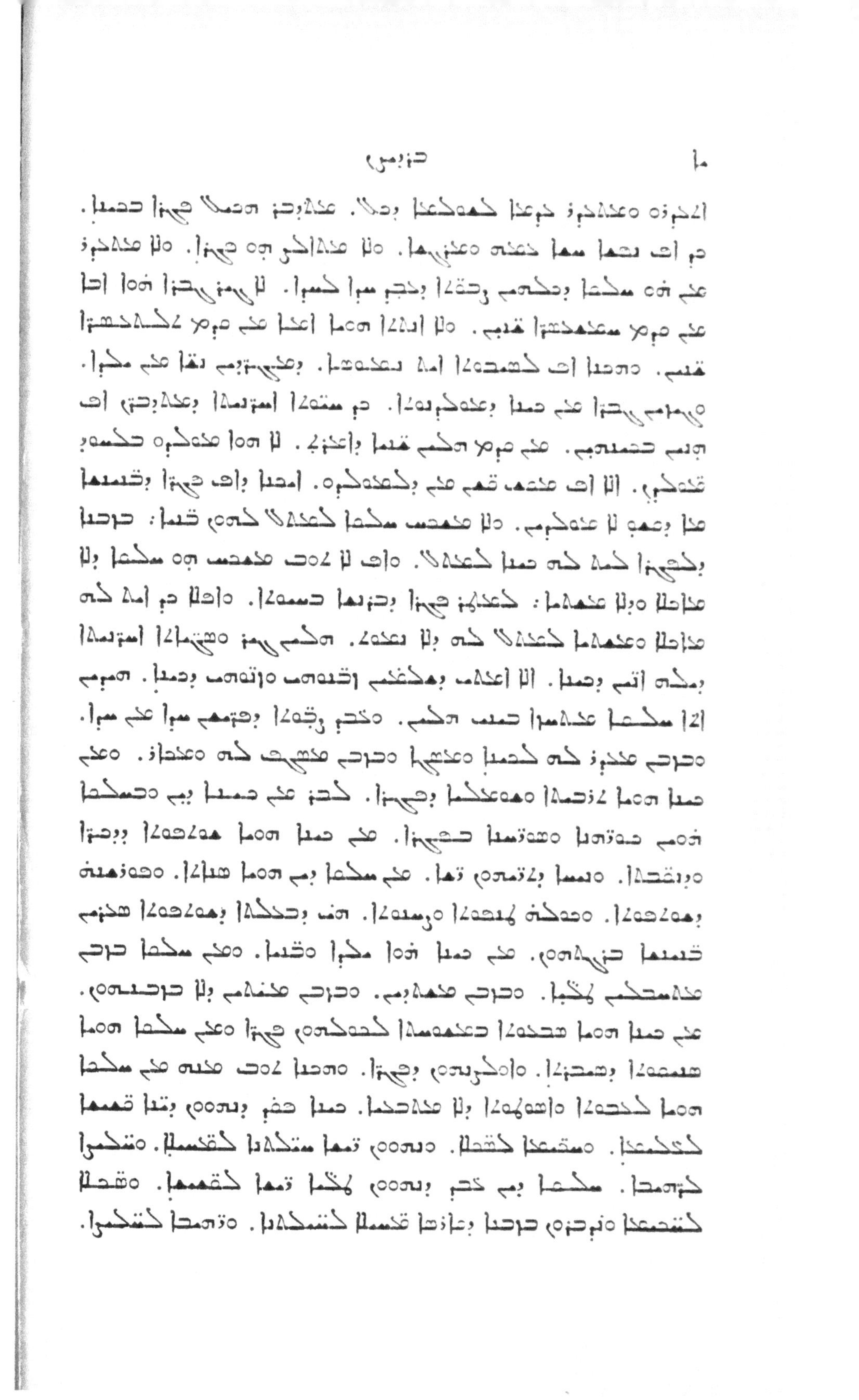

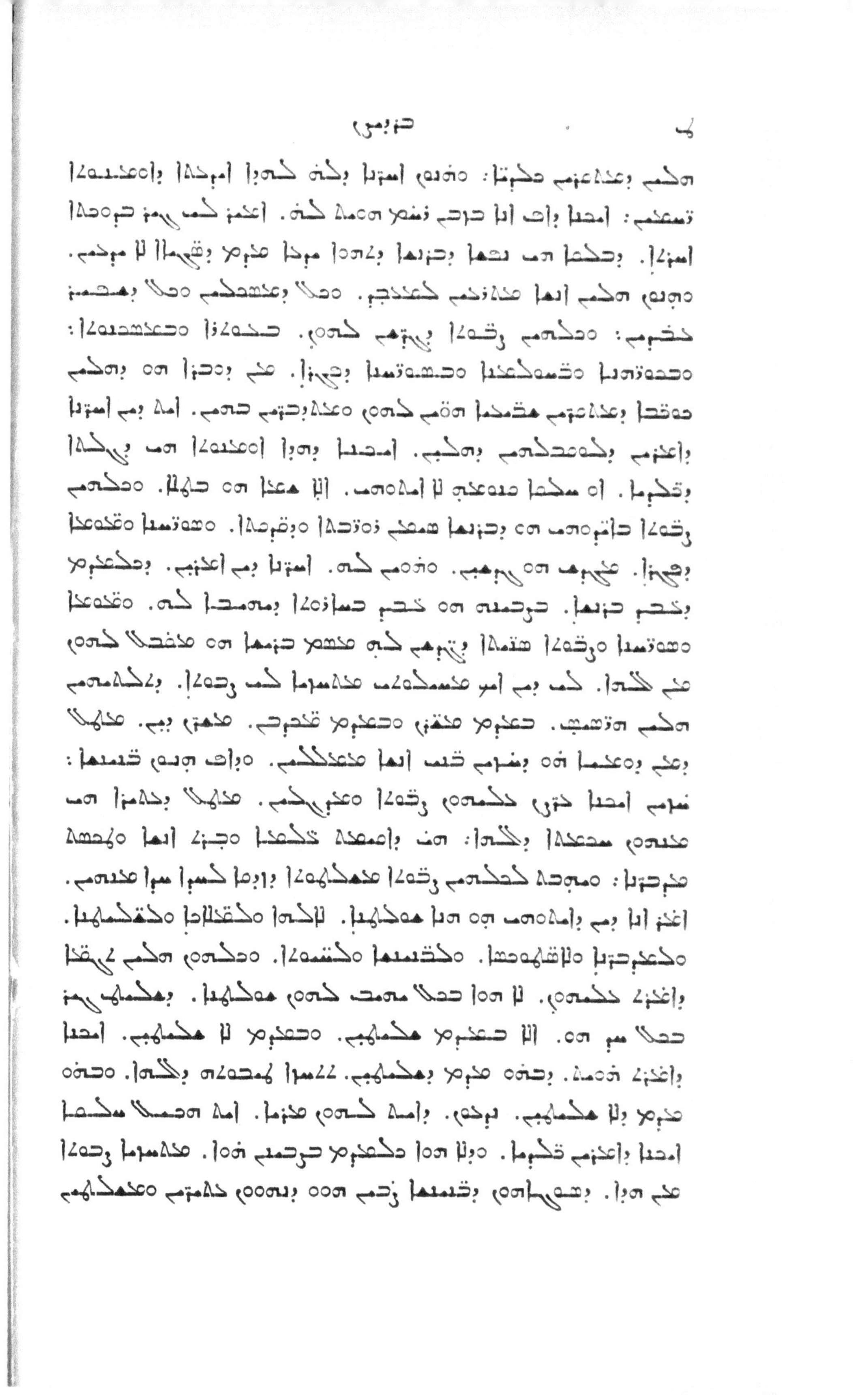

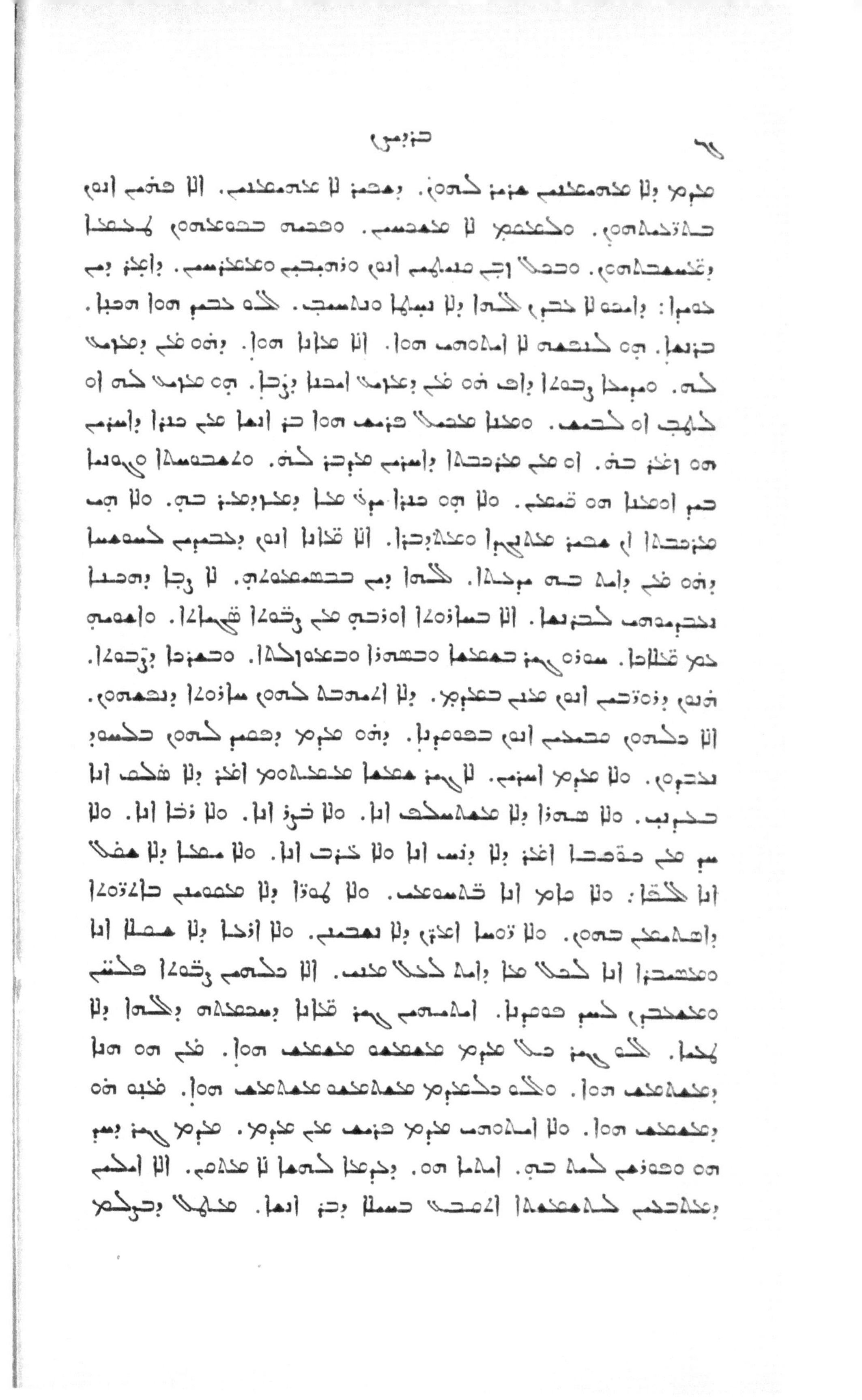

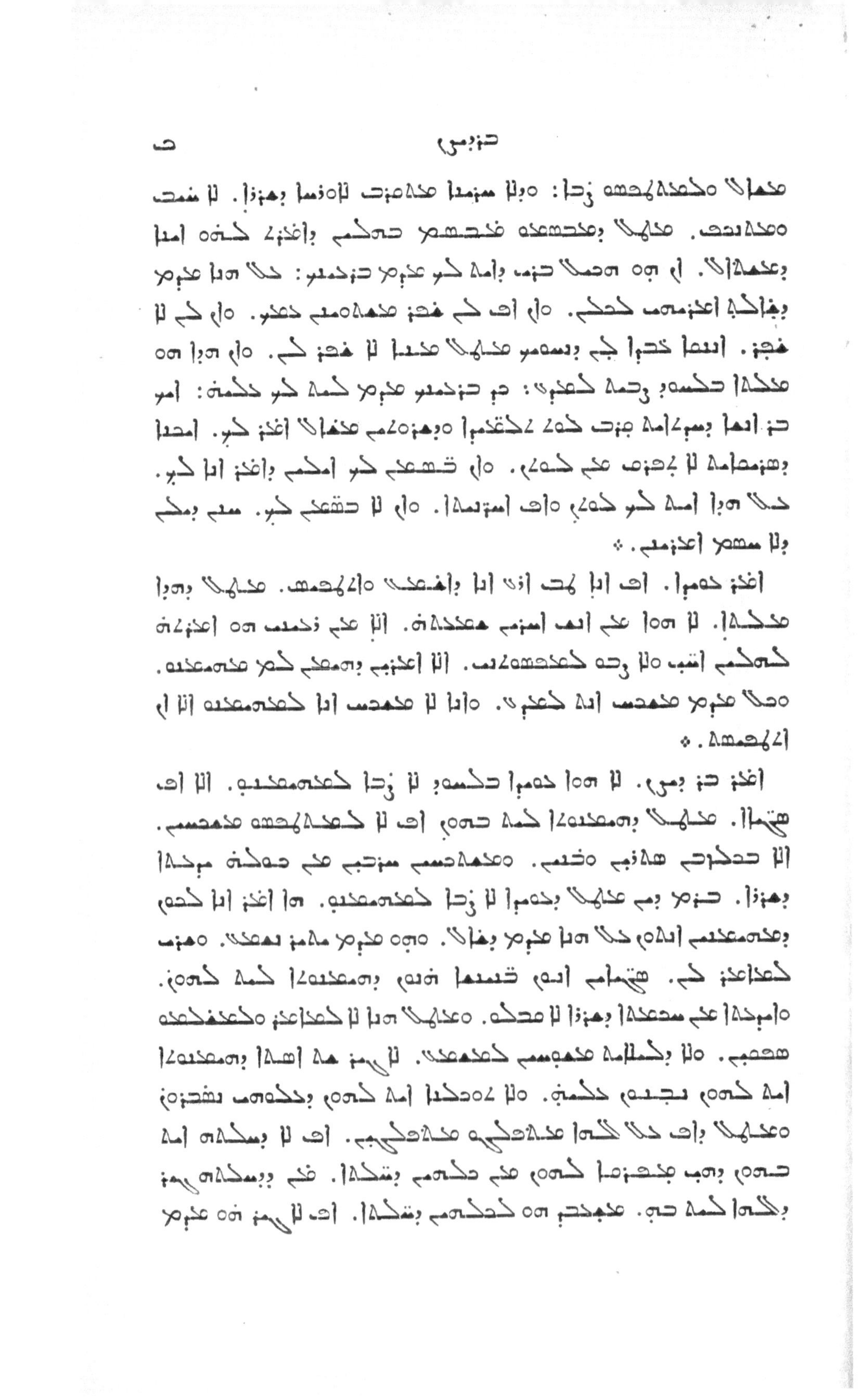

ܣܠܐ ܘܝܩܐܘܐ
ܕܐܠܘܐܠ ܀

WORKS BY REV. W. CURETON.

I.

كتاب الملل والنحل : BOOK OF RELIGIOUS AND PHILO-
SOPHICAL SECTS, by MUHAMMAD AL-SHAHRASTANI : now first edited
from the collation of several MSS. 8vo. London. For the Society for the
Publication of Oriental Texts. 2 Voll. 1842, 1846.

II.

שרח ספר קינות : TANCHUMI HIEROSOLYMITANI Commen-
tarius Arabicus in LAMENTATIONES : e codice unico Bodleiano literis He-
braicis exarato. 8vo. Londini, apud Jac. Madden, 1843.

III.

عمدة عقيدة اهل السنة والجماعة : PILLAR OF THE CREED OF
THE SUNNITES ; being a brief Exposition of their principal Tenets, by
AL-NASAFI. 8vo. London. For the Society for the Publication of Oriental
Texts. 1843.

IV.

CATALOGUS CODICUM MANUSCRIPTORUM ARABICO-
RUM, qui in MUSEO BRITANNICO asservantur. fol. Londini, Impensis
Curatorum Musei Britannici. Pars. I. 1846. Pars. II. 1852.

V.

VINDICIÆ IGNATIANÆ: or, The Genuine Writings of St. Ignatius, as exhibited in the Syriac Version, vindicated from the charge of
Heresy. 8vo. London, Rivingtons. 1846.

VI.

ܐܓܪ̈ܬܐ ܕܦܨܚܐ ܕܩܕܝܫܐ ܐܬܢܐܣܝܘܣ : THE FESTAL LETTERS OF
ST. ATHANASIUS, discovered in an Ancient Syriac Version, and edited
with a Preface. 8vo. London. For the Society for the Publication of
Oriental Texts. 1848.

VII.

THREE SERMONS, preached at the Chapel Royal, St. James' : The
Essential Connection of Christian Faith and Practice, being Two Sermons
delivered on Sunday, Feb. 27 ; The Revelations of Christianity with respect
to Temporal Polity, preached on Wednesday, March 22. 8vo. London,
Rivingtons ; Oxford, Parker, 1848.

VIII.

CORPUS IGNATIANUM. A Complete Collection of the Ignatian Epistles, genuine, interpolated, and spurious, together with numerous Extracts from them as quoted by Ecclesiastical Writers down to the Tenth Century, in Syriac, Greek, and Latin. An English Translation of the Syriac Text, with copious Notes and Introduction. Royal 8vo. London. Rivingtons. 1849.

IX.

FRAGMENTS OF THE ILIAD OF HOMER, ftom a Syriac Palimpsest. 4to. London. Printed by order of the Trustees of the British Museum. 1851.

X.

The Third Part of the ECCLESIASTICAL HISTORY OF JOHN BISHOP OF EPHESUS, now first edited. 4to. Oxford. At the University Press. 1853.

CPSIA information can be obtained
at www.ICGtesting.com
Printed in the USA
BVHW031208310122
627640BV00004B/179